Leading from the Middle

Part of the American Council on Education,
Series on Higher Education
Susan Slesinger, Executive Editor

Other titles in the series:

Learning to Lead by James R. Davis
The "How To" Grants Manual, Seventh Edition by David G. Bauer
Higher Education Assessments by Gary L. Kramer and Randy L. Swing
Leading the Campaign by Michael J. Worth
Leaders in the Labyrinth by Stephen J. Nelson
Academic Turnarounds edited by Terrence MacTaggart
Managing Diversity Flashpoints in Higher Education by Joseph E. Garcia
  and Karen J. Hoelscher
The Art and Politics of Academic Governance by Kenneth P. Mortimer
  and Colleen O'Brien Sathre
Strategic Leadership by Richard L. Morrill
Leadership Legacy Moments by E. Grady Bogue
The Indispensable University by Eugene P. Trani and Robert D. Holsworth
Peak Performance for Deans and Chairs by Susan Stavert Roper and
  Terrence E. Deal
Presidential Transitions by Patrick H. Sanaghan, Larry Goldstein, and
  Kathleen D. Gaval
Changing Course, Second Edition by Peter D. Eckel
Searching for Higher Education Leadership by Jean A. Dowdall
Other Duties as Assigned edited by Mark P. Curchack
The "How To" Grants Manual, Sixth Edition by David G. Bauer
Leaders in the Crossroads by Stephen James Nelson
International Students edited by Maureen S. Andrade and
  Norman W. Evans
Faculty Success through Mentoring by Carole J. Bland, Anne L. Taylor,
  S. Lynn Shollen, Anne Marie Weber-Main, Patricia A. Mulcahy
Leading America's Branch Campuses edited by Samuel Schuman
Beyond 2020 by Mary Landon Darden
Out in Front edited by Lawrence V. Weill
Community Colleges on the Horizon edited by Richard Alfred, Christopher
  Shults, Ozan Jaquette, and Shelley Strickland
Minding the Dream by Gail O. Mellow and Cynthia Heelan

Leading from the Middle

A Case-Study Approach to Academic Leadership for Associate Deans

Tammy Stone and Mary Coussons-Read

Published in partnership with the

AMERICAN COUNCIL ON EDUCATION
Leadership and Advocacy

ROWMAN & LITTLEFIELD PUBLISHERS, INC.
Lanham • Boulder • New York • Toronto • Plymouth, UK

Published in partnership with the American Council on Education

Published by Rowman & Littlefield Publishers, Inc.
A wholly owned subsidiary of The Rowman & Littlefield Publishing Group, Inc.
4501 Forbes Boulevard, Suite 200, Lanham, Maryland 20706
http://www.rowmanlittlefield.com

Estover Road, Plymouth PL6 7PY, United Kingdom

Copyright © 2011 by Tammy Stone and Mary Coussons-Read

All rights reserved. No part of this book may be reproduced in any form or by any electronic or mechanical means, including information storage and retrieval systems, without written permission from the publisher, except by a reviewer who may quote passages in a review.

British Library Cataloguing in Publication Information Available

Library of Congress Cataloging-in-Publication Data

Stone, Tammy, 1961–
  Leading from the middle : a case-study approach to academic leadership for associate deans / Tammy Stone and Mary Coussons-Read.
     p. cm.—(Series on higher education)
  "Published in partnership with the American Council on Education."
  Includes bibliographical references and index.
  ISBN 978-1-4422-0464-5 (cloth : alk. paper)—ISBN 978-1-4422-0466-9 (electronic : alk. paper)
  1. Deans (Education)—Case studies. 2. Universities and colleges—Administration—Case studies. I. Coussons-Read, Mary Elizabeth. II. American Council on Education. III. Title.
  LB2341.S833 2011
  371.4—dc22   2010051262

∞™ The paper used in this publication meets the minimum requirements of American National Standard for Information Sciences—Permanence of Paper for Printed Library Materials, ANSI/NISO Z39.48-1992. Printed in the United States of America

To Carroll Reichen, Jim Read, and
Tim and Harriet Coussons for all their support

Contents

Preface		ix
1	Academic Leadership for Associate Deans: Tool Kits and Case Studies for Maintaining Your Sanity	1
2	Are You Ready to Visit the Dark Side? Considering Becoming an Associate Dean	9
3	Stepping Up to Leadership with Your Head and Your Heart	23
4	Working with the Realities of Your Dean's Leadership and Management Style	35
5	Changing Behavior in a Culture of No Accountability	51
6	Something Old, Something New: Working with Department Chairs and the Faculty as an Associate Dean	63
7	Communicating Effectively: Say What You Mean and Mean What You Say	71
8	Dealing with Conflicts between and within Units	77
9	Trouble in Paradise: Dealing with Departmental Dysfunction	89
10	The Inmates Are Running the Asylum: Getting Hostile and Unproductive Faculty and Staff on Board	101

11	I Know Your Parents Think You Are Brilliant, but You Still Have to Follow the Rules: Working with Students in an Atmosphere of Entitlement	113
12	Call Me When the Fire Trucks Have Left: Defining and Responding to Crisis	123
13	Meet and Greet: Making Connections outside Your School	133
14	Adapting to Change While Keeping Your Sense of Humor	143
15	Burning the Candle at Both Ends: Drawing Boundaries and Defending Balance	149
16	Moving On: Life after Being an Associate Dean	159
17	Lessons Learned: Distillation of the Principles of Leading from the Middle	173
References		183
Index		187
About the Authors		189

Preface

We decided to write this book, in part, out of desperation. More specifically, when we took our positions as associate deans, many situations arose for which we had no previous experience or training. Additionally, as Gilan and Seagren state so eloquently, "Research validates that leading from the middle is no easy task" (2003, 21). Being good scholars, we fell back on our faculty skills and went looking in the literature for guidance. We were dismayed to find that although there were numerous guides on how to be a good dean and how to be a good chair, no such tome existed for the position of associate dean and the transition from faculty or chair to that of associate dean. Therefore, we set out to write the book we wish we could have had when we took on our positions.

First, a note on terminology is necessary. Many colleges and universities use the titles of both "associate" and "assistant" dean. At some institutions, associate deans rise from the faculty tracks and assistant deans come through parallel staff tracks; at other institutions, the opposite is the case. At still other institutions, associate and assistant deans are not distinguished from one another in the same way, and both positions are considered to be administrative. In order to take on these administrative positions, faculty positions (and rights and responsibilities defined under contracts or collective bargaining agreements) must be suspended. We write from the position of faculty who still maintain faculty status when they move into that middle level in the dean's office (regardless of the title), which is common at many institutions. For ease of conversation, we use the term "associate dean" throughout this book for this position. There is definitely that bias in our writing, particularly in sections dealing with balancing faculty roles with administrative roles. One of the reasons we take this approach (other than the fact that we are both faculty with the extra administrative title of associate dean) is that faculty are not trained to take on the types of duties faced by associate deans, and they often have had very limited exposure to the types of situations with which they will deal. Additionally, there is a certain amount of distrust of administration by most faculty, as well as a devaluing of the skills required to carry out administrative responsibilities (Raines and Squires Alberg 2003)—hence the frequent references to having "gone to the dark side." Conversely, individuals who rise to the position through the staff ranks often come to the job with an arsenal of skills that faculty lack. We can learn much from them. Despite this obvious bias based on our personal experiences, we feel that many of the situations we describe and the advice we give are appropriate for people who come to the job through either the staff or faculty tracks.

A second note on terminology is also necessary. Although both of us work at Research I Comprehensive Universities that are divided into a series of schools and colleges, many of the situations we describe may arise regardless of the type of institution (teaching vs. research, comprehensive vs. four-year). We all must deal with student issues, faculty conflicts, and dysfunctional units, and we have to do this while achieving some level of balance in our own lives. Thus, we will refer to the academic unit served by the associate dean as a "school" or "college" and the broader institution as the "university."

We have structured this book into a series of modules encompassing different types of situations in which associate deans may find themselves, and we freely give advice on how to handle them. Most modules contain one or two fictional case studies to better illustrate the challenges and issues under discussion. None of these examples has occurred in exactly the way it is described here, but bits and pieces of them have. The result is an amalgam of common issues. The point of the case studies is not to recount history but to present situations that frequently come up in the life of an associate dean. These are then followed by suggested ways of dealing with each issue. We do not give pat answers, but rather present a series of issues, questions, and suggestions you should consider in the process of deciding how to handle a situation. Additionally, we provide references to sources in areas where we think you might want to dig a bit more deeply, such as conflict management and communication styles.

The added difficulty for many contemplating the move from a faculty position to the dean's office is that the job frequently entails a considerable increase in responsibility but ambiguous power at best. Whereas staff positions often come with detailed job descriptions and reporting lines, the roles of associate dean that are filled from the faculty ranks are often more ill defined and more dependent on the personality of the dean they serve and the culture of their school and university. Collectively, we have served as associate deans with four different deans, and the nature of our job was radically different under each depending on the personality of the dean to whom we answered and whether he or she was an internal or external hire. The nature of your dean's management and communication style and your relationship with the dean will flavor how you address many of the issues we discuss. Therefore, we start out with a discussion of how individuals come to the job of associate dean and the relationship you may have with your dean. These discussions necessarily set the tone for the rest of the book.

Our hope is that this book will serve as a reference and a source of support for current associate deans and as a window into these jobs for faculty who may be considering taking on such a role. There is undoubtedly an aspect of "I wish someone had told me *that*!" in some areas of this book. But happily, we believe we have a real opportunity to share some of the good, the bad, and the ugly of taking on the challenges of leading from the middle and excelling as an associate dean.

Chapter 1

Academic Leadership for Associate Deans

Tool Kits and Case Studies for Maintaining Your Sanity

Given all of the books that have been written to aid deans and chairs in their positions, you might ask why we need yet another book on academic administration. The answer to this, of course, is that the job of associate dean is sufficiently different from other positions in its scope, roles, and ambiguous authority that it warrants its own treatment.

What do we really mean by this? What we have noticed in our own careers—and learned through talking to other associate deans from around the country at national meetings—is that the position of associate dean is ambiguous at best. Frequently, the charge of the job is to ensure smooth day-to-day running of the school and attending to various details that enable the dean to concentrate on the larger issues of strategic planning, fund-raising, and the role of the school within the larger university and community context. In other words, associate deans may enforce policy, ensure classes are offered, aid faculty in making it through the tenure process, settle fights between chairs and their faculty, negotiate conflicts between departments, and address student complaints about the faculty and student disciplinary issues, to name just a few specifics. They frequently do these tasks without authority or power of their own and almost always with no training in administration or in the conflict management, negotiation, and coalition building skills needed for the job. Further, in their new roles, associate deans must relearn many of the skills they thought they had mastered in their faculty careers. Specifically, they must figure out new ways to balance not only their personal with their professional lives but also their faculty with their administrative roles. Dealing with enormous time demands, deadlines, and scheduling conflicts are common problems for all staff and faculty, but they may be even larger problems for associate deans. Additionally, they must switch from primarily focusing on their academic field of study (a skill for which they have been rewarded through the tenure and promotion system) to broadening their knowledge of the institution at large and of other members of the academic community. They must learn how to take a broad view of issues, incorporating the needs and goals of fields beyond their own, as they move from the department to the school as a whole. While doing this, associate deans must still maintain their position in their own field of study. This requires that as associate deans they explicitly distance themselves from their home departments while maintaining a foothold in their fields of study.

This book is designed to help faculty make the transition to administrator and acquire the skills to do so successfully. It discusses a collection of skills that combine to form the tool kit that is needed by associate deans. Faculty members are not trained in all these skills, which are, in many ways, contrary to the behaviors and activities for which they have been rewarded in their careers up until this time.

We hope that the tool kit you acquire by reading this book will help make the position of associate dean not only manageable but also rewarding. For example, as an associate dean, you will need to deal with stressful situations such as complaining students, disruptive faculty, and mixed messages from your dean. We hope we can share with you the rewards of helping students in need, reengaging unproductive faculty, and developing programs to make your school or college better. You will find case studies in these chapters to illustrate how these tools can be used, as well as the consequences for not acquiring these skills.

Are there experiences you can use from your previous work as faculty members that might help as you move into the position of associate dean? Yes, there are. Many of us have been chairs, or we have chaired major committees in our professional organizations. Others of us have administered large grants and interdisciplinary projects. Although some of these skills are transferable, there are major differences about being an associate dean that we all must recognize and deal with. The major difference is that the majority of our time is now spent with people trained in completely different academic fields from ourselves. This is obvious in the case of large, heterogeneous schools (like schools of liberal arts and sciences) but comes into play in smaller, more homogeneous schools as well as associate deans' work across schools on issues of concern to the campus as a whole. Thus, we cannot use a reference to the commonality of our field as a starting point in coalition building, negotiation, conflict management, etc. Those of us who are chemists must learn to talk to the poets. The individual trained in business management must now work with the physicist. The public policy expert must work with the anthropologist, and the sociologist must talk to the musician. This fact requires that we take a much broader view and distance ourselves from our previous positions and disciplines. Sometimes this will mean that you must make a decision that your home department will not be happy with, but the broader goals and welfare of the school must be paramount in your decision-making process. The associate dean who cannot move from being primarily a member of a particular department to being a leader for the entire school in both his or her decisions and his or her way of dealing with others will have a great deal of difficulty adjusting to this new role (Hoppe 2003; Lucas 1998; Plater 2006; Strathe and Wilson 2006).

Unfortunately, the transition from faculty member to administrator is a difficult process for many individuals because universities are notoriously bad at creating succession plans and providing mentoring and career development. Additionally, it is often assumed that you have all of the skills necessary for the job and are all-knowing about the nuances of policy and procedure the second you walk through the dean's office door. We hope that the tool kits we discuss, the case studies we present, and the advice we offer about common issues that may arise in the position of associate dean will help you find your own balance and your own way of dealing with the conflicts and tensions that arise in the job. One of our goals in writing this book is to aid you in moving from managing the office of associate dean to "leading from the middle," while maintaining both your sanity and balance in your career. Doing this requires that we explore the differences between management and leadership, as well as an understanding of how individuals both above you (the dean) and below you (the faculty, staff, and students) view your position and how you can change, or at least manage, these views to make the position of associate dean rewarding and manageable.

MANAGING VERSUS LEADING

One of the fundamental principles of this book is that there is a difference between managing and leading. To us, managing is ensuring that the day-to-day activities necessary to keep the school running in its same path continue and that deadlines are met. Without a doubt, associate deans do a fair amount of managing; in large part this occurs so that the dean is freed of these responsibilities and can undertake leadership roles. Leadership involves activities that effect change. Despite the managerial responsibilities of the position of associate dean, we also believe this position can and should be one of leadership—hence the title of the book. This does not mean that we are advocating that you ignore your dean and attempt to develop a new strategic plan for your school on your own. Rather, in the implementation of a strategic plan, you may be responsible for the details of various policies that must be worked out to pave the way for the changes outlined in the plan. In order to accomplish such a task, coalitions must be built, efficiencies must be created, and new initiatives and programs may be developed. From time to time, existing units may need intervention during such processes to bring them into the fold and manage changes that are happening. Each of these activities requires leadership, and it is these leadership tasks that this book is about. In selecting skills to combine into the tool kits that we talk about here, and in using the case studies to illustrate these tool kits in action, the issue of *leading* from the middle is paramount.

THE EVOLUTION OF A DEAN

How you go about leading from the middle is dependent, to some degree, on your dean and his or her style and agenda. Is your dean a leader or a manager? What is your dean's communication style? How does your dean envision working with the members of the dean's office? Was your dean hired from outside the institution or did he or she rise through the ranks of the faculty? All of these factors will affect your everyday life; they are dealt with extensively in chapter 3. It is important to remember, though, that your dean's attitudes, priorities, and way of interacting are likely to change through time. Woverton and Gmelch (2002) have argued that deans (and to some degree associate deans) go through very specific stages as they adjust to their positions, though how long each stage takes differs for each person. The first stage concentrates on understanding the larger structural issues, starting with the school itself and then moving on to the larger university in which it is housed, including the strategic plans of both. How long it takes to gain in-depth knowledge of these issues depends on whether the dean was hired in an external search or from within the existing faculty ranks, as well as how effectively the upper administration communicates these issues to the schools. Next, deans get to know the individuals involved, starting with the members of the dean's office and continuing with the key players in other departments and support offices throughout the institution. After this settling-in period, deans can move into setting priorities, building support, and developing new initiatives. That means that it is important to reevaluate your dean's communication, management, and leadership style periodically and to check for shifting opinions and priorities. That might make you feel as though you are aiming at a moving target, but it is important to remember that we all grow into our positions, and our views and experiences influence the way we interact and lead. This is just as true for your dean as it is for you.

WORKING WITH FACULTY, STAFF, AND STUDENTS

The remaining chapters in this book concentrate on situations that may arise as you work with the faculty, staff, and students. These chapters concentrate largely on helping you develop the skills and tools necessary to function as a leader in situations fraught with conflict and stress. In particular, how do you tell if something is really a crisis, and (whether it is a crisis or not) how do you tell whether it will and should significantly affect your reaction to the situation? As we noted above, the case studies provide occasionally humorous introductions to these and other issues. We follow the cases with strategies and advice for making decisions to address these situations and to help you move from a purely managerial perspective to one of leading from the middle.

COMMUNICATION

Communication is a complex and multifaceted activity that is an essential skill for you to develop and hone during your job as an associate dean. First and foremost, you need to learn to communicate in new ways. This is a central topic in many of the chapters. Effective communication can make the difference between a good outcome and a train wreck when you are dealing with passing information through the layers of an institution. For example, how can you ensure that those with whom you are sharing information understand and are absorbing what you are trying to say? And how do you manage the conflict that inevitably arises any time multiple people are involved in a planning activity or in the execution of a project? Communication for associate deans goes beyond "getting a message out" clearly and concisely. It also means using the way we communicate to build consensus for a new initiative, to motivate unproductive faculty and staff to higher levels of performance, and to mitigate conflicts between individuals and/or units. In fact, conflict management is a major portion of the job for most associate deans. In addition to thinking carefully about how we communicate (the words we use, the tone, and the method of delivery), we must also understand how others communicate. Sometimes this requires some detection skills, as we decipher not only their words but also their priorities and agendas so that we can tease out the underlying root of an issue.

TIME MANAGEMENT

As faculty move into administration we also must learn to manage our time in new and different ways. Tied to this, the boundaries between the personal, the academic, and the administrative must be negotiated. Investing time and energy in all three of these areas, while still maintaining your sanity and occasionally getting some sleep, presents new challenges. For example, when you become an administrator, others suddenly have access to your calendar for scheduling meetings. The result is that you may come in on a Monday morning expecting to spend the day grading papers or working on a manuscript because your day is free of meetings only to find your calendar has been populated with four new meetings to deal with the "crisis" that arose over the weekend. Your dean may present you with last-minute projects that suddenly become your top priority. Often, these new projects appear at the same time your classes are creating their heaviest workload, you are facing a deadline for an article, and issues in your personal life demand attention. There are ways of setting priorities, maintaining research time on your calendar, and leaving the office before midnight every day while you are an associate dean, but you must think about time management in a very different way.

BUILDING YOUR TOOL KIT

Our hope is that this book will provide some perspective on some of the issues you are facing as you consider stepping into "real" university administration by becoming an associate dean, including challenges you'll face when working with your dean, faculty, staff, and students and the question of how being an associate dean fits into your present career and influences your future career. The book is framed in terms of the processes of inquiry that we've found useful over our years as associate deans and is intended to help you develop a long-term strategy for dealing with complex and often intractable issues through observation, collaboration, and professional conduct. We pose a series of questions that are worth asking when you encounter a particular situation or one like it, and we then go on to offer some strategies and tools you may want to employ to help move through the situation and resolve it. Many of the techniques and strategies can be applied in numerous situations, but the nuances of using them to navigate various challenges can be adjusted based on your understanding of the people, principles, and policies that may be involved. The strategies are flexible but consistently focus on developing solutions that preserve your integrity and credibility and foster collaboration and positive problem solving to the degree that it is possible. We have both found that using this process of applying tools based on observation and data gathering is a powerful approach to dealing with tough situations that allows you to come home at the end of every day (okay—*most* days) and say to yourself, "I did my best today and I have no regrets about the way I handled X, Y, and Z." Using this process to understand, for example, your own growth and that of your dean and institution will go a long way toward helping you get the most out of being an associate dean and will prepare you well for whatever comes next in your career.

Chapter 2

Are You Ready to Visit the Dark Side?

Considering Becoming an Associate Dean

How do you know you are ready to make the leap into the realm of school administration? And once you do, how will your world and your relationships with others in the school change? This book deals with different aspects of the latter question, so it is only appropriate we start with a chapter about deciding whether to make the leap or not, and if the time is right to do so.

Although much of this book is focused on the pitfalls, perils, and perplexities of being a successful associate dean, a fundamental premise of ours is that being an associate dean can be a critical, formative, and incredibly valuable step in your career. We hope that after reading this book you opt to take the leap, if it fits with your own goals and aspirations. If you are in an associate dean job now, we hope that you appreciate that even your struggles are making contributions to your professional development and that the work you are doing is essential to the students, staff, and faculty of your school and university.

In many institutions, associate dean is one of the first "real" administrative positions faculty may take that exposes them to the real inner workings of a school or university. As department chairs, faculty see some of the sausage being made, but much of the background and complexity is still off-limits to them; they are largely seen as "faculty," while associate deans are typically viewed as "administrators." The great thing about being an associate dean is that you can immerse yourself in all the doings of the school and university and learn a ton, while being somewhat shielded from the slings and arrows of the massive responsibilities that come with higher administrative positions. In other words, you get a lot of exposure to the issues and challenges without having to shoulder all of the responsibility. Even better, when and if you decide to, you can simply return to the faculty and relatively easily resume your life as a teacher and a scholar—since, hopefully, you have continued to retain some activity in these areas. This step is fundamentally different from becoming a dean, vice chancellor, or provost because in those positions, for example, it is virtually impossible to maintain any real scholarship or research program, and classroom teaching is usually out of the question due to the immense time commitment and responsibilities that go along with these jobs. Basically, being an associate dean is a great way to get your feet wet in higher education administration without having to make the shift totally from being a faculty member to being a full-time administrator. If administration is something you are attracted to, this may be the perfect foray. Here are some of the things you will gain from being an associate dean:

1. *You will learn how things really work.* As faculty members, we often think that there is some seat of power or war chest of endless funding that is controlled by the deans and upper administration on the campus. Although it is possible that this is the case at some institutions, at many it is not, and as an associate dean, you will learn the real processes and issues faced by administration daily. The perspective this gives you as a member of the institution is a great benefit; your view becomes broader and more whole, which will serve you well regardless of whether you climb the administrative ladder or not.
2. *You will meet many people you would never meet otherwise.* As an associate dean, you will not only get close to the dean, but also meet other deans, vice chancellors, provosts, vice presidents, presidents, chancellors, and potentially, members of your institution's governing board and your counterparts in dean's offices all over the country. The networking opportunities afforded by being an associate dean are great, and it is also a wonderful way for people in your institution and beyond to learn who you are, what you can do, and why you are so fantastic.
3. *You will have the opportunity to develop your leadership and management skills.* We will talk more about being a leader versus being a manager later in the book, but both sets of skills are critical if you are going to advance as a competent and respected administrator. As an associate dean, you will have the chance to cultivate both of these skill sets, and again, whether you move up or not, this will be time well spent.

4. *You will develop great conflict management skills.* This may not sound like something to strive for, but really it is. Regardless of what sort of associate dean you become, the position will without a doubt challenge your ability to avoid, work through, and resolve many kinds of conflicts. You will be exposed to many different types of tussles, and by the end of your tenure in the job, you will be seasoned at dealing with all kinds of difficult situations and conversations.
5. *You will become an expert at time management.* You will have multiple types of pressure on your time as an associate dean—meetings, conferences, projects, reports, and task forces, as well as things like research, teaching, grant writing, and the like. This list does not include any of your personal commitments and goals. Considering all of this, you will emerge from your position as an associate dean with excellent time management and organizational skills.
6. *You will have a stronger curriculum vitae (CV) in terms of administrative experience.* Being an associate dean is a great addition to your CV, whether you become a higher administrator or not. The position shows that you have the trust of your institution and faculty, the skills to do a complex job, the leadership capabilities to make things happen, and the ability to take on considerable responsibility successfully.

Although this is not an exhaustive list, these are some of the primary and very tangible benefits you will gain from taking on the challenge of being an associate dean. The job will do wonders for your professional skills and confidence—in other words, it is really worth doing if it is the right time for you and if it fits with your personal and professional goals.

All the great things you can gain from being an associate dean, of course, can come at the cost of other things. For example, all that time you are spending doing faculty development and evaluation work in the dean's office is time you are not spending writing manuscripts and grants or teaching in the classroom. Those retreats you are attending for budget and strategic planning are eating away at weekend time with your family and friends. Although this may work for some people, it may not work for you. Some people find themselves taken by surprise by the degree to which associate dean's work eclipses other aspects of professional and personal time. Part of the degree to which this occurs is a function of how well you set and maintain boundaries between aspects of your work and your personal life, but even if you are a master at doing that, you should expect that the job of associate dean will impinge on some aspects of your life.

TO BE OR NOT TO BE AN ASSOCIATE DEAN?

It is flattering to have your chair or others say things like "You would be a great associate dean—you should apply for that position" or for your dean to say "I have talked to lots of folks around the college and it is clear that you are the right person for this job. I hope you will apply for the position." When you are asked to think about taking an administrative position like associate dean, it is essential to think about several things before accepting. These jobs are tremendously rewarding and can be terrific for developing your career, but they can also put pressure on other parts of your life. It is really important to think about all these pieces before plunging into a position as an associate dean, and to go into the job with your eyes open. One thing that sometimes happens to faculty members when they are approached by the dean in the manner stated above is that they accept the job first and think things through later. This is totally understandable. It may be tempting to say yes to an opportunity to become an associate dean without stopping to really consider what it means for your career in both the short and long terms. Consider this case study.

Associate Professor Smiley was an up-and-coming leader in the faculty in her college with a strong research and grant-funding record, a teaching award, and a reputation on her campus for being a fair, hardworking person with a real dedication to the college. The year after receiving tenure, she served as interim chair for her department, and as that appointment ended, she was approached by Dean Leechmore to serve as the associate dean for difficult affairs in her college. The position, although very important, was undoubtedly the most demanding and complex of the associate dean jobs, and it was for this reason, said Dean Leechmore, that Professor Smiley was "the perfect person with the perfect temperament and values" for the job. Dr. Smiley admired Dean Leechmore, was flattered by his offer, and was attracted by the extra pay, and thus she quickly accepted the job. She eagerly plunged into the work, dealing with many difficult and complex processes, situations, policies, and conflicts. She was very successful in her work, but gradually she found herself asking the dean for more and more teaching offloads to accommodate her work as an associate dean, and she began regularly declining invitations to submit abstracts for conferences and offers of collaboration from colleagues in her area of research. Associate Dean Smiley simply found that the demands of her position and the unpredictability in her schedule associated with dealing with the crisis of the day created real problems for her regarding the amount of time and energy she had available to prepare classes, meet with students, hold regular office hours, write grants, collect data, and go to professional meetings.

By the end of her second year as an associate dean, Smiley was doing no classroom teaching at all, and by the end of her fourth year in the job, she had not published a peer-reviewed paper since taking the position. As Smiley entered her fifth year as an associate dean, she prepared her dossier for promotion to full

> professor, and although she was concerned about her lack of grant funding and slowed publication rate, she figured her lack of teaching would be offset by the massive service she had been doing as associate dean and that her promotion bid would succeed. Unfortunately, her department, school, and university were not able to support her candidacy for full professor, citing stagnation in her teaching and scholarly work. Associate Dean Smiley was crushed by this development, and found herself worrying that, due to the gap in her publication record, she would never get promoted to full professor, a primary goal for her career.

This may seem like an improbable case study, but in our experience, it is all too common. It is not that it is impossible to get promoted to full professor while serving as associate dean (we were both successful in doing so), but it is certainly much more challenging due to the demands on your time and it takes some serious planning and thought. Taking on the job of associate dean will bring with it tremendous benefits to you and your career, but it is not without cost. Weighing these is key to deciding when to take the job and, later, when it is time to leave (see chapter 16).

YOUR GOALS

Being an associate dean is a rewarding and challenging job, but given the potential it has for stalling your professional progress in terms of scholarship and possibly promotion and the toll it can take on your personal life, it is important to go into the job with your eyes open and recognizing the costs and benefits of taking on such a position. Acknowledging this, we suggest that you spend some time mulling over the following questions before you accept the position.

The first thing to ask yourself is where you are in your career. This can be an especially critical question if you have not been promoted through the ranks to full professor and if that is a goal for you. In Associate Dean Smiley's case above, she was dismayed to find that the demands of being an associate dean had derailed her bid to become a full professor. It is not that Smiley will never be successful in her promotion bid, but in her haste to accept the job in the dean's office, she did not stop to consider how being an associate dean might impact her ability to get promoted. If this is an issue for you, you may wish to delay taking the job until after you have been promoted. You can be sure that there will be other opportunities in the dean's office if this one does not work out. To help you decide, take careful stock of your research, teaching, and service and talk with people "in the know" to see how close you are to being competitive for promotion. If you are essentially ready to go, taking the job may not be such a big deal. If you do take on the position of associate dean prior to promotion, be really brutal about negotiating for research and faculty activity time when you take the job. Get in writing, for example, that you will not be in the dean's office at all on Mondays and Thursdays so you can continue your growth as a faculty member. The caveat here is that often the fingers of the dean's office have a way of prying this time away from you. In our experience, this is not likely to have the hoped-for outcome, so be aware of this from the beginning and plan for it.

Of course, it is possible that becoming a full professor is not a particular goal for you. If this is the case, then none of the above really applies. We would, however, caution you about not setting this as a goal for yourself; many higher-level administrative positions like dean, for example, require that you be a full professor, and in our experience, it is not uncommon for people to regret later in their careers not having been promoted to full professor.

The second thing to ask yourself is where you are in your personal life and to identify your goals in that area. If you have a partner or spouse, are a parent or plan to be, are caring for aging parents, or are a caregiver for someone who is ill, or if you have a large commitment to outside activities or hobbies, it is worth thinking about whether the time pressures of being an associate dean are compatible with those aspects of your life. Although it is certainly true that being a dean or vice president, for example, puts substantially more pressure on your personal life and time than being an associate dean, there are times when even being an associate dean will demand some unexpected long hours, weekend work, or curtailed vacation and personal time. Both of us had substantial personal and family responsibilities outside of our jobs as associate deans, and we can assure you that juggling all those aspects of our personal and professional lives was difficult at times. This can be particularly challenging if you are a parent, especially of young children, or a caregiver for a spouse or parent. As an associate dean, it can be very difficult to absorb days when a child is home sick from school or to make parent-teacher conferences or doctor's appointments. Again, it is not that it cannot be done or that it is not worth taking on the challenge of being an associate dean, but it is important to clarify your goals and expectations prior to your decision.

SOMETIMES "NO" IS THE RIGHT ANSWER

Finally, ask yourself if being a university administrator is a goal for you. When most of us decided to become professors, we said to ourselves, "I will *never* be an administrator! What a lousy way to spend a career when you could be teaching and in the lab (studio/field/etc.)!" As time passes, however, some of us learn that in fact, we have aspirations to become leaders and realize that we could actually make a positive contribution as administrators at the department, school, and/or university levels. For some, this is a reluctant realization and for others, an exciting one. If you are reading this book, you've certainly gotten the message, internally or externally, that you have the potential to be a good administrator and that you should consider taking this road. Having said that, it is important to consider whether it is your goal to become an administrator or if it is more a case of the institution or others asking you to become an administrator. For many individuals, these two things merge, but for some, they do not. Consider the following case study.

> Professor Marter was a respected member of the English faculty with an international reputation as a poet and a local reputation as an even-handed senior faculty member with a knack for resolving conflicts among faculty and factions. Associate Dean Haddit had resigned from the dean's office after three hard years of service, and Professor Marter was surprised to get a call from Dean McPressure asking him to please apply for the position. Dean McPressure told Professor Marter that the position would certainly not impede the progress he was making on a new volume of poetry and that he could count on having at least two days per week to focus on his scholarship. Dean McPressure reminded Professor Marter that he was given a substantial raise in the previous year and that it was essential that senior faculty members in the college lend their talents to supporting the college's needs and mission. Reluctantly, Professor Marter agreed to serve and started his career as an associate dean. Although effective in his position, Associate Dean Marter found himself longing to return to his life as a faculty member and missing interactions with his students and colleagues. After less than a year, he approached Dean McPressure to tender his resignation. Dean McPressure, although disappointed, was supportive, as Associate Dean Marter is a valued faculty member. As he began to think about finding a replacement for Associate Dean Marter, Dean McPressure reconsidered the approach he used to recruit Marter, realizing that he might be better off looking for strong faculty who were actually interested in administration rather than twisting the arms of strong faculty who were not so inclined.

The point here is that although Professor Marter was a good choice for associate dean, he basically did not want to do it and agreed to serve under pressure from the dean. It is not uncommon for upper-level administrators to approach faculty and encourage them to serve in an administrative position, and if you are a faculty member on the receiving end of this "encouragement" as Professor Marter was, it can be tough to say no even if in your gut you know it is not the right choice for you. If you are approached by someone to be an associate dean, or if you are an associate dean being encouraged to take on a larger administrative role, be sure you are clear on what you want for yourself and when you want it. Even if the school or university has been very good to you, do not allow yourself to be pressured into taking a position that does not make sense for you. Here are a couple of ways you can respectfully handle this situation.

1. *Delay.* It very well may be that although the position in question is not a good fit for you right now, you know it will be in the future. Sharing this with whoever is encouraging you is a good idea as it lets that person know that you are both interested in the future and thoughtful about your own goals, abilities, and career trajectory.
2. *Decline.* If you are relatively sure that the position you are being asked to consider is not going to be a good fit for you in the foreseeable future, simply decline clearly and respectfully. You really do not need to explain yourself, and although it may not seem like you would ever be interested in the job in question, be careful about saying "never." Things may change in a way that would make an administrative job attractive to you at some point, and saying that you would never consider taking such a job may come back to haunt you in the future. In other words, the less said the better, but be respectful.

The take-home message here is to consider (and possibly take) this opportunity with your eyes open to what the job will mean, good and not so good, for your career and life, and whether all this is a good fit for you right now.

A few final pieces of advice seem fitting here. If you are on the fence about taking an administrative job now or in the future, do not be shy about talking to former associate deans and deans, current associate deans, department chairs, any senior mentors you have, and importantly, some people who have not made the leap into administration but seem like they would be good at it. Ask them to tell you about their experiences, how they made the decision to go into administration (or not), and looking back on their decision, what they are glad they did and what they would do differently. Ask and listen in these conversations rather than telling them about your fears, worries, and uncertainties (unless one of them is a really trusted friend). Be aware that what you say may be broadcast and may come back to haunt you at some point, so be judicious in what you share and with whom. It is also important to remember that if an administrative position is coming your way now, others are likely to in the future. If the timing of the job in question does not meet your personal and professional goals at this point in your life, it is fine to respectfully decline and keep the door open for the future. If you find yourself in this situation, consider sharing some of your professional and/or personal goals when you meet with your dean or others to decline the offer. Being able to state and stick to your goals reflects very well on you and also lets people know that you are thoughtful and deliberate about your career and your life. For example, you might tell your dean, "Although I can certainly see myself as an associate dean one of these days, it is important for me to get promoted to full professor and let my children get a little older before I take on the responsibilities and time commitment of that position. I hope you will keep me in mind for future positions, and thanks again for thinking of me." Becoming an administrator is a service job, but it is not one you are obligated to take. Take on these exciting and rewarding roles when and if they are attractive to you and fit with your life goals.

APPLYING FOR THE JOB OF ASSOCIATE DEAN

So you've decided to go for it and apply for the position of associate dean. How do you approach this transition and what should you expect if you are successful in making the transition? The question "Are you ready to visit the dark side?" is only partly in jest; becoming an administrator will create change in not only your career and its trajectory, but also your relationships at your institution. When you move into an administrative position such as associate dean, you move from a peer position with other faculty to one in which your decisions affect their lives, be it through merit reviews, assigning classrooms, policy decisions, space allocations, or any number of other activities in which associate deans are involved. Most faculty members will understand that these are important jobs and although they may not like an individual decision you make, they will respect you and appreciate you for doing the job. Others will fail to understand what you are doing and why you are doing it; some will accuse you of being power hungry and out of touch; still others will feel as though you have become the enemy who stays up late at night thinking of ways to make their lives unbearable (no, we are not making that one up).

Regardless of how any single individual reacts or interprets your action, your relationships with others will change. As an administrator you need to look at the bigger picture and consider the ramifications of your actions on the entire school rather than the benefits to a single individual or department, which is typically how we are trained to think as professors, faculty members, and even department chairs. Further, the goals of faculty and staff are different from the goals of administrators, and sometimes those goals come into conflict. For example, faculty and staff will rightfully tell you that they are "in the trenches" and really understand why additional investment of resources in their area is the obvious priority. As an administrator, however, you have to look at the needs of the entire school and make objective judgments about how and where investment of scant resources will have the biggest impact, even if the decision you make is not popular. The major difference, therefore, is that while faculty and staff see the "trees," you have to see the "forest." As a result, and if you are doing your job well, boundaries will almost inevitably get drawn by faculty and staff; individuals on the other side of that line are occasionally seen as the enemy. To be successful as an administrator in general and an associate dean in particular you must avoid the us/them mentality on your part, but you should not be surprised when it is applied to you. Suddenly, colleagues who used to praise you for your research productivity and innovation will tell you that only faculty who cannot do research go into administration. Alternatively, faculty colleagues may tell you (in all sincerity) that you do not know what it is like to be a faculty member balancing teaching and research—despite the fact that you have done that job. These statements are made despite the fact that at many universities, associate deans continue to carry on their faculty roles while also serving as administrators. This contradiction demonstrates a disconnect between faculty perceptions and the reality of life as an associate dean.

Another interesting perspective is the reaction of search committees to people applying for administrative positions. Both of us have sat on numerous search committees for high-level administrative positions in which members of the committee discounted an applicant with considerable administrative experience because they did not like the applicant's research (either the topic or level of productivity). Additionally, we have been amazed when faculty stated that anyone who actually seeks out administrative positions at the chair or associate dean level and has worked to build up the skill sets necessary for higher level administration is obviously power hungry so should not be hired. Given the job these individuals will be doing, this is an interesting perspective; logically, such a person should be an ideal candidate rather than one who is dismissed. These types of reactions are likely to be based more on distrust of administration (because of the differing goals and perspectives of faculty and administrators) and a view of administrators as having gone to the "dark side" rather than on the qualifications of the particular candidate. There is not much you can do about these attitudes while you are applying for an administrative job, but you should be aware of them and be ready to answer them both in a job interview and in your early days in the job.

To help you do this, we recommend you create a personal mission statement for the position. Now, we can hear the moaning and see the eye-rolling over the recommendation of a personal mission statement even as we say it—the cry of "How corporate!" is ringing in our ears. So given this predictable reaction, why do we still recommend it? There are a couple of reasons (and these are discussed below), but the paramount one is that a job that consists solely of reacting to the latest crisis is exhausting. So, what is a personal mission statement? We are suggesting that you think about what your role is, what your short-term and long-term goals are for the position, and how these tie directly to both the job description and the strategic plan of the school (assuming that both those elements exist). Do not just think about it; actually write it down so you have something concrete to which you can refer. One way to approach this strategy is to develop a statement that addresses both your "faculty life" and your forays into "the dark side." One strategy is to think about how these two perspectives are complementary, and we would argue that this complementarity is necessary to being an agile, compassionate, and realistic leader in higher education. When you write your statement, set goals, define your role, and define benchmarks for how you will know you are doing your job well. Understand that the longer you are in the job, the more the job will change, and so you should also periodically update your mission statement. What are the benefits of doing this? They are the same benefits the school gets from its mission statement and strategic plan. Specifically, it gives you a goal to shoot for, a path to head down. In so doing, it allows you to lead rather than manage and react to the latest crisis. It will not guarantee that crises that must be dealt with yesterday will never arise—they will. But it will allow you to put them into a broader context so that you can deal with them in a consistent manner.

On a more personal level, a clear view of your role and goals helps you figure out what skills and strengths you already have and which areas you need to develop more strongly. For example, you may have strong analytical skills and be detail oriented but may never have dealt with negotiation and conflict management. This book is about helping you explore these skills and gather tools that will allow you to do the job of associate dean more effectively—tools that you will carry on to your next administrative position. However, we do not argue that your personal mission statement will stand alone and suggest that you may wish to seek out a mentor who can help you develop the skills you currently lack in your tool kit (more about that later). Finally, you need to remember that in moving from a faculty position to an administrative one you are moving from a position of considerable autonomy where it is easy to pretend you do not have a boss, to one in which you have a direct report to a supervisor (i.e., your dean). That means periodic evaluations. If you can state what your goals were for the previous year and what you have done to accomplish them, and what your goals will be for the next year and the steps you will take to accomplish them, the evaluation process is simplified considerably.

TOOLS AND TAKEAWAYS

The take-home message here is to go into considering and possibly taking this opportunity with your eyes open to what the job will mean, good and not so good, for your career and life and whether all this is a good fit for you right now. To summarize key pieces of advice:

1. *Expect to be seen differently*. Know that when you do become an administrator your colleagues will see you differently. This occurs to varying degrees, but the general theme is that now that you are an administrator, you are no longer a "real" faculty member. This perception may impact the degree to which even close colleagues are comfortable confiding in you about things and/or the way in which your opinions, motives, and actions are interpreted by faculty. This is not necessarily something you can do anything about, but it can be surprising and disappointing when it happens if you are not anticipating it.
2. *Ask around*. If you are on the fence about taking an administrative job now or in the future, don't be shy about talking to former associate deans and deans, current associate deans, department chairs, any senior mentors you have, and, importantly, some people who have not made the leap into administration but seem like they'd be good at it. Ask them to tell you about their experiences, how they made the decision to go into administration (or not), and looking back on their decision, what they are glad they did and what they would do differently. Ask and listen in these conversations rather than telling them about your fears, worries, and uncertainties (unless the person is a really trusted friend); again, be aware that what you say may be broadcast and may come back to haunt you at some point, so be judicious in what you share and with whom.
3. *Be patient*. Remember that if an administrative position is coming your way now, others are likely to in the future. If the timing of the job in question does not meet your personal and professional goals at this point in your life, it is fine to respectfully decline and keep the door open for the future.
4. *Be clear*. If the above is true for you, consider sharing some of your professional and/or personal goals when you meet with your dean or others prior to taking an administrative job. Being able to state and stick to your goals reflects very well on you and also lets people know that you are thoughtful and deliberate about your career and your life. For example, you might tell the dean, "Although I can certainly see myself as an associate dean one of these days, it is important for me to get promoted to full professor and let my kids get a

little older before I take on the responsibilities and time commitment of that position. I hope you'll keep me in mind for future positions, and thanks again for thinking of me."

Becoming an administrator is a service job, but it is not one you are obligated to take. Take on these exciting and rewarding roles when and if they are attractive to you and fit with your life goals.

Chapter 3

Stepping Up to Leadership with Your Head and Your Heart

Congratulations! You have applied for, been offered, and decided to take on the job of associate dean. The challenge appeals to you, you feel like you have an idea of the good and not-so-good parts of the job, you have written your personal mission statement and shared it with the dean, you have assessed your skills and at least thought about who would be a good mentor even if you have not approached him or her yet, and the job fits with your personal and professional goals. In short, you feel ready. Despite all this preparation, however, there is a little voice in the back of your mind saying, "What on earth am I doing? I have no idea how to be a leader! I have never done anything like this before." It is one thing to decide to take on the challenge, but another to really step into the role, to feel confident about your abilities and doing your best, and importantly, to ask for what you need as you negotiate for the position to make sure that you have the resources and support you need both to do the job well and also to live your life as a faculty member, if necessary, and as a person with a life outside of work. This chapter deals with how to step up to leadership, both in the way you think about yourself and in what you ask for to support you in your new role. You know you can do this, but how do you step up and lead at this new level that you've never encountered before?

To get it all done, you have to lead by example, work with others to see what is possible, and together, chart a course that gets you, your colleagues, and your school to the next level. To help you do this, we want to introduce several themes here that will be reiterated throughout the book. These are things you need to think about, keep in your mind, and rethink often as the job evolves if you are to lead successfully from the middle.

ACADEMIC LEADERSHIP: AN OXYMORON?

Part of the reason it may feel intimidating to take on a substantial administrative leadership role is that the skill set that makes people good managers and leaders is pretty much contrary to what we are taught to do as faculty members and professors. It is one of the great contradictions of academic life. Specifically, as professors, we are trained from early in our graduate careers to think independently, to expect essentially to be left alone to do our teaching and research, and to work as part of a group only when it benefits us and as long as it does not detract from our "independence." When we become junior faculty members, we are told to avoid serving on committees in favor of getting our own independent grants, papers, and creative works produced. As members of an academic department, especially in tough economic times, we are part of an effort of "circling the wagons" to protect our own department's needs and goals and to try to extract all the resources possible from the school, even at the expense of another department. Finally, through training and development as a faculty member, a key aspect of our lives is that we really do not have a "boss" per se. Of course, we are beholden to our chair and the dean to do our jobs, but no one really pays attention to where we are at a certain time or how we spend our time as long as we are getting our teaching done. No one dictates what we will do or how we will do things. As one of our colleagues once put it, faculty members are "a loosely connected affiliation of free agents." Faculty members also have tendencies toward anarchy tied to a distrust of the administrative hierarchy. Being a professor affords tremendous opportunity and freedom, and the academic mindset is cultivated to expect independence, autonomy, and flexibility. Once tenured, professors have guaranteed employment as long as they continue to do their jobs reasonably well, and they cannot be terminated except for cause, dereliction of duty, or financial crisis.

Of course, all this changes the minute you become an administrator. Many experience considerable culture shock because of the change. If you are an associate dean, all of a sudden you do have a boss you have to report to on a regular basis. Your dean will tell you what you are to do, may tell you how to do it, and can redirect you to redo it or to do it another way. Frequently, you will be expected to account for your time and keep regular hours. The dean's office staff will want to know where you are during work hours. Some deans expect even more, such as availability after hours, on weekends, and on holidays (see chapter 12). Moreover, your administrative appointment is typically "at will," and you can be terminated from it at any time. Of course, you have your faculty position to fall back on, but termination is always a bit hard on the ego. These are all adjustments to a world of work that academics are not used to, but they are part and parcel of the working world outside the university.

More important, however, is the fact that many of the things you are expected to do and need to do well to be an effective leader and administrator are actually contrary to the independent, self-focused mindset of the typical faculty member. Good leaders do not think of themselves first but think of the group or the organization as the focus of their efforts. Strong academic leaders are able to facilitate discussions and help diverse and often contrary groups find common ground to reach a solution to complex problems. Effective associate deans are sometimes required to squelch their own frustrations and individual desires about outcomes in the school in favor of working to observe objectively, to analyze, to connect, and to support the decisions of other groups. These skills are typical of good managers and leaders but are neither fostered nor rewarded in the typical training we receive as students or faculty. In fact, faculty members who use these skills may be punished or their accomplishments delegitimized, as they are required to demonstrate independence to achieve tenure and promotion. In other words, the transition into a leadership position requires a change in mindset, accepting a different set of constraints on your time and independence, and being open to thinking about things in a fundamentally different way.

EMBRACING THE "SHIFT UP"

Another aspect of the change in mindset that is needed as you move into administration—and a difficult aspect of taking on a major leadership challenge for many—is the psychology of "shifting up." By this, we mean you need to think differently so you can meet the challenges that you face, have faith in your own ability, and project that confidence. To accomplish this shift, you must do several things. First, you must believe in yourself. If you do not, others will not believe in or have confidence in you and, therefore, will not follow your lead. Second, you must acknowledge the things you are nervous about in terms of your new role. It is natural to be a little leery of taking on new things; change can be hard. To be successful in administration, however, you must find a way to overcome the anxiety and move forward. One way to do this is to recognize the skills you have—what you are good at and what you like to do. Alternatively, you also need to recognize the skills you lack—what you are bad at and what you hate to do. Chances are your job as associate dean will require that you tackle at least some of the things that you think you are bad at or hate, so figuring out what skills you need to develop is an important step. Third, be proud and confident in yourself, but do not be arrogant. Arrogance really annoys people and guarantees that you will have difficulty building consensus.

What do you have to do to make the shift up? This is where the "head and heart" part comes in. Although this may feel like the busiest time of your life, it is more important now than ever to get your head and heart in alignment as much as possible to prepare yourself for the challenges and successes ahead. In addition to the attitudinal issues mentioned above, you also have to figure out a few things about yourself. In our experience, regardless of the particular issue, there are four actions you have to take and decisions you have to make constantly.

The first thing you need to do is to "know your own center." Okay, we hear the groans about spewing pop psychology even as we say this, but hear us out. Chances are, you have been in academia long enough to know a few things about yourself, your school, and your university, including the good, the bad, and the ugly. Stop and think about these, because how you define them will affect how others react to you, and thus, how you do your job. Specifically, think about what your core values are and what is totally nonnegotiable. For many of the issues you will face, you will have to ask yourself, "Is this the hill I am willing to die on?" as a leader. In other words, what are you willing to expend your political capital on and what are you willing to compromise on? This is important because political capital is a finite resource, and if you never compromise (thus rebuilding your store of capital) you will quickly run out of it. Frequently, our "hills" revolve around protecting what we see as vulnerable populations or the reputation of our unit. The hills you are willing to die on may be different from those of others in your office, school, and university, because they define who is vulnerable and what affects the unit's reputation differently. So you need to know what your values are and act accordingly. These are the things you find yourself thinking about in terms of black and white or right and wrong with little middle ground. Other issues may be important to you, but you tend to think of them more in terms of shades of gray. For things that you decide are in that gray category and thus are negotiable, you should work toward compromise with others.

Second, you need to think about the things that make you angry or emotional in the workplace and become very conscious of them. What are your buttons that others may push, to which you are likely to have an immediate and negative reaction? It is never a good idea to make a decision or deal with a difficult situation when you are truly angry. Take the time to listen to your body and mind, and if you feel your emotions heating up, take a break and delay the discussion or decision until you are 100 percent calm. Despite what people will try to tell you, there is almost never a "must do right now" issue. Virtually everything can wait at least half an hour. A good stalling line you might use to buy you that half hour is "let me look into that and get back to you." This lets everyone know you are not blowing them off but also gives you time to cool down, reflect, and possibly research the situation.

Third, although you will have a personal mission for the job and goals in mind, be open to talking about these with the dean and modifying and/or changing their priority to match the dean's strategic vision. Additionally, be willing to work with a team to secure both the school's and your own goals. Remember, there are numerous ways to go about creating change in your organization, but in order for the change to be well received and supported in the long run, you as a leader need to engage in a collective process. The staff and faculty with whom you work on initiatives need to feel valued and should be encouraged to share their ideas, concerns, and analyses of the issue to implement new ideas. If you go it alone, you may stall out alone. Conversely, by engaging and encouraging others on your team to help in the creative process of problem solving, you will tap into a productive atmosphere and expand the possibilities.

To make this process work for you, you have to develop the ability to be open to the outcome of such group sessions and not be attached to a specific strategy. That is not to say, however, that you should not be committed to achieving the ultimate goal. As a leader, you can state the goal, throw out some ideas you have, and then honestly open the conversation up to your team(s) on a course of action. They may come up with a better solution. You should direct them a bit, but if they are going to buy in and help you get where you want to go as a leader, they have to feel they are part of the process.

Fourth, know what resources (time, money, personnel) you need to accomplish the job and the goals you have, as well as the goals the dean has set for you, while still maintaining balance with your faculty role and personal life. These resources will not be the same for everyone and need to be negotiated when you start the job. For example, do you need to set time aside to be away from the dean's office for teaching or research? Do you need a set schedule in the office or a flexible schedule that allows you to telecommute? Do you need staff support? Do you need an operating budget that is solely under your control? Some of this you will have negotiated before you took the position of associate dean. However, the longer you are an associate dean the more likely it is that new projects and responsibilities will be added to your plate. When you are asked to take on a new project, make sure you know what conditions and resources you need to accomplish the job and on which you can compromise. When you figure out what it is you need, ask for it, and be prepared to negotiate. If there is something you really must have (for example, being able to leave at 3:00 when necessary to pick up your kids from school), hold firm and explain that you cannot accomplish the goals the dean has set out without them. In doing so, however, be prepared to let go of "nice to have" things that you can, in reality, do without.

POSITIVE CHANGES AND YOUR ROLE IN THEM

So far we have talked about the things you should think about before or at least soon after accepting the associate dean job and the things you should ask for to make you successful. Much of the rest of this book is centered on problems that may arise during your tenure as an associate dean with which you will have to deal. After all, you do not need advice when everything is going well. We do not want to leave you with the impression that the job is nothing but crisis management, however. You will have many wonderful experiences in this position: you will help students in need find resources that will allow them to stay in school, you will develop successful new programs, you will help faculty find funding for new and innovative research, and you will craft policies that allow you and your school to flourish. We want you to celebrate these accomplishments. Your school and university are better for your role and the people you help are truly grateful. This section is about some of these rewarding experiences, the positive impact you can have on the individuals you help, and how you can make them happen. This help frequently comes in the form of mentoring (both formal and informal) or facilitating conversations. You have undoubtedly served as a mentor in your academic field to students and younger colleagues. In your new role as associate dean, you will be asked to serve as a mentor in additional areas as well. The following case study is an example.

Various faculty members in a number of different departments in the College of Mathematics and Science have been meeting informally with each other and with faculty in the College of Education for some time to talk about mathematics and science education at the university level over coffee, lunch, and in other informal venues. The faculty members in the College of Mathematics and Science are interested not only in providing the best possible mathematics and science education for their undergraduate students, but also in preparing their PhD students to teach in university settings. Additionally, they share research interest regarding pedagogy with their colleagues in the School of Education. Although these conversations are interesting philosophical exercises, they have

> not progressed much beyond this point. The faculty members involved very much want to formalize these relationships by working on curriculum issues together as well as applying for grants to produce research papers on these topics. Unfortunately, they cannot seem to move beyond the philosophical stage. Enter Associate Dean Facilitator. Even though Associate Dean Facilitator has not been part of these discussions and does not do pedagogy-based research, he has a remarkable impact. Within a year of Associate Dean Facilitator's participation with the faculty members in the two schools, three grant proposals have been submitted and new assessment programs have been implemented that have resulted in new classes as well as changes in the way existing classes are taught. Moreover, several papers are being developed for publication, and an air of excitement permeates both colleges.

What has Associate Dean Facilitator added to the equation that was missing before? How can the addition of an associate dean to the equation bring about these positive results in such a short period? As an associate dean, you will often find yourself in the position to be a catalyst for this type of positive change; it is what most of us hope to do when we come into the job. The suggestions we offer below may help you in this process.

We do not think we are overstating the case when we say that most academics are not the most organized people in the world. In many cases, that is really the understatement of the year. The stereotype of the absent-minded professor exists for a reason. Academics may be enthusiastic and dedicated to the idea of interdisciplinary collaboration (as in the example above), and they may be very good at organizing their own particular research projects, but when it comes to getting a group of people together and moving into new areas they are often challenged. An associate dean can have a tremendous impact just by getting everyone in the same room and talking. We are *not* saying that as an associate dean you need to become responsible for managing other people's schedules or helping them get organized or that you should, for example, change your research to a topic you are not interested in just to make a collaboration or new project move forward. Rather, we are saying that with a minimal investment of time and organizing skills, an associate dean can get the ball rolling to get the right people together in the same room at once and can broker a conversation that gets people to hear others' perspectives and find common points of interest. Think of it as mentoring on the group level.

At the first meeting Associate Dean Facilitator simply called people together in the same place and at same time to talk about interests and activities. The agenda item for this meeting was brainstorming of projects to find areas of common interest. He encouraged everyone to talk, wrote the ideas on the board, and grouped common themes together. You would be amazed at the visual impact that resulted from having all the ideas up on the board for everyone to see. Once everyone saw all the ideas and possibilities and knew the range of interests (as well as the overlap in interests), groups of people began to naturally sort themselves out and began conversations among themselves. To maintain the momentum, Associate Dean Facilitator ended the meeting by talking about next steps. He asked the people associated with each idea or group of ideas what they would like to do with their common interest: work on a grant proposal or a curriculum proposal, write an article, and so on. His assistant then made a list of the topics mentioned and who would work on each. This list was sent out to the group via e-mail after the meeting to reaffirm the direction they were heading. About two weeks later, Associate Dean Facilitator checked in with each group to see how they were doing, and he did so again in another two weeks. Some ideas died on the vine and others took off. This vignette demonstrates that frequently faculty members simply need someone to help get them together, get them organized, and nudge them periodically for ideas to take off. With relatively little effort on the part of Associate Dean Facilitator (a little group mentoring about organization and facilitating some meetings), a major change occurred in the interaction between the faculty members of the School of Mathematics and Science and the School of Education, and a slew of new initiatives were launched.

In addition to the type of group mentoring noted above, associate deans frequently are asked to mentor a variety of individuals on a personal level. Minimally, associate deans concerned with faculty affairs are expected to monitor the progression toward tenure of the junior faculty. If this is part of your job, you can consider it an exercise in bookkeeping, where you check off each step as a faculty member goes through it, or you can reach out and be more active. In other words, you can shift from monitor to mentor. We realize that the majority of the mentoring of junior faculty occurs at the departmental level, where research and teaching expertise related to the specific fields exists. That being said, do not forget that you are now a senior member of the faculty and part of the administrative hierarchy. That means you have considerable expertise in how your individual school works as well as how your university works. You have been through the tenure process yourself and have likely evaluated tenure dossiers both within your home department and at higher levels of evaluation. You know what individuals need to do and what needs to be in a dossier, even if the junior faculty member is in a different academic field. Also, remember that most junior faculty are at least somewhat nervous (and others are downright paranoid) about the tenure process. Simply checking in once a semester for the first several years with a new faculty member to ask how things are going and if he or she has any problems lets the faculty know the dean's office cares about them and their careers. It has the added benefit of aiding in faculty retention. Consider holding workshops to explain the mystery of the tenure process or the elements of a good dossier for the junior faculty. You can have a positive impact on a young scholar's career by simply sharing your institutional experience and knowledge.

Your mentoring activities will almost certainly not be restricted to junior faculty. Not long after taking on the job of associate dean you will find the department/division heads seeking you out for advice, first on policy issues and then eventually on how to deal with difficult personalities or sticky problems within the department. This is a testament to the trust and respect they have for you, even if no one says it. It is important to take these conversations seriously. If issues can be solved early on, many of the situations we talk about later in this book will not arise. These conversations may start out as a gathering of information or fact checking on a policy, but they can easily evolve into a mentoring relationship over administrative issues.

As you are in your job longer and become better known within your university, regionally, and even nationally, requests for administrative mentoring will become more explicit and extend beyond your school. Individuals will call and ask you to join them for a cup of coffee to get your take on an issue or ask your advice. In taking on the role of mentoring for a senior faculty member, staff member, or administrator, you need to remember that mentoring of someone in a senior role is very different from mentoring a junior faculty member working toward tenure. To start with, senior people already know a great deal, so do not start with the basics or you will sound patronizing. Second, the individuals talking to you are generally your peers rather than people you oversee in some way, and you need to interact with them accordingly. Indeed, one of the benefits of peer mentoring is that the relationship can easily be reciprocal; you can ask them for advice or talk through an issue as well. Third, senior faculty members (even if they are new to administration) generally contact different individuals for different kinds of advice, resulting in a far-flung mentoring network. This is a good thing because it brings in a broader perspective. It also means that sometimes your advice may not be the advice they follow. You need to remind yourself that when this happens it is not because they do not value your opinion. If this were true they would not have talked to you in the first place. Rather, everyone is different and different solutions work for different people. Remember, your goal in mentoring is *not* to re-create yourself but rather to help individuals achieve their own goals even if these goals are something you would never strive for yourself. Remember to celebrate their successes with them and congratulate them, even if the solution they chose was not the one you offered.

KEEPING YOUR CHIN UP AND NOT WRITING THE RESIGNATION LETTER

Now that you are an associate dean with a bit of experience under your belt, you have a clear view of your role and the skills you need to improve to accomplish your goals. Aside from reading this book, how do you get these skills? And how do you survive the times when crises arise that you must deal with while maintaining an optimistic view of your job and your university (and occasionally the world at large)? In other words, how do you keep your chin up and avoid the overwhelming desire to chuck it all and resign from the position when times get hard? These moments are more common when you are new to the job (and wondering what you've gotten yourself into) and tend to occur even more frequently when you are charged with breaking in a new dean who's been neither a dean nor an associate dean prior to becoming your dean. Again, this can be a great experience in which you learn how to work with someone new. Undoubtedly, you will learn a lot from your new dean, but there will be moments that will, to put it mildly, try your patience. Given all this, what can you do to support yourself and not lose your cool?

It is crucial to find someone you can vent to when you get very frustrated, even if it is only your dog on your evening walk. Rather than your dog, though, we actually recommend you find someone who will listen when you need to vent but will not attempt to solve the problem for you, as well as individuals who will help you problem-solve and do a reality check when you need some help. In other words, find a good mentor for yourself. You may think that mentors are just for junior faculty and once you receive tenure and are promoted to full professor that you should switch from the role of mentee to mentor. At some level, this is true, and you will serve as a mentor in your position of associate dean. But you need to remember that you yourself are heading into new and uncharted waters in terms of administration. We would argue that mentors are good at any point in your career, although you need them for different reasons when you are senior than when you are starting out. As you become more established, you tend to switch from mentors who are senior to you to those who are your peers. The fact is that there are times in any job when you will be bombarded by people unhappy with a decision you have made or actions you have taken, as well as times when you question your own skills and abilities. Additionally, there will be times when you just do not know how to handle a situation and you will need to talk it through with someone. Going back to your personal mission statement and having someone to talk with about these situations will help you make it through the tough times and avoid writing that resignation letter.

A mentor can be anyone with whom you are comfortable talking who can give you insights on the issues you are facing. Common people to tap into include other associate deans (either in your own school or in another school on your campus), your dean, individuals who were in your position previously, or other individuals in administrative positions (at your own university or at other universities). If you work through the issue rather than resigning, you will learn something new about yourself, your school, and your university—and what is better than being paid to learn something new?

In addition to finding a mentor, we recommend that you take time to learn who the players are, what the policies are and who knows them, and what political dynamics shape interactions in your school. You may already know some of this information, but chances are you actually only know part of the system, even if you have had other leadership positions, simply because you have not dealt with all the issues you will deal with in this job. Interestingly, many in your school and the university will assume you have perfect knowledge the second you walk in the door. It is okay to indicate that you will research the problem and get back to people once you have all the information you need. The caveat here is to make sure you do get back to them, even if it is just to say that you are still looking into the problem.

You also need to take time to understand the dean's office structure and the staff. You may feel you know this because you have been in the school for a considerable length of time. In reality, however, large portions of the dean's office operate invisibly to the faculty. Things just get done, and most faculty members never stop to consider who did what and how hard they work to make things happen. Do not discount the staff both in the dean's office and throughout the school. They are often unrecognized but in many ways, they are the ones who keep the operation going on a day-to-day basis.

Finally, much of the work you do will be behind the scenes, which means you will live most of your life as an associate dean as an unsung hero. When you are in the position of having to enforce policy or to intercede when someone is behaving badly, you may be vilified. In other words, it is important to remember Stephen Trachtenberg's advice in the *Chronicle of Higher Education* on retiring from the administration: "Do not expect gratitude. If you receive it, you are blessed to be working with exceptionally good and humane colleagues" (2007, 59). Although you should not expect gratitude, you should always express gratitude to those who help you in your job, especially staff who are frequently ignored and rarely thanked. You will be amazed how much you will be appreciated and how much people will be willing to help you in return for this small courtesy.

So you will be glad you took the job if you want to affect the direction of the school and affect a larger group than just your department. Remember that as associate dean, people will be upset with you occasionally, you must work collaboratively rather than in an independent setting, and you can expect interruptions and frequent changes in direction. Additionally, you must tell your dean what you think but be willing to enforce the policy or goal the dean chooses, even if it is not the one you suggested. If you can't accept these facts of life, you will be miserable in the job and probably ineffective. If you can accept them, we believe you will find leading from the middle as rewarding as we do.

TOOLS AND TAKEAWAYS

There will be days when you are really glad you took this job and other days when you'll wonder what on earth you were thinking. Remembering a few things will help you make the most of both kinds of days and help you get as much as you can out of your experience as an associate dean.

1. *Expect a learning curve.* Remember that the skill set that made you an effective faculty member is not necessarily the same skill set that will make you a successful administrator. You'll need to consciously shift from being independent and perhaps a bit competitive to being collaborative and willing to let others take credit for things.
2. *Embrace your inner leader.* Have confidence in your ability to do this job and remember that you were selected for this position because you are capable and people respect your abilities. If you want people to think of you as a leader, you must think of yourself that way first and have your words and actions reflect your confidence.
3. *Know you are helping.* Even though it may seem thankless and things may not always go as you hope or plan, know that the work you are doing with your colleagues is making positive changes in the institution. Be prepared to help see changes happen but to let others take credit for the outcome. You are a facilitator who empowers others to create the future they want.
4. *Take a deep breath.* On the days when you feel like writing your resignation letter, step back and remember the big picture of why you wanted this job and what you are getting out of it. Find and use a good mentor who can serve as a sounding board and who can help you find an outlet for frustration. Also remind yourself that the job is not forever, and that you can do anything for a relatively short period of time, so meet your obligations and make the best of even the bad days—they may be some of the best opportunities for growth you'll have

Chapter 4

Working with the Realities of Your Dean's Leadership and Management Style

> God, give me the patience to accept the things I cannot change, the courage to change the things I can, and the wisdom to know the difference.
>
> —The Serenity Prayer

Expectations are not unreasonable things to have when taking on your position as an associate dean, but they are likely to be somewhat altered by the day-to-day realities of the job. For example, an understandable expectation that many of us have when coming into the dean's office is that we will have the opportunity to observe and learn from an effective leader—our dean. We expect that we will work for someone who has vision, is strategic, has clear priorities, has a well-defined and empowering management style, and is fair, equitable, and transparent in decision making. We look forward to being part of a dean's office that is characterized by clarity of priorities and process, and working for a dean who values us as partners in the growth of the school and as trusted colleagues in navigating the slings and arrows of budget cuts; unspeakable acts of stupidity by faculty, staff, and students; and the whims of the upper administration and governing board. We enter the dean's office with expectations that our job will be hard and sometimes unpredictable, but that on the whole the job will be gratifying, satisfying, and rewarding, and that despite the hardships we may face, we will be working with a respectful and respected dean who values our efforts and hard work. We expect, not unreasonably, that we will be on the same page as our dean, and that our dean will say what he or she means and mean what he or she says. We expect that, when tasked with a job, we will be empowered to do the job without interference. We expect reliability, leadership, honesty, and responsibility from our dean. We expect that our dean's goals will be defined, his or her vision will be clear or at least clearly evolving, and that our hard work, even in the face of changing pressures and perhaps external forces, will be appreciated and rewarded.

It is wonderful to have such expectations, and happily, most days and encounters with your dean will live up to these expectations in large measure. Also, we know when entering the associate dean role that sometimes our expectations may need to be shifted to meet new and unexpected demands imposed by changing institutional priorities. What happens, though, when these expectations are not met due to shortcomings or quirks in the dean's leadership or management style? This chapter starts with the Serenity Prayer as a nod to the fact that once the reality of working with your dean sets in, you will sometimes have to accept inconsistencies of management and leadership that may challenge your expectations of the job. Making adjustments in your own expectations and in the way you engage with your dean and approach your tasks can make the difference between a reasonably productive, albeit challenging, time as an associate dean and an exercise in frustration.

LEADERSHIP VERSUS MANAGEMENT

Many of us come into our first administrative experiences thinking of leadership and management as synonymous, or at least tightly coupled, in the academic context. Good managers have people who are willing to follow and work with them, which makes them leaders, right? The fact is, however, that management and leadership are not the same, and it is the rare person who is good at both at the same time. Learning to distinguish between these two concepts and sets of capabilities will be critical for you both in managing yourself as an associate dean and in working effectively with your dean.

A key feature of managers is the fact that they have and claim authority based on the role they play. They are charged with certain responsibilities and are required to carry them out, and they evaluate the people they supervise with regard to how well they perform tasks. Managers are given marching orders by others in many cases, and they work to realize the goals set by an organization rather than setting goals themselves. In other words, managers are primarily tactical in their approach; they have a job to do, and they work with others to get the pieces of the job done to deal with short-term problems and issues. Further, a good manager is someone who can effectively organize people to accomplish tasks on a day-to-day basis, hold those people accountable for their work, and provide them with positive and, when necessary, negative feedback to influence future performance. Management is a skill set that is greatly needed in schools and universities, and it is important especially in the fast-paced environments in which most of us work and live. Being able to organize people to accomplish tasks can be a great asset. Unfortunately, however, most individuals cannot operate without a leader with a vision and the ability to set the goals of the unit.

Leaders are more strategically focused than managers. Rather than merely implementing the wishes of others, they set the goals for the organization and have the personality, vision, and confidence to inspire and motivate the people who work for them. Good leaders are skilled in reading and understanding what motivates others as well as in seeing the "forest" rather than just the "trees" of a situation. They are able to bring people together to set strategic goals and priorities, establish a path to those goals, and embark on the path with them. Although a manager has authority based on his or her role, a leader's authority is innate and influences how he or she approaches situations. Leaders also are focused on change, and they are able to see that empowerment of the people who work for them through clarity of priorities and process is critical for long-term personal and organizational success. In other words, leaders set the path for the next five to ten years, and managers ensure efficient day-to-day running of the operation. A catchy statement to help you remember the distinction between leadership and management is "Leadership is doing the right thing, and management is doing things right." Leadership and management ideally go hand-in-hand; great leaders who lack management skills are limited in their ability to succeed, just as managers without leadership qualities are hamstrung in their progress. Ideally, your dean will be a good manager *and* a good leader, able to manage and delegate day-to-day tasks and deliver results, while at the same time able to plan for change and think strategically about the big picture. It is the rare person for whom both leadership and management come easily and at the same time, and there lies the rub.

GETTING REAL ABOUT YOUR DEAN

The primary factor that will determine your ability to weather the small and large storms that come along with the job is how well you can work with your dean's strengths and challenges as a leader and manager. This involves not only knowing what your dean's priorities are, but also knowing his or her leadership management style—for better or worse.

The character, goals, habits, and expectations of your dean essentially determine whether your time as an associate dean will be a period of great growth and learning mixed with a relatively smaller amount of inevitable frustration, or a period of great frustration mixed with a relatively smaller amount of growth and learning. The vast majority of deans create the atmosphere of the former, but occasionally, due to the dean's actions, we experience the latter. To illustrate this point, consider this case study.

> Associate Dean Smith is asked by Dean Jones to convene a committee of faculty members to review a set of grant proposals submitted by faculty for research seed money. Smith and Jones have been working together for less than a year, and this is a new grant program in the college that Jones asked Smith to develop and spearhead. Dean Jones indicates that the priority is to "be tough" in the reviews and only fund the proposals that are really strong in the committee's view. Dean Jones expresses her commitment to quality and rigor, and she tells Associate Dean Smith that she is in charge of the whole review and reward process. Associate Dean Smith takes Dean Jones at her word, spends a great deal of time developing the grant announcement and publicizing it, and finally, forms the review committee. Associate Dean Smith and the committee spend many hours carefully reviewing the applications, ranking them, and meeting to discuss the merits of the various proposals. In fact, Associate Dean Smith spends so much time organizing this process that she has to put off a writing project from some recent research. Dean Jones unexpectedly decides to attend the committee's final meeting at which they are going to make decisions about which grants to fund, and Associate Dean Smith looks forward to the dean seeing how seriously she and the committee have taken Dean Jones's charge and the results of their hard work. The meeting convenes and the committee makes its decisions about the proposals. Dean Jones then chimes in and indicates that she had read all the proposals and is not going to fund three of the proposals ranked highest by the committee. Rather, she intends to fund three other grants, two of which were from members of her home department and are not supported by any members of the committee. Dean Jones then leaves the meeting. As they are packing up, the committee expresses its frustration with the process and blames Associate Dean Smith for wasting their time. Associate Dean Smith feels frustrated that a process she allowed to supplant her research plans ended in this way. Further, she feels foolish and micromanaged, having been publicly countermanded by the dean and having been the architect of a process she put in place in good faith that ended up wasting her colleagues' time.

What were Associate Dean Smith's expectations going into this situation? What has she learned about herself and her dean through this interaction? Could she have gathered information regarding the dean's preference prior to this episode to avoid this outcome? Smith understandably initially felt empowered by Jones to create and run this new grant process, and she expected her hard work and that of her faculty colleagues to be viewed in a manner consistent with the message Jones verbally expressed to her about her goals for the process. Smith took Jones at her word that quality, equity, and fairness were of fundamental importance to her in this grant competition. Given that Jones had indicated that these were really important to her, Smith expected that she would act in a manner which supported what she had said. Jones, on the other hand, acted in almost exact opposition to what she had originally stated to Smith, making Smith feel undermined, unsupported, and foolish. Clearly, Dean Jones has a tendency to favor her own department in her decision making, and despite the instructions she gave to Associate Dean Smith, she wishes to retain a high level of control over decision making in the dean's office, at least in the area of faculty grant fund distribution.

One important component that Smith must consider is the degree to which this was a simple leadership failure as opposed to the unlikely possibility that it was an intentional power play on Jones's part; either is possible, and understanding which situation is occurring is essential. In the case study above, Dean Jones clearly and blatantly favored her own department. In other cases, a dean may not even be aware that his or her behavior is or could be perceived as biased, although it may not be intentional. In such cases a dean may honestly believe that a choice is just and correct, even though from the outside, it appears arbitrary and unfounded in principle or process. Either reason for bias is bad, admittedly, but being able to tell one from the other is important, as it helps distinguish between well-intentioned but biased decision making and calculated favoritism. In the end, Smith is now a sadder but wiser associate dean, who in the future will anticipate micromanagement and bias on some issues and take action to mitigate these behaviors. Given that they had been working together for less than a year prior to this incident, Associate Dean Smith might not have been able to predict the outcome; we all get blindsided on occasion. Through careful observation and gathering information about Dean Jones's priorities, biases, and management style from the start, however, Associate Dean Smith might have detected tendencies in Dean Jones's behavior that would have helped prevent or at least mitigated the outcome.

For Associate Dean Smith and for all of us in the associate dean role, the style and behavior of the dean has a major impact on the quality, or lack thereof, of the associate dean experience. Accumulating and applying knowledge about your dean, setting some "soft" goals of your own for the job, and getting clarity on your personal boundaries and professional aspirations is essential to making your time as an associate dean what you want it to be for your own career. The key is finding a way to reconcile these things. At the core of your challenge are the sentiments laid out in the Serenity Prayer. This chapter addresses each of these key aspects of working with your dean and discusses how to integrate them to increase your effectiveness as an associate dean and meet your own goals.

ACCUMULATING AND APPLYING KNOWLEDGE ABOUT YOUR DEAN

To work with your dean successfully, you need information about your dean in four areas: expectations, priorities, possible biases, and management style. The "expectations" and "priorities" aspects feed into the leadership profile of your dean, and the interplay between these and "biases" and "management style" can do a great deal to help you navigate the waters ahead. Knowledge in these areas is best obtained from direct conversation, but in reality, a combination of discussions about these areas and careful observation will provide what you need. It is important for your dean to know that you want to understand all these aspects of how he or she operates in order to ensure that you are able to be effective in your associate dean role. Although it may feel awkward, consider setting up an appointment with your dean when you come into the associate dean role or when you get a new dean to have a conversation about these issues and to ask questions regarding them. Beyond that, be a keen observer and look for additional pieces of information as you interact with your dean and as he or she works with others in and beyond the college.

Expectations

Whether you are a new associate dean or in an associate dean position when a new dean comes on board, it is essential to get a clear vision of your dean and of his or her expectations for you in your associate dean role and in your role as a faculty member. There are a few things that will affect the direction of this discussion, including what sort of appointment you have and the degree to which you are still engaged in faculty activities. If your appointment as an associate dean is a 100 percent administrative one, the discussion is simpler: your sole responsibility will be to the dean's office and to your associate dean work, and there should be no expectations for teaching or scholarship for annual merit reviews and evaluation.

Most likely, however, your appointment as an associate dean will be for some percentage of your time and effort, with the remainder being devoted to faculty work. In this case, it is critical to make sure of a few things. For example, if your appointment is 50 percent in the dean's office and 50 percent faculty, it is important to discuss with your dean and your department chair how you will be evaluated for merit and salary adjustments each year. Related to this is the importance of discussing with your dean his or her expectations for how your time will be spent. Clearly, if your associate dean position is 50 percent time, you will be expected to spend half of your workweek (theoretically, a forty-hour week) doing associate dean work and the remainder doing faculty work including teaching, research, and working with students. How will this time be partitioned? The fact is that for many associate deans, the position is essentially a full-time one regardless of how contracts are written, and the responsibilities of the position tend to expand to fill all the available (and unavailable, for that matter) time. If you are expected to continue doing faculty work, discuss with your dean when you will be doing associate dean work and when you will be doing faculty work. Ideally, you will be able to block periods of time during the "forty-hour week" that correspond to the relative percentages for associate dean and faculty work. Put these blocks of time on your calendar as appointments, and honor them. It may work well to partition a day or a couple of afternoons each week, for example, for research and teaching work, and then diligently protect those blocks of time from the tasks of your associate dean position. If others have the ability to put appointments on your calendar and frequently invade time marked *research*, try putting the name of an individual important in the history of your field on the calendar instead. Others will be less willing to overschedule your time if they see you are dealing with something or someone specific.

The key to this arrangement is that your dean and others in your office respect these blocks of time as equally important to your work as associate dean time. Discuss the arrangement of your schedule with your dean as you are planning your schedule to make sure that what you plan works for him or her; be flexible as to the days and time blocks allotted. Try to get a commitment from your dean to support you in holding your faculty time harmless. Of course, sometimes there will be a bona fide crisis that will require you to give up some of this precious time. Decide in advance what circumstances will dictate giving up your allotted time. Will you only do it when your dean asks you to give up the time, or will there be other circumstances that you will allow to impinge on these times? Of course, it is important to remain flexible and responsive, but do not be quick to give up your faculty time. If you have faculty responsibilities, you will need to be very protective of this time and not allow it to be usurped without a really good reason.

Priorities

What is at the top of the "to do" list for your dean, formally and informally? You have numerous tasks on your plate, but everything you do as an associate dean should support your dean's priorities. Formal priorities, for the purpose of this discussion, are those that everybody knows or should know about, that are the focus of much faculty and staff energy and effort. Commonly, these will be things like "increase grant funding" or "foster diversity in our curriculum." Some of these formal priorities may be written down in a strategic plan at the school level or set out by the upper administration. Have a conversation with your dean about which of these "hard targets" he or she wants to tackle first, and in what order attention should be directed toward each one. If there is a strategic plan in place when your dean comes in or when you come into the dean's office, explicitly ask your dean which parts are at the top of his or her list. Although the university may list several things that are strategic initiatives, different schools and deans will, due to the strengths of their units, emphasize things in a different order.

A key piece here is getting a sense from your dean about what will be his or her approach to setting formal strategic priorities for your tasks and for the school. This is a place where seams in the leadership veil may become clearer; the tactical demands of the job may make it difficult for your dean to clearly articulate or develop strategic goals that will be a hallmark of his or her time as the leader of the college. Although this is frustrating, understanding the difference between leadership and management, especially for new deans, can be very helpful in finding ways to work with your dean and getting your dean to a place of focusing on long-term priorities for his or her administration.

Knowing about your dean's informal priorities may be even more important, frankly, than the formal ones. Informal priorities are often not written down, but are overarching principles and philosophies that flavor all of the dean's actions and decisions and should also affect how you handle situations, including working toward the formal priorities. Informal priorities may be things like "foster accountability in faculty evaluations," "hold chairs accountable for making sure faculty meet service responsibilities," or "create a culture that supports non-tenure-track faculty as well as tenure-track faculty." Again, ask your dean about these more nebulous, but very important, parts of his or her vision. In addition to asking these questions, pay attention to the topics your dean brings up independently. Are certain themes common in schoolwide faculty meetings or in the dean's communication with department chairs? Are other initiatives discussed only when someone other than your dean asks about them?

Possible Biases

This issue is awkward but very important. In the case study above, Dean Jones clearly was biased in favor of her home department. This is not something Associate Dean Smith could have learned in a conversation.

No dean is going to come right out and say, "I know I'm supposed to treat all my departments equally, but my home department is more deserving of support than the others, so I'll always put them first." Alternatively, your dean may think a particular kind of research or creative activity is more valuable than another or one form of delivery method is preferred to another in terms of classroom instruction. In an ideal world, your dean would not have any biases that affect his or her decision making, but we are all human and bias is frequently present due to our backgrounds and frames of references. In some cases these biases are blatant (as in our case study) and in others they are much more subtle. In either case, it is important to keep your eyes and ears open for possible biases in your dean and plan accordingly so that you can either point these out or circumvent them and thus minimize their impact on your work as an associate dean and as an effective member of your dean's team.

Careful observation is generally the best way to sniff out possible biases in your dean—and in others, for that matter (Davis 2003). For example, when you are in a situation in which you are discussing the strengths and weaknesses of various units in the school, does your dean de-emphasize the shortcomings of some departments and exaggerate the strong points of others? Do funding or hiring decisions favor some units and faculty over others for no clear reason? Are low-enrolling classes rarely cancelled in some programs while courses in other areas are cancelled for similar enrollment shortfalls? These and other types of clues may suggest bias in your dean that may affect decision making and create unexpected challenges in your work as an associate dean.

Management Style

Learning your dean's management style is critical to developing an effective working relationship. Although you can ask your dean to describe his or her management style, everyone's response in such situations is going to be something like "I am a collaborative leader. Consensus building is critical for me, and I work hard to make sure that communication lines are open and decisions are made in a cooperative manner." No one in his or her right mind would answer that question with "Well, first I tell everyone that I really care about their views and opinions, ask them to do a bunch of work and come to several meeting to discuss views and suggest some possible strategies and actions, and then I completely ignore all of their input and do whatever I feel like" or "I do not trust anyone else to do things right so I'll be micromanaging you to within an inch of your life." The best way to learn your dean's preferred management style is through observation and interaction. The ways in which your dean speaks, interacts, plans, and makes decisions with you and others are the best indicators of his or her preferred management style. For example, does your dean react first and get the facts later, or is he or she slow to react, collecting information before rendering a decision? Does your dean tell you what he or she is doing or thinking along the way (i.e., think out loud) or hold this information closely until after he or she has made a decision? Does your dean love a crisis or make provocative statements? Does he or she like to chit-chat and want to connect on a personal level, or does your dean keep it strictly business?

Although there are numerous books and "systems" characterizing management styles in the corporate world, there are two basic types of management styles that seem to be most common in higher education (Bryant 2005; Buller 2007).

1. *Democratic*. This is the style virtually all leaders in higher education claim to use, as it honors the academic tradition favored by faculty of gathering data, discussing it, considering options, and then collectively making a decision. In this situation, the dean's style emphasizes facilitation and management; he or she empowers those under him or her to "own" the decisions and agrees to accept the decisions made through this process. There is extensive communication in both directions in the organization (top down and bottom up), and an environment is created in which subordinates (associate deans included) feel ownership for the decisions that are made and thus responsibility for following through on them.
2. *Authoritarian*. In contrast to the democratic leader, the authoritarian manager makes all the decisions by himself or herself or, at most, keeps the information and decision making among the senior management, such as the dean and associate deans. In the higher education model, this shuts out the role of faculty and departments in favor of an entirely top-down communication approach. As a result, the dean and sometimes, by extension, the associate deans are viewed as either dictators or micromanagers. Clearly, this model can create frustration and a lack of investment among subordinates, but it does ensure that there is a great deal of consistency in the decisions that are made. Few authoritarian managers admit that this is their style, engaging in the appearance of democratic process, but in the end, making the decision centrally. The results of this chain of events are evident in the case study above.

Once you know your dean's preferred leadership style, what do you do? Clearly, working with a democratic dean will be a more rewarding experience in many ways, as it provides an opportunity for real discourse and exchange of ideas; you and your colleagues will have ownership of the decisions that are made, although the process of making the decisions will take longer. Working for an authoritarian dean can be incredibly frustrating, especially if the dean believes that he or she is democratic but in reality is not. Figuring this out can save you and your colleagues a great deal of time and energy. Key to this process is determining issues over which you have complete control versus things over which you have no control or only partial control (Chambers 2004). You should always attempt to place your greatest effort in areas of total or partial control—that is, put the words of the Serenity Prayer into action. For example, had Associate Dean Smith known that Dean Jones was, in fact, an authoritarian dean, she still could have engaged the faculty review committee but have greatly limited the amount of time and energy she required them to put into the process. She could also have framed the committee as "advisory" to the dean, and indicated that Dean Jones would be making the final decisions on funding. The upside of working for an authoritarian dean is that decisions tend to be made quickly and with a degree of predictability that may not occur with a more democratic process.

Back to Associate Dean Smith and Dean Jones

So what could Associate Dean Smith have observed, asked, and learned about Dean Jones that could have prevented the mess she ended up with? The two had been working together for a year, in which time Associate Dean Smith could very likely have surmised that there might be issues with bias and a tendency toward authoritarian leadership. These pieces of information could have given her the chance to approach the task of the grant reviews differently so that she could meet the goals set out for her by Dean Jones, but also protect herself and her faculty from wasting time and energy and garnering ill will from them. In summary, collecting information, obvious and not-so-obvious, about your dean's spoken and unspoken priorities and style provides a backdrop in front of which you must accomplish your work as an associate dean; do not forget that the backdrop can change the way things look and are perceived, for better or worse.

AM I TALKING TO MYSELF HERE?

Regardless of what you figure out about your dean's expectations, priorities, biases, and management style, and no matter how well meaning your dean, your ability to steer him or her away from a rocky coast is sometimes limited, especially early in a new dean's tenure in the job. To put it bluntly, sometimes people do amazing things that backfire and end in disaster, even after you have told them that the line of action they were suggesting was problematic. The longer you are in the job of associate dean, the more likely this is to happen, if for no other reason than you become aware of history (of policy, strategic aims, relationships, etc.). If your dean is wise, he or she will see the importance of understanding these histories and taking them into account in his or her policy decisions and strategic planning. After all, as Coffman (2005) very rightly points out, administrators who fail do so not because they are stupid but because they are out of sync with the culture and history of their school or university. That being said, it may take a while before your dean realizes he or she is missing the relevant history or that there even is one. During this time, you must sometimes be willing to let your dean fail or embarrass himself or herself; there are some lessons we all must learn on our own, as the following case study illustrates.

The bylaws of the School of Arts and Letters have not been updated since the college's founding forty years before. Needless to say, they are now out of date. Besides the references to departments that no longer exist and ignoring new ones that have been created in the last forty years, there is no discussion of the structure of the school, how promotion and tenure will occur, or how new curricular programs will be approved. Furthermore, there is no ethics committee and no way for students to appeal academic decisions. For all intents and purposes, the bylaws are so out-of-date that the school needs to start from scratch. In an attempt to get the process going, Dean New Ann Eager has decided to task the two most senior faculty members in the school to create a first draft of the bylaws that can be distributed to the faculty. Because this is such a burdensome task, she has decided to give the two faculty members a course release and to award them a stipend during the academic year that is equivalent to 10 percent of their respective salaries.

When Dean Eager announces this at a staff meeting, Associate Dean Old Hand gently points out that the faculty compensation policy that is part of the collective bargaining agreement of the university will not allow this type of compensation. Second, he points out that the two faculty members in question have a long-standing feud going back twenty years involving accusations of one taking credit for the other's work without due credit, which might make working together and producing a document in a reasonable time period difficult to achieve. Finally, he points out a third problem that might arise. Since the faculty members come from the two largest departments (both in the humanities) in the school, some of the other departments/faculty in the school (particularly the faculty in the sciences) might feel as though their views are not represented. Dean Eager thanks Associate Dean Old Hand for his comments but states that she has gotten to know the faculty involved, likes them both immensely, and feels there will be no problem. In fact, she has already made the offer to the faculty members in question and they have accepted. She will personally meet with them once a week for the next four months to ensure that the first draft of the bylaws is completed by the end of the fall semester. Finally, she asks Associate Dean Old Hand to fix the compensation issue with Human Resources.

What can Associate Dean Old Hand do? The compensation issue may be the easiest to deal with, particularly if he has a contact in the HR department with whom he is used to working. Having that relationship already established allows Associate Dean Old Hand to pose a question in a manner in which the dean and the school are not immediately branded for breaking the faculty contract and coming up with possible solutions. For example, is there a way to ask for an exemption to the compensation rules that would allow the stipend to be paid? If not, would compensation in the form of a faculty development fund that could be used for travel to conferences, TAs, or some other activity tied to research be allowed? Finally, could they receive the stipend as summer salary and be within the rules of the collective bargaining agreement? The other two issues (i.e., the feud between the faculty members and the perception of the smaller science departments) might be more difficult and will depend on the history of the relationship. If there is long-standing distrust between faculty members or units it may be that there is no good solution. Rather, we need to let people try to work it out; sometimes they surprise us and actually succeed. Other times, the relationships will follow the same course as we have seen in the past. If there is no potential to harm a student and other bystanders (such as other faculty and staff) who might be caught in the cross fire, it may be best to let the new dean experience the frustration and fail personally. There are some lessons we only truly learn by experiencing them firsthand.

Let us state right up front that we are not arguing that you always take the stance of assuming something new will not work, even if a version of it was tried in the past and failed. As we stated above, sometimes people will surprise you and rise above past difficulties. Rather, what we are arguing is that the history of policies and relationships can and should help shape current and future actions. People are products of their histories and tend to evaluate new ideas within the frame of their past. Therefore you need to be cognizant of this fact if for no other reason than it helps you think about the approach you might take in presenting a plan of action, suggesting a collaboration, or just anticipating problems or objections that might be raised. At the most general level, we all need to be aware of our unit's story and develop sensitivity for when it will come into play. Further, no one will ever be completely aware of all past events, so it is probably more accurate to say that you need to be aware that history is important, and if you do not know the history of a specific event or idea, you should know whom to ask and be willing to do some research to educate yourself. To say that you should be aware of history is a broad statement, encompassing a large number of areas.

So what kinds of histories do we need to know and how will they help? The case study above suggests at least three types of histories are important: policy, interpersonal relationships, and interunit relationships. As in the case study, we will start with the policy side of things first. By understanding not just the policy (or portion of a collective bargaining contract) in its current state but how it came to be, we gain a better understanding of what issues a policy is designed to correct. This knowledge gives you insights into what warrants an exception or the legitimate alternatives that may be possible. Further, if changes to the bylaws have been attempted in the past and failed, Associate Dean Old Hand might be able to inform his dean of the types of objections that were raised so these can be dealt with from the beginning. For example, perhaps there had been an attempt to institutionalize a committee for grade appeals to which a student could appeal directly. In the past, objections were raised because the committee structure bypassed conversations with the instructor and chair of the department and students complained that individuals who knew nothing of the course content were making grading decisions. This seems like a legitimate complaint on the surface, and so Associate Dean Old Hand might suggest to Dean Eager that the process requires the student to work with the instructor and then appeal to the chair of the department before he is eligible to approach the committee. Further, the committee could consider a mechanism to review previous decisions and arguments for why the grade appeals should be denied, as well as the student's proposal.

The interpersonal and interunit relationships are probably the most difficult ones with which to deal. Depending on the nature of the past relationship/conflict, the individuals involved may view all interaction through the lenses of those past interactions and assign intent (usually negative) that is not present. For example, Associate Dean Old Hand may try to point out to Dean Eager that in the past, conflict has arisen when the two senior faculty write something in common. The result is that one accuses the other of doing no work but taking credit for the work done by the other. Dividing up the task so that they work on different parts of the bylaws rather than both working on the same section together may avoid some of the problems.

Similar processes can be followed when it comes to the issue of interunit conflict. In other words, if Associate Dean Old Hand can help Dean Eager understand and anticipate the concerns that some groups would have regarding the actions of others, it can help Dean Eager decide how to present the bylaws in such a way as to alleviate these fears. For example, if the chemistry department, in the past, has had space taken away from it to accommodate growth in the English creative writing program, it may consider English a "predatory" unit (don't laugh, that perception is out there more often than you think). Given that any bylaws tend to ensure that all units have a voice in decisions affecting the entire college, Dean

Eager may want to begin a presentation of the proposed bylaws to the faculty by reinforcing that all units (or groups of units—e.g., sciences, social sciences, humanities) will have representatives on standing committees.

In other words, Associate Dean Old Hand's knowledge of the history of interactions within the college can help the new dean a great deal in presenting new initiatives to the faculty and staff of the college so that they get a fair review. If Dean Eager does not wish to listen to Associate Dean Old Hand's advice it can be frustrating, but it is her right. Associate Dean Old Hand needs to be willing to let the situation take its course. The best you can do in that position is to warn people of possible pitfalls to avoid. That being said, however, sometimes you have to be willing to let people make their own decisions (even if you think they are making a mistake). Sometimes things will work out, and other times the initiatives will fail. If no student or other vulnerable person is hurt, it is sometimes best to let people make their own mistakes and thus learn from them rather than trying valiantly to fix the problem for them.

TOOLS AND TAKEAWAYS

We have said a couple of times that relationships are a large part of what makes your work as an associate dean possible and effective. One of the most critical relationships is the one you have with your dean. Hopefully, it will be characterized by sunshine and butterflies at least most of the time, but here are some tips to remember for when the going gets tough.

1. *Expectations should be flexible.* Although you may have an ideal picture in your mind of what your relationship with your dean should be and how he or she should perform and treat you, let go of these as soon as it is evident they do not match up with reality. It is not that expectations are bad to have—on the contrary, we think they are good to have—but they need to be adjusted to align with the realities of your situation. If your new dean comes in and immediately is faced with making a 15 percent midyear budget rescission, for example, do not expect him or her to have much time to tell you are doing a great job.
2. *You are only human.* This is important to keep in mind not only about yourself, but about your dean as well. As hard as people try to do the right things, sometimes they make honest errors or are so busy that it is hard for them to take the time to say "thank you" for a job well done. Give your dean (and others you work with) the benefit of the doubt, and resist the urge to assume that people have bad motives when things go awry. Most people in higher education got there be-

cause they want to teach, do research, and support others in getting a great education. These are noble motivations that are likely to connect you somewhat with all the people with whom you work.
3. *Have your dean's back.* A big part of your job as an associate dean is to shield your dean from problems and conflict so he or she can attend to larger strategic issues in the school. Do what you can to intercept problems and solve them yourself before involving the dean. Also do your best to help the dean (especially a new dean) navigate the political waters at your institution. If you have been around for a while, you probably know the back story on many issues and relationships and can save the dean some headaches by sharing these in a professional, "need to know" basis.
4. *Know when to let go.* Although you should do what you reasonably can to help your dean and others when difficult situations arise and you should be collaborative and open to options and suggestions that others may have, there is a point when you have to just let go, even if you are concerned that the outcome will be bad. Make every effort to help and be a team player by making suggestions and offering solutions to a problem that you can help correct, but when and if these are repeatedly declined, stop trying to push and let the chips fall where they may, provided no one will be harmed by the possible bad outcome. Remember, you cannot fix everything, and trying in the face of consistent opposition frustrates everyone, including you.

Chapter 5

Changing Behavior in a Culture of No Accountability

As faculty, we often enter the job of associate dean with a view of our university as a community that values fairness and hard work and rewards accomplishments. We know of exceptions to this, of course, but we believe they are rare. Once in the job, however, we sometimes discover that the community does not always live up to this ideal. This is problematic for us as associate deans, as often part of our job is taking part in faculty evaluations. The following case study illustrates this frustrating situation.

> Professor Dormant has been with the university for seventeen years. When she arrived, she was a solid teacher and had a sound research record in her specialty, quadralinear behavioral physics. As a member of the Behavioral Physics Department, Dormant was an active departmental citizen and a clear contributor to the department and the school. Then she got tenure. Once she received tenure, Professor Dormant stopped writing grants, her teaching evaluations stagnated, she stopped attending conferences, and she rarely trained graduate students. Her participation in departmental, campus, and professional service became less consistent, and Professor Dormant has published only one additional peer-reviewed paper in the ten years since receiving tenure. Professor Dormant's department has rated her performance since tenure as "exceeding expectations" despite her record and despite the fact that she has stopped holding regular office hours and often misses department meetings. As a result, Professor Dormant has received consistent merit raises that exceed the school average, and she recently passed her post-tenure review with flying colors due to the dependence of that review on departmental merit ratings.

> Dean Disbelief, who is new to the school, is alarmed by both Professor Dormant's merit raises and post-tenure review outcome given her dismal record since tenure and calls the chair of the Behavioral Physics Department, Dr. Ovine, into his office. When the dean asks Dr. Ovine why Professor Dormant has been rewarded for such poor performance, he is told that as chair, Dr. Ovine feels she has no choice but to give everyone high merit ratings. After all, Behavioral Physics is a small department, and if someone got upset, it could be uncomfortable. "I have to live with these people, you know," says Dr. Ovine. Ovine goes on to say that since Professor Dormant has expressed a desire to teach only on Mondays and Wednesdays between 10:00 a.m. and 1:00 p.m., she will be bumping Assistant Professor Diligent from that slot to accommodate Professor Dormant's wishes.

The greatest source of both benefit and frustration for school and university administrators is the independence of the faculty. On one hand, the latitude they have in how they teach, do research, and produce creative work is a core source of the vitality and relevance of higher education and results in innovation, entrepreneurship, and the generation of new knowledge and creative works. On the other hand, this same independence means that for the most part, university administration cannot dictate to faculty what they will do, how well they will do it, or even how much of it they will do once they receive tenure. At unionized schools, this situation may be further exacerbated by the nature of the collective bargaining agreement. Of course, the exceptions to this statement exist in cases of dereliction of duty, misappropriation of funds, frank insubordination, sexual harassment, and discrimination against students. In most cases, faculty in this situation are meeting the minimum requirements of their contracts by showing up to teach classes and documenting some level of research-related activity and service, but an objective evaluation of their productivity shows that they are far from producing an acceptable amount of scholarly work, positively impacting students and curriculum, and serving the university and the profession commensurate with a typical 40-40-20 faculty contract. It is rare that such mediocre performance meets with any consequences except for continuing to receive a full paycheck with annual raises and receiving ratings of "passing" to "strong" on annual evaluation/merit ratings.

The reasons a culture that lacks accountability becomes established in schools and universities are complex. Among the sources of this pattern of turning a blind eye to poor faculty performance are fear of retribution against chairs and administration by disgruntled faculty; lack of administration support for departments and chairs who do enforce standards; a desire to avoid conflict; and a general unwillingness to define clear merit expectations for teaching, research, and service at the department level. As in our case study above, many department chairs see no value in calling unproductive faculty on the carpet for not pulling their weight because first, there are really no consequences for doing so in many merit processes unless the behavior is egregious; second, as department chairs they have few "carrots or sticks" to reward or discourage faculty performance; and finally, if a slack faculty member were to be dinged on merit, the increasing disenchantment of that person is likely to negatively affect the atmosphere within the department and make the chair's life more difficult. Moreover, from an administrative standpoint, it may be difficult to hold department chairs responsible for really addressing faculty performance; there are often few real rewards for being a department chair, and coming down too hard on chairs may make an already difficult and often poorly compensated job even less appealing.

As an associate dean, you will often find yourself dealing with various manifestations of this culture of lack of accountability, and from time to time the pervasiveness of this culture may be the bane of your existence. You should not, however, ignore it. Rewarding poor performance encourages this behavior, and it is hard on the morale of those who actually work hard. What, then, can you do to help your department and dean address and rectify poor faculty performance? The good news is that there are processes that can be implemented to gradually create more accountability for faculty by rewarding solid performance and stopping the reinforcement of poor performance by faculty and department chairs. It takes time, however, and changes should not be expected to occur overnight. Additionally, what we present in the rest of this chapter describes an ideal set of steps and actions and makes the assumption that the faculty will be on board and will embrace these changes. If this does not happen, have a look at subsequent chapters in this book on how to deal with resistance to change, various personality types, and unproductive faculty and staff.

THE MERIT PROCESS

Ideally, the mechanism for modulating faculty behavior should be the annual evaluation/merit review process. In theory, this process objectively examines the quality, sometimes quantity, and impact of each faculty member's research, teaching, and service. The dean's office must set the tone for expectations and conduct of the merit process, and as an associate dean, you may be the person in charge of this process before it reaches the dean. This is a place where the dean must be the heavy and send the message to the whole school that the evaluation/merit process has to have teeth, that poor performance will not be rewarded, and that there will be negative consequences for poor performance and rewards for excellent performance. Departments should have clear evaluation/merit criteria that have been discussed, ratified, and approved by the dean, and there should be an agreed-upon way of applying these criteria each year. What should happen is that faculty are evaluated each year on how well they are meeting the expectations of their department based on these criteria, and they should receive a merit rating that reflects this performance. The salary increment a faculty member receives should reflect this rating or, if merit-based pay increases are not part of a collective bargaining agreement, rewards that are available, such as lab space, office upgrades, and preferential teaching times should be distributed to faculty members based on performance. Within a department, one would expect to see a range of faculty performance, with some faculty being rated as excellent, others as very good, some as average, and some as below average, for example. Faculty should be able to expect that the evaluation/merit system has teeth and that their ratings are meaningful. Department chairs, when faced with discussing their faculty's ratings at evaluation/merit review time, should be able to justify their ratings based on the criteria and the objective measures of faculty performance.

The reality, of course, is that often the merit process goes awry for a number of reasons, some of which are illustrated in the case study above. The most common problems are that the review criteria in a department are vague, weak, or nonexistent. Alternatively, the criteria exist, but chairs are unwilling to apply them. Both of these factors can contribute to what some refer to as the Lake Wobegon effect, in which all faculty appear to be above average. Clearly this is not the case. So what can be done to support departments in remedying these two problems? We suggest a two-step approach, and it is likely that as an associate dean you will be involved in both of these steps.

First, there needs to be a review and revision of the merit evaluation criteria for each department. The edict for this needs to come from the dean or the provost on the campus (usually in the form of sunsetting all existing criteria within a certain time frame and replacing them with new ones), and there must be clear direction for what the outcome of the revision is expected to be. For example, the provost may set some requirements for new criteria such as that they be benchmarked against an agreed-upon group of peer institutions, or that new merit systems have a numerical component of some type. One way of approaching setting such goals is reminiscent of the way institutions have, from time to time, addressed concerns about classroom grade inflation. Knowing that not all students are above average and that the expectation is not that most of a class of introductory chemistry students, for example, will receive a B or better in the class, universities may mandate that grade distributions in such classes conform to an expected grade spread in which roughly half the class gets a C or better and the remaining students score below a C.

There are two ways to accomplish this task: first, the difficulty of the class material and evaluation can be ratcheted up; and second, a curve can be used that normalizes student performance such that average performance is pegged to a grade of C regardless of numerical score. A similar approach can be suggested to departments. The easiest and fairest path is the former, in which it takes more accomplishment (as well as clear definitions of accomplishments) to receive higher ratings, because everyone has the opportunity to step up their activities. The dean's office (often an associate dean) can work with departments to revise their review criteria according to this criterion by creating and writing down clear, objective achievements that will be necessary for different levels of faculty performance in teaching, research, and service. A review of these criteria by experts in the field at another university can be used as a check if necessary. As an associate dean, you may be charged with working one-on-one with departments to make these revisions.

Second, department chairs need to be held accountable for the evaluation process. Once the criteria are up to snuff, the next step is actually applying and enforcing them. As in the case study, department chairs are often hesitant to apply criteria to their faculty with any stringency. In extreme cases, the hesitancy may be caused by fear of retribution, but more often it is due to worries that, especially in small units, annoying a faculty member may result in that person becoming difficult, intractable, and contrary in many ways that can make the department chair's already frustrating job even harder. This is understandable, of course, but it can be remedied with the support of the dean. At a national meeting of deans and associate deans, we asked a seasoned dean how he had addressed the problem of merit in his school, which had seen a 400 percent increase in external grant funding over a five-year period. The dean replied that he had accomplished this by bringing together a group of department chairs who "had the guts" to enforce standards. He said he had gradually removed weak chairs and replaced them with new people, whom he rewarded for taking a stand on merit. Over several years, these actions resulted in a team of chairs who were of like mind with the dean regarding faculty expectations and in a merit system that resulted in merit ratings (and commensurate raises) that rewarded the productive and withheld rewards from the unproductive.

How can such a transformation occur in a short time frame and without removing most of the chairs in a school? Deans can begin to create this transformation through doing two things: first, rewarding chairs for being tough at merit time by giving them, in turn, high ratings and rewards for their performance as chairs; and second, backing up these chairs in the event that they face retribution from disgruntled faculty. At many universities, department chairs have a two-part evaluation, half related to their faculty achievements and half to their administrative activities. If this occurs, the deans should have a separate pot of money (or other resources) they can use to reward chairs who enforce standards in their departments. Deans can be explicit from the start that a major part of their evaluation of chair performance will be the application and reinforcement of the merit process. Deans should also broadly and frequently state to faculty at large that merit is a priority for them and that performance will be measured and rewarded (or not) based on objective criteria. Consequences for poor performance must be publicized and meted out by the dean, not the department chair, and can include reporting of inadequate performance to the provost, letters documenting poor performance added to the faculty member's personnel file, and no raises in years when performance is poor. Alternatively, highly productive faculty should receive praise, letters of thanks, and public accolades. Finally, deans need to publicly let faculty know that they have department chairs' backs on annual reviews, and that strong merit criteria and solid faculty performance are required by the school.

As an associate dean, you are likely to be the conduit of both the evaluation/merit process documents and conversations between departments and the dean, and the first line of defense when it comes to complaints and angry faculty. It is critical for you to get your dean to back you as well as the department chairs, as you are the gatekeeper between the dean and the "madding crowd." You will learn quickly if your dean will back you up by supporting your efforts in dealing with the evaluation process and faculty performance issues, and in resolving complaints on behalf of the school. In later chapters we discuss strategies for dealing with a dean who does not back you up or support you. In an ideal world, this is a situation you will not face.

POST-TENURE REVIEW

The other mechanism through which faculty performance, ideally, can be modulated and accountability increased is through post-tenure review (PTR). Most institutions have some form of PTR, and these processes vary in their intent and effectiveness. We argue that meaningful PTR, tied to a strong annual evaluation process, can begin to create a culture of accountability that serves everyone well.

At its simplest, PTR is a multiyear version of the annual evaluation/merit process, often involving a retrospective evaluation of the last five years or so by the faculty member under review, his or her department or department chair, and some level of review at the dean's level. As an associate dean, you may be charged with the dean's-level review or may oversee a committee that does these reviews. The results and quality of these reviews are frequently dependent on the annual evaluation/merit process, so it is important to view them as interdependent.

The outcome of PTR, just as the outcome of annual evaluation/merit, should have meaningful and positive consequences for strong faculty and negative consequences for poor performers. For example, some institutions offer PTR grants that are given to support faculty for doing well in this process. These monies can be used to support a graduate student assistant, for professional development, or for travel to a conference. Alternatively, faculty "failing" the PTR process may be subject to a remediation plan which, if unsuccessful, can lead to sanctions including reduction in rank, pay, or dismissal for cause. Again, sticking to the plan of rewarding the performers and punishing the slackers is easier said than done and depends on your dean's ability to be tough and fair.

THE ISSUE OF INCIVILITY

As noted above, one of the reasons department chairs may be hesitant to give negative evaluations is fear of the unproductive faculty member's reaction. In a small department, one unhappy or disgruntled faculty member can create an uncomfortable environment for all members of the department, as the following case study illustrates.

> Associate Professors Tweedledum and Tweedledee of the Department of Marginal Scholarship do not like their new department chair. The new chair, Associate Professor Steamroller, admittedly has some clear ideas on how things should be changed and knows he needs to learn some leadership skills to realize his vision of improving the department's reputation and productivity. He has the right ideas but is overbearing in his approach. Associate Professors Tweedledum and Tweedledee, both of whom squeaked by for tenure and are notoriously unproductive faculty, mount an active campaign to create problems for Department Chair Steamroller. Among their antics are telling the non-tenure-track faculty that Steamroller plans to eliminate all of their positions, urging them to complain to the dean about unfair treatment, and intimating to their undergraduate classes that Chair Steamroller is censoring them from discussing controversial topics in class. The indignant students start a petition to the dean demanding Chair Steamroller's termination on the grounds of impinging on the academic freedom of Associate Professors Tweedledum and Tweedledee. When Chair Steamroller approaches the dean to ask for help in reprimanding Associate Professors Tweedledum and Tweedledee for their actions, the dean tells him that his only real recourse is to "kill them with kindness" and stay above the fray. In short, unless he can ding them on PTR or wants to file a hostile workplace complaint against them, which the dean indicates is likely to fail, Chair Steamroller simply has to put up with the situation.

The above discussions of merit and PTR fail to address one of the most frustrating and destructive aspects of lack of faculty accountability—rude, disrespectful, and sometimes malicious behavior. Often the people who engage in these types of shenanigans are not stars, but rather are weak performers who, rather than spending time on teaching and scholarship, put their energy into being destructive. What can be done to discourage these kinds of behaviors?

One of the most effective ways of dealing with incivility is peer pressure. Faculty within the department or school can pressure the bad actor(s) to cut it out. Ideally, someone (at least the chair) has the guts to pull the person aside and tell him or her to change the behavior. It is not uncommon, however, for departments to be unwilling to confront a toxic colleague until the smear campaign he or she has started has done considerable damage. When this happens, it will fall to you as the associate dean to clean up the situation. In these cases, the best strategy is not to simply lambast the bad actor, but rather to explain to the person how his or her behavior negatively affects his or her colleagues, the students, and the department. It is useful to ask what is generating the bad behavior and to try to learn what is at the core of the acting out. A common reason for such behavior is fear that changes may be happening that will leave the bad actor behind (i.e., increasing research expectations necessary for merit raises). If it is possible to find the cause of the acting out, solutions can be explored.

If this strategy does not work, the second strategy is to do damage control. Aspects of this are presented throughout the book, and frequently, a flexible and long-range strategy for reducing the amount of destruction that can be caused by such incivility is necessary. If, however, it gets to the point that the department becomes dysfunctional, please read chapter 9.

GOLDEN BOY/GIRL SYNDROME

A final way in which we have seen lack of accountability come into play is through a phenomenon we call the golden boy/girl syndrome. Someone you work with in the school or in the dean's office has been singled out by the administration as exceptional and deserving of special consideration and, perhaps, additional perks and compensation that you and others do not receive. Golden boys and girls, for reasons unknown to you and others who work on a day-to-day basis with them and see what they do (and importantly, do not do), are viewed by the administration and some faculty as wonderful and very competent people who can do no wrong. A different set of rules seems to apply to these people; during tight budget times, they receive perks removed from others, and although others are required to be accessible on weekends and evenings, golden boys and girls are exempt. Of course, if these people were really doing a remarkable job and working hard, their reputations would be deserved and understandable, but in the case of golden boys and girls, the anointed ones are not pulling their weight. They are just really good at saying the right things to the right people, appearing to be busy at key times while producing very little, and promoting themselves shamelessly. In the meantime, you have your head down, working your tail off, playing by the rules, and you expect to be rewarded for doing that. Instead, the golden boys and girls receive larger raises, more budgetary resources in their areas, and additional professional development resources and staff to help them with their jobs—and they are loudly and publicly praised. What on earth are you supposed to do when you find yourself in a situation like this? How do you keep up your morale, remain a team player, and cope? Here are some suggestions for first, reality-checking yourself and your perceptions, and second, finding ways to keep from going nuts over the frustration created by golden boy/girl syndrome.

Having said that, we present one large caveat before launching into the rest of this chapter: you should be spending the *vast* majority of your time doing your job and furthering your own career by working diligently and with integrity and spending very, very little of your time and energy thinking about the golden ones. The reality, however, is that these situations can create a considerable amount of frustration for you and be totally demoralizing. From time to time, you may need to step back and deal with the effects of golden boy/girl syndrome.

Like it or not, there are times when our perceptions about situations like this are not correct. There may be information we do not have. Perhaps the decision to anoint the golden boy/girl is not coming from your dean but from someone higher up in your university. Although it may be difficult, do your best to do some fact-finding before you conclude that Steve or Jane is a golden boy or girl with no justification. Here are some questions to ask yourself in this process: Is it possible that you are not aware of the things Steve or Jane is doing and that he or she is, in fact, really contributing in ways you do not see? See what you can do to answer this question without wasting too much time. Also, is it possible that forces outside your office have determined the status of the golden one? Listen to water-cooler conversation and check in with colleagues. The fact is that sometimes people are in this position because of some political or litigious situation beyond your office environment. This, of course, is not good, but sometimes it is simply a fact of life. Knowing that this may be the case may help you look at your boss's situation in a different light.

So let us assume that you have concluded that indeed, Steve or Jane fits the "golden one" definition and that you are getting the short end of the stick as a result. What can you do? Well, as tempting as it may be to complain about it (more about that later), your first and most effective strategy is to focus your attention away from the injustice at hand and do everything in your power to elevate yourself. Concentrate on doing a fantastic job, acting professionally and courteously, and distinguishing yourself as the person Steve or Jane is purported to be—an invaluable, incredibly competent member of the organization who deserves recognition. Here are some tips on how to accomplish this.

First, make every effort to get along well with your dean, your colleagues, and especially Steve or Jane. Although this last one is hard to swallow, the fact is that since your boss favors Steve or Jane, alienating the golden one may very well jeopardize only your own career. Second, stop fretting about the injustice of the golden boy/girl syndrome and the special relationship Steve or Jane has with your dean or provost and start improving your own relationship with those same people. Step up to the plate. Help others, even Steve or Jane. Do outstanding work. Make suggestions for improvements and offer to implement them. Be consistently professional, pleasant, and supportive of your boss and your coworkers. Third, do not focus only on your own responsibilities. Look for and even ask for opportunities to take on more responsibility and to learn about other aspects of the school and university. Of course, do this only when and if you are knocking everything on your plate out of the park and truly have the capacity to increase your workload and responsibilities and excel at doing so.

The basic mantra we have been repeating so far is "keep your head down, work hard, and keep your mouth shut" when dealing with the golden boy/girl syndrome, but at some point there may be an opportunity to bring up your concerns about the injustice you see—and about the fact that you are being passed over for promotions and raises in favor of Steve or Jane. There may come a point where despite your best efforts, you find your morale so low that you are on the verge of leaving or inappropriately confronting the situation. If you find yourself in this position, there are some things to consider before you throw yourself on your sword, which is, potentially, what you will do when you broach this subject with your dean.

Are you prepared to face the possible consequences of a poor outcome of this conversation? What if this results in further rewarding of Steve or Jane at your expense—or in your termination? Be sure this is the hill you are ready to die on, because you may have to, despite your best efforts to be professional.

Can you have the conversation without venting your anger? If not, do not have it. You should only bring this up if you are confident you can remain calm, cool, and collected through the conversation, otherwise the dean's focus will be on your meltdown and not on what you said.

When you have the conversation, frame it in a nonconfrontational way if at all possible. For example, instead of saying, "Why did Jane get a big raise last year and this year, when I did not? If you look at her productivity and mine, you can clearly see that I am far more effective than she is, I always step up, and she is always asking others to do her work and then taking credit." Instead, say, "As much as I hate to bring this up, I need to talk with you about something I am having a hard time understanding. I suspect I do not have all the information, but I am hoping that after talking with you, I will have a better understanding of what is going on and can put my concerns aside." Then respectfully bring up your concerns and have a conversation about what you can do in the future, if anything, to put yourself in a better position. This conversation may not lead where you hope it will (e.g., your getting a better raise on the spot or getting a satisfactory explanation), but you will have carefully and respectfully stood up for yourself.

As totally and incredibly aggravating as the golden boy/girl syndrome is, and justifiably so, your primary job is to take care of yourself and your own career. Basically, act like someone your boss would want to promote and assign more responsibility to rather than spending time and energy stewing about how screwed you are because of the golden one. If you really cannot tolerate the situation, you have to find a way out. That being said, remember that golden boys and girls exist everywhere. Given this, ask yourself what you want for your career, your school, and your university and what the best way is to get there.

TOOLS AND TAKEAWAYS

It is unfortunate that a culture of poor accountability can develop within a department, school, or university when it comes to evaluating faculty performance. This typically is more of an issue after the tenure point when the pressure to perform well to achieve that goal is no longer in place. As an associate dean, it is likely that you will be involved in faculty evaluation and also in helping departments and the college revise, create, and implement policies that are focused on developing processes that support faculty and departments in doing the quantity and quality of work expected of them. This component of faculty affairs can be frustrating, but it is also a place where you can really make a positive impact as an associate dean. Here are a few things to keep in mind as you navigate these issues.

1. *Understand the reasons*. A culture of poor accountability does not occur in a vacuum. Often there are reasons that encourage and support

it. Take the time to listen to faculty, chairs, and administrators about their perceptions of how and when faculty evaluation fails, and use this information to shape your actions in changing the culture.
2. *Word from the top*. Ideally, improving faculty evaluation and accountability should be publicly encouraged and supported by people who are upstream from you. This is an instance in which having the top of your institution say "This is important" is critical to your success, especially if raises are distributed and approved above the school level. If that is the case, important distinctions in performance that are made by the school may be diluted by decisions to base the raise process on something besides merit at the university level.
3. *Do not reinvent the wheel*. There are many solid merit and PTR systems and approaches out there, so there is no need for you and your departments to start from scratch. Use the Internet, your colleagues, and professional groups to gather some documents that you can use as a starting point for your discussions.
4. *Accept that there will be "injustices."* Despite having solid merit systems and PTR processes, you may find yourself dealing with golden boys/girls who, despite poor performance, get rewarded because they are buddies with the dean, play golf with the provost, or are perceived broadly to be fantastic even though there is no support for such a perception. When these people are rewarded by your dean or others outside of the process of faculty evaluation that you are in charge of overseeing, think twice before you raise the flag about such actions. As an associate dean, you have to pick your battles carefully, and when you do, you should be prepared to fight them all the way. Ask yourself if this is the issue for which you are willing to really fight or if it is one you can let lie.

Chapter 6

Something Old, Something New

*Working with Department Chairs and
the Faculty as an Associate Dean*

Serving as an associate dean requires dealing with challenging issues, some of which are familiar and others that are unique to the job. Regardless of your specific responsibilities as an associate dean (personnel, faculty affairs, student affairs, research, curriculum, etc.), you will work with department chairs and the school faculty a great deal of the time. For example, your dean will expect you to implement his or her policies, keep department chairs informed about actions in the school, assist chairs in communicating these actions to their faculty, and work with departmental faculty. You will be expected to work with faculty and departments to increase research funding, improve research performance, develop curricular initiatives, assess learning outcomes, and perform mentoring activities. Department chairs and individual faculty and staff are likely to contact you to find out about policies or request exceptions to them. You may be asked to help develop curriculum or other new programs. Additionally, others may ask you about how the dean may react to certain proposals or other issues in the college.

Many faculty become associate deans after serving as department chairs and developing some skills in communicating and working with faculty in their home departments. Becoming an associate dean, however, requires the development of additional skills and strategies for communicating with members of the school beyond those used by department chairs. Two factors make this communication pathway challenging for associate deans relative to the way department chairs and deans communicate with each other. First, associate deans typically have both faculty and administrative appointments, and as such may continue to be involved in scholarship and teaching in their academic departments in a way that is not possible for the dean, who has a full-time administrative appointment. Second, the power differential between associate deans and department chairs is smaller than is it between the dean and the department chairs; department chairs know that although associate deans are part of the dean's team, when push comes to shove, the dean, not the associate dean, is often ultimately in charge of important decisions and resources and may act against the associate dean's suggestions. This combination of blurred boundaries and ambiguous power puts associate deans in a new state of "leading from the middle" as compared to what is experienced by department chairs, and that position creates challenges to leadership that can be hard to navigate.

BLURRED BOUNDARIES

Associate deans must enforce policy and sometimes communicate unpleasant news to members of the school, both down to the staff and faculty and up to the dean. This situation can get particularly interesting because at most institutions, associate deans are faculty with administrative responsibilities; they still teach, work with students on research projects, and do their own research. In other words, they think of themselves as faculty, and as a result, are confident that they understand the positions of faculty and even department chairs. However, that is not how the faculty and department chairs may view them now. Individuals new to the job of associate dean are often surprised when department chairs no longer view them as faculty colleagues but rather as administrators who have lost perspective on the needs of chairs and departmental faculty. In fact, associate deans are sometimes told by department chairs and faculty that they are the problem, and they may be held personally responsible for every new school or university policy with which faculty and chairs are unhappy. This is because many, if not most, department chairs and faculty think of associate deans as faculty who have fully "gone to the dark side" of administration and no longer have any idea what it is like to be a faculty member or deal with the challenges of chairing a department (Bryant 2005; Dowdall and Dowdall 2005; Strathe and Wilson 2006).

A core feature of being an associate dean is that relative to being a department chair, whose primary focus and loyalty is communicating within and on behalf of a single academic department, associate deans must not only appreciate the perspectives of other disciplines in their school, as noted above, but also learn to communicate with people in these other disciplines. That is, in order to be fair, effective, and engaged, associate deans must be able to bridge communication and philosophical gaps among disciplines and groups in order to accomplish the dean's goals. Seeing the broader view of the school as a whole means that occasionally associate deans must go against the wishes of their home department, while still remaining members of the department faculty. This puts them in a position very different from department chairs who, while having one foot in both the administrative and faculty camps, still act from the perspective of their own department and their field of training.

AMBIGUOUS POWER

Added to the fact that associate deans simultaneously serve and are expected to communicate as both faculty and administrators, their position is one of considerable responsibility but with ambiguous power. The associate dean is frequently charged with "making things happen" without further guidance. How you handle these situations depends to some degree on the dean's personality, agenda, and communication style, but also on your own. Inherent in making this work is to respect and remember the way that department chairs and their faculty see the world and developing ways of balancing that perspective with the need to complete the tasks you are given. The following case study illustrates the interplay of these factors.

> The College of Natural Disaster will soon be undergoing its accreditation review and still lacks an outcomes assessment plan for its core curriculum. Associate Dean Worker Bee is assigned the task of getting the faculty together and producing an assessment plan during the fall semester that would then be implemented in the spring semester. Knowing that, the faculty are somewhat resistant to the idea of outcomes assessment, since they feel that simply giving students grades is sufficient. Associate Dean Worker Bee sets about convincing the faculty that outcomes assessment is something they should want because it helps their students. He holds a series of brown bag meetings to talk about assessment, and gradually the faculty start to see its value. They appear excited and engaged about the process. However, no one steps forward to write the first draft of the plan. Because the deadline is looming, Associate Dean Worker Bee takes it upon himself to write a draft and then distributes it to the faculty governance bodies of the college for comment. Unfortunately, these groups are not thrilled with the draft, but they are still excited about the idea. As a result, they start a massive rewrite at the meeting, changing almost everything Associate Dean Worker Bee has written. At the end of the meeting he leaves with a heavily marked-up copy and a dazed look in his eyes.

> Later that afternoon, the dean follows a loud thumping noise to the associate dean's office and finds Associate Dean Worker Bee banging his head against the drywall with a draft of a letter of resignation on his computer screen. The dean calms Associate Dean Worker Bee down and refuses to accept the resignation letter. Despite this, Associate Dean Worker Bee never manages to regain his enthusiasm for outcomes assessment, and a large picture has been hung to hide the dent in his office wall. The plan remains as it was after the committee meeting for several more semesters and the faculty no longer talk about assessment as a good thing.

Associate Dean Worker Bee started out by holding a very promising set of brown bag meetings but for several reasons failed to succeed in his mission in the end. What if you find yourself in his shoes one day? What can you do? First, since as an associate dean you may no longer be viewed as a "real faculty member," you may have trouble getting faculty and departments to follow your lead if you do not have the overt support of the department chairs and dean. Second, because your power as an associate dean is ambiguous at best, you often need to rely on charm, logical arguments, presentation of information and data, reference to campus policy, and occasional nagging (use this one sparingly or people will stop listening) to make things happen. Which of these techniques you choose to use in a given situation is determined by the culture of your campus, rules and policies that govern your actions, and your personality (Bryant 2005; Buller 2007; Hoppe 2003; Strathe and Wilson 2006). One of the reasons the job of associate dean can be very frustrating is that you cannot accomplish much on your own; rather, you need collaboration and consensus to move the mission of the school forward. This is frustrating because many of us were trained to work alone, and as faculty we usually did. This position requires an entirely different approach. Additionally, consensus building takes a considerable amount of time and often involves private rolling of eyes, gnashing of teeth, and an overwhelming desire to just do it yourself. However, when you succeed at making the group effort work, it can be incredibly rewarding and you can see change for the better due to your actions.

Exactly how you manage to develop group consensus depends on your own personality and communication style. Because associate deans almost always rise through the faculty ranks at their institution, it is difficult for them to change suddenly and communicate in totally different ways. The faculty and staff of the school know you and will be immediately suspicious if you suddenly start acting in a different manner. You may be faced with backlash, resistance, and immediate suspicion of administrative conspiracy and cover-up. No matter how good the idea, if the individuals you are trying to convince to participate do not believe you are telling them the truth, the whole truth, and nothing but the truth, you will not succeed.

To succeed in the position of associate dean you have to understand your own leadership and management styles as well as your strengths and weaknesses. Perhaps more importantly, you must be able to see the big picture and to separate yourself from the issue. Associate Dean Worker Bee succeeded at the beginning of the process through the brown bag meetings that engaged the faculty and changed the view of the assessment process in the school. In the end, however, he failed because he forgot the other aspects of working collaboratively and could not separate his feelings from criticism by the faculty.

THE KEY: FACILITATING RATHER THAN MANAGING

At the core of success in dealing with department chairs and their faculty in your role as associate dean is to find a way to let the faculty and departments own the process and outcome you are charged with helping them complete, to be minimally directive to them in your interactions (just enough to keep them on the path), and to praise and lift them up when they have met the challenge.

The key here is to switch from manager to facilitator. Department chairs tend to function more as managers, as the decisions and quality of work produced by their departments are often part of their own evaluation as chair. It is understandable that department chairs are highly invested in the outcome of faculty work in their units. On the other hand, associate deans are expected to act as agents of change but not to implement the changes themselves. As an associate dean, your charge is likely to be to provide a framework for department chairs and their faculty in making substantive decisions and implementing the changes that *they* want. Thus, you cannot become so attached to a particular way of doing, explaining, or describing an issue that you feel that disagreement with your perspective about the plan is equivalent to attacks directed at you personally; this reaction is that of a manager who owns and feels responsible for the outcome. For example, if you have written a first draft of an assessment plan as a starting point for a unit and have put it out for public comment and discussion like Associate Dean Worker Bee (a necessary step in engaging people in the process), you have to remove your ego completely from the process. That is the role of facilitator, and it requires that the faculty take responsibility, as they should, for the outcome. This has the happy side effect of relieving some pressure from you as associate dean.

We realize that what we are telling you is difficult to do; as academics, our egos are closely tied to the scholarly works we write and the research designs we develop. We often transfer those feelings over to administrative proposals we submit to the faculty. If you do not change the way you view what you write as an administrator, however, you will become very upset when faculty groups insist on different wording, goals, data collection methods, and procedures. Your job (and your contribution to the process of improving the institution) is to get the appropriate people engaged and involved in the process, not necessarily to ensure that everyone agrees with your perspective. This does not mean that you cannot have ideas about how things should be done. You should have these and you should express them. But you must also be open to other ways of doing things and you must remove your ego from the details of the process.

FAIR TREATMENT IS KEY

Given your position in never-never land, with one foot in the administrative/school camp and another in the faculty/department camp, how do you figure out what to do when push comes to shove? You must be consistent in the way you treat individuals and units; you cannot show favoritism or have different rules for different individuals or groups. Additionally, you need to remember that what little power you have is limited and tenuous.

The only true authority you have is existing policy applied fairly and equally to all. Your power is limited to the power of persuasion and your ability to get buy-in from the faculty and staff by communicating a shared vision of what is good for the school and the belief that what benefits the school also benefits the individuals and units that constitute it (Berryman-Fink 1998; Bryant 2005; Coffman 2005; Hoppe 2003; Plater 2006). In other words, policy and process are your friends. Do not ignore them. Not all students, staff, and faculty are aware of the policies, however, so you must make an effort to explain your actions in light of them. More specifically, make sure that everyone knows the policies and processes, that everyone knows why they exist, and that the policies and processes are applied consistently to all. In addition, provide information on how to go about changing policies and processes if they become unfair or unworkable. This reduces conflict and increases your credibility. People may not like your decision, but they know what it is based on and that it is not merely your whim. In other words, they may be angry with you for a while, but they will respect you and understand in the long run why you made the decision you made.

Does that mean you should never vary from policy? Although there are always extreme circumstances in which this is warranted, we want to encourage you to make these instances extremely rare. Once you waive a policy you have set a precedent that others will hear about through the campus rumor mill. If you do not waive the policy for the next individual who asks (even if the circumstances are different), you will have the appearance of treating people differently, and accusations of favoritism and capriciousness will abound (Bryant 2005; Hoppe 2003). In other words, give great thought before deviating from policy, do so only after considerable consultation, and follow your decision with clear communication so that the exception is not setting a precedent.

TOOLS AND TAKEAWAYS

Working with diverse groups of faculty and staff can be trying and difficult as an associate dean because you are essentially caught in the middle between faculty and staff and upper administration. Moreover, you may find yourself with lots of responsibility but little authority, so your power to accomplish things and decide things may be ambiguous, not only to you but also to others. A few simple things can help you accomplish what you need to with faculty and use the authority you do have to make the most of your time as an associate dean.

1. *Accept your position.* Although it creates challenges, get comfortable with the fact that you are in between the faculty and the upper administration. Consider turning your frustration about this, when it occurs, into an opportunity to bridge the two worlds.
2. *Facilitate rather than manage.* When working with faculty groups on a task, do what you can to support them, and expect that they may change or rewrite some of what you put together. Remember that your job is to start the ball rolling, not to get it all the way down the hill.
3. *Be fair.* Even though you are straddling the fence between your department and administration, resist the urge to do anything that favors your own unit over others. When it comes down to it, as an associate dean, you work on behalf of *all* the departments in the school rather than only your own.
4. *Use policy as power.* As an associate dean, you may have ambiguous power to accomplish things, but when it comes to policies you are charged with implementing or enforcing, your power is clear. Use written procedures to back up your decisions and help others understand that decisions you make are driven by policy, not personal whim. Policy is your friend, and it is a great communication tool to clarify muddy issues as they arise.

Chapter 7

Communicating Effectively

Say What You Mean and Mean What You Say

In addition to implementing policy and setting processes in place, associate deans are expected to function as a communication portal to the staff, faculty, department chairs, and the dean in an attempt to facilitate discussions and manage conflict resolution. Your experience in higher education probably has already taught you that effective communication is essential to maintaining good working relationships; the good news is that often this is easier to achieve than you may realize. For example, when faculty members or department chairs contact you about an issue, you should acknowledge the contact, even if it is to direct faculty members to someone else (such as their department chair) or to say you need to research the issue and it might be a while before you can provide an answer. Check back periodically to let them know you are still working on their issue until you find an appropriate solution or answer. Failure to acknowledge their query causes great frustration for faculty and staff; makes the dean's office appear distant, out of touch, or incompetent; and can lead to conspiracy theories about why you will not answer them on this issue and what you are up to (no, we are not making that last part up). It is also important to realize that the way you respond to a situation has the potential to help it spiral out of control in lightning fashion. The following case study illustrates the impact of different communication styles.

> The chair of the Department of Political Controversy contacts Associate Dean Communicator through e-mail about a rumor that is circulating on campus. Because of a severe budget cut from the state legislature and the very controversial nature of the Department of Political Controversy on another campus in the state university system, the department chair is worried that the provost and dean have decided to eliminate the department by eliminating budget lines and possibly publicly embarrassing the department. Associate Dean Communicator immediately responds via e-mail that she does not think that is the case but that in her meeting with the dean later on she will let him know that this rumor is out there and that the department has asked about it. The dean confirms there are no plans to eliminate the department and Associate Dean Communicator calls the department chair with the reassuring news.
>
> Two weeks later, a faculty member in the Department of Political Controversy at another campus (who happens to have dubious credentials and less than stellar scholarly productivity) makes an inflammatory public statement resulting in the lead story on the evening news and numerous editorials in the paper. The editorials demand that the state legislature investigate what the Department of Political Controversy on your campus contributes to the education of the citizens of the state and calls for its elimination in these tough budgetary times. Associate Dean Communicator immediately talks to the dean, knowing how nervous the chair of the department on her own campus is, and they decide that the best defense is a good offense. They decide to collect vitae of the members of the department so that they can immediately deflect negative inquiries and demonstrate the high quality of their own faculty. At the end of this meeting Associate Dean Communicator contacts the chair, and since she knows he is in class at the time, she sends an e-mail. In an attempt to defuse the tension, she takes a lighter approach in asking for the vitae and assures the chair there is nothing to worry about, this is just a precaution. By 8:00 the next morning, Associate Dean Communicator has every social science chair in the school in her office wanting to know why she is persecuting the Department of Political Controversy by demanding vitae as though they need to justify their existence. The dean and the provost call wanting to know what the devil she told the chair, because they have over a hundred e-mails from alumni of the program.

How did an action that started out proactive and supportive turn so terribly wrong so quickly? Associate Dean Communicator had every intention of being supportive, and collecting the vitae was a way to have information with which to brag about the wonderful contributions of her faculty and demonstrate the importance of the department. She thought she communicated well and attempted to use humor to defuse a very tense situation. However, she underestimated several things: (1) how nervous (and perhaps justifiably paranoid) the chair of the department was, (2) the difficulty of communicating nuance through e-mail, (3) proactive steps the chair might have been taking on his own to improve the perception of his department, and (4) the fact that associate deans are perceived as part of the administration rather than as part of the faculty. In such an "us versus them" climate, every action is suspect and subject to multiple interpretations.

Waiting to talk to the chair in person would have been a better strategy given the ambiguity of e-mail as a medium of communication. A face-to-face conversation would have allowed Associate Dean Communicator to pick up on visual cues of panic that could be addressed immediately. Additionally, pulling the chair into the conversation on goals and strategies that Associate Dean Communicator had had with the dean would have made the request seem less like an administrative dictate and more like a team effort to support the department, as it was intended.

FACING DOWN: TALKING TO DEPARTMENTS, STAFF, AND FACULTY

This case study highlights both the importance of the manner in which we communicate and the fact that associate deans are often perceived very differently from how they perceive themselves. Although you may still think of yourself as predominantly faculty, the faculty and department chairs may think of you in a very different light, as noted in chapter 5 and elsewhere (Berryman-Fink 1998; Coffman 2005; Hoppe 2003; Lucas 1998; Plater 2006; Strathe and Wilson 2006). Specifically, the faculty and chairs are likely to lump you and other administrators together in tough times and may be highly suspicious of your motives. Further, it is your responsibility as an associate dean to understand both faculty and chair perspectives and fears and to translate them up to the dean as well as translating the dean's perspective down to the staff, faculty, and chairs. Many guides for department chairs talk about chairs having to straddle the concerns of the department versus the concerns of the wider institution (e.g., Gmelch 1998), but associate deans have the added responsibility of having to enforce policies and procedures and participate in the allocation of resources. As a result, their actions may be perceived as harmful by staff, faculty, and departments, even when they make their best efforts to protect programs and mitigate cuts. The need to enforce policies and procedures and the responsibility to allocate resources inevitably sets up tensions and conflicts between departments and the dean's office (Lucas 1998) and can cause considerable stress for the associate dean caught in the middle. This tension means that if you wish to be successful in the position of associate dean, you must treat all individuals and all units equally, even if that action results in comments from your faculty colleagues about how you used to be so much more reasonable before you went into administration.

Being fair to all is not always an easy principle to follow but is absolutely essential. One of the reasons it may be difficult to follow is the manner in which people may attempt to interact with you. We want to stress that the vast majority of staff, faculty, and chairs are dedicated and fair-minded individuals. They understand the constraints under which you work and your need to enforce policy. Unfortunately, about 90 percent of your time will be spent on the 10 percent of staff and faculty who do not understand your constraints and lack the perspective to see the larger picture. When you are sure that a situation is about to expand beyond your control (e.g., calls made to the dean, provost, chancellor, president, board of regents, etc.), you should always give your dean a heads-up. Deans do not like to be blindsided. However, unless you know all the personalities involved well, you do not always see these crises coming and are sometimes as surprised as the dean. In particular, some faculty and staff may attempt to manipulate you in the arguments they use when presenting an issue to you. They may make assumptions about you because of your gender, age, disciplinary training, etc. If their requests are denied, they may become doubly upset because their intellectual acuity that placed you into a particular box proved incorrect. Academics do not like their assumptions to be proven wrong. Likewise, you may be confused by their reaction and that of the people above you when they complain to them about you.

FACING UP: TALKING WITH YOUR DEAN

How much the dean relies on you to communicate faculty views to him or her depends to a large degree on whether the dean was an external hire or promoted from within the unit. In the case of the former, the dean will often need you to fill him or her in on campus culture and the history of relationships between individuals and between departments. The history of relationships often informs the dean about motivations and the likelihood of the individual or group following through on proposed initiatives. Deans who are promoted from within will often know much of the background but may still need insights on what faculty members are thinking about a particular issue as the dean is dealing with a problem or rolling out an initiative. Thus, it is important to think about the ways you interact with staff, faculty, and chairs in your school.

When dealing with difficult issues, the ideal process is to share and discuss the information you have with your dean. After you present all of the information to the dean (including all e-mails regarding the issue), the two of you together should decide how to handle the situation. If the dean decides to take the lead but you are still subjected to vitriolic phone calls and e-mails from the outraged individuals, there are several ways to handle the situation: (1) ignore it, (2) confront it with a standard response regarding unprofessional behavior, or (3) subvert it. By subverting it, we mean that these arguments are often internally contradictory and may contain threats and bluffs. Point out the inconsistencies to your dean and call their bluff. Regardless of which of these options you attempt, make sure your dean knows what you are doing. Remember the number one rule: deans do not like to be blindsided.

WORKING WITH STAFF AND FACULTY GOVERNANCE GROUPS

In your attempts to implement existing policy, to change policy, or to create new policy, clearly communicating and working with staff and faculty governance groups is crucial. The nature, structure, and relative power of staff and faculty governance is highly variable from campus to campus and can be heavily impacted by whether your institution is unionized or not. If it is, the nature of the collective bargaining agreement must be considered in all your discussions and decisions. As a faculty member, you probably participated in only a portion of the governance system, so you must put a priority on gaining a picture of all of the committees in your school, their responsibilities, and their roles in various aspects of personnel, budget, planning, program development, curriculum, and campus life. Being well versed in the school's bylaws is only the first step, because each campus and each committee has its own culture and way of doing things. Visit these committees, introduce yourself, and listen. These groups can contribute considerably to your ability to develop, implement, and communicate policies. They should be brought into discussions early and often in a respectful and appreciative manner. Not only do you need buy-in from these groups, but also they can provide important insights and new ideas to help you attain strategic goals.

Administrators who choose to ignore governance groups or to treat them as irrelevant do so at their own peril, for staff and particularly faculty can easily derail strategic plans and policies they do not believe in or about which they feel they were not consulted. They may refuse to participate and may actually develop methods to circumvent them. Often, there is little you can do to stop this behavior once it begins. Administrators succeed not because of how smart they are, but because they successfully negotiate within their school culture and understand the decentralized and democratic nature of higher education and the role of governance on their campus (Bryant 2005; Coffman 2005). Work with and communicate with governance groups as much as possible—they can play a big part in your success as an administrator or make your position untenable. It is your choice.

TOOLS AND TAKEAWAYS

Communication in general is extremely important. Remember that one of your true sources of power in the position of associate dean is the power of persuasion. That means that you must think carefully about how you communicate.

1. *Play it straight.* Jokes and sarcasm may have worked wonders to reduce tension as a faculty member but can take on very different meanings when you are speaking for the dean's office.
2. *You are being watched.* Comments that no one would have taken notice of before now may take on considerably more importance and can be interpreted in ways you did not intend (Palm 2006) by individuals who are distrustful of administration, especially if they are being asked to do something they do not want to do (remember, you now represent the dark side).
3. *Use humor as a tool.* Is humor ever appropriate? If used correctly, it can reduce tension. But you must consider all of the different interpretations that your statements can have, and be wary!
4. *Be careful with the e-mail.* Remember that e-mails (either in their original form or in an edited form) can be forwarded to anyone and everyone. That means there are probably turns of phrases that may be fine in a one-on-one conversation on the phone or in person that can explode on you in e-mail. As a general rule, never say anything in e-mail you would not want to see as a headline in the morning paper. You want to avoid having a phrase or communication that was intended to defuse a situation actually inflame it because it was taken out of context.

Chapter 8

Dealing with Conflicts between and within Units

In other chapters we discuss dealing with difficult personalities, conflict resolution, and even the possibility of taking control over dysfunctional units. These discussions deal with how we react to things after they blow up. It is, of course, preferable to deal with conflicts between individuals and groups before they get to this point, when relationships are still salvageable. This requires cutting through the rhetoric and the poor communication of others and bringing the individuals together so that they see the situation as win-win rather than win-lose. These situations can occur between units or between individuals within units. The focus of this chapter therefore is developing and implementing preemptive measures to deal with conflict before it reaches the boiling point. We will begin with conflict between units and next move to conflict between individuals.

CONFLICT BETWEEN UNITS: SPACE WARS AND E-MAILS OF MASS DESTRUCTION

It is a fact of life that in higher education today, we are always short of space, time, and money, and in many cases these are zero-sum-gain situations (i.e., if you give one of these to one group they have to be taken away from, or at least withheld from, another). For the most part, everyone is aware of this and tries to work within the constraints of the reality in which we live and to be team players. However, when friction between units arises, it is almost always over these issues. The following case study illustrates these tensions.

> Landlock University is surrounded by densely packed urban development and cannot acquire additional land or buildings. Accordingly, there is a severe shortage of space. Associate Dean Jones receives a call from Professor Eager, chair of the Department of History, with the exciting news that they have received a major external grant to collect oral histories from long-term residents of the city in which they are situated—but they need space to conduct the interviews. This is exciting news indeed, particularly given the difficulty of receiving large externally funded grants in the humanities and the ramifications the project has for public outreach by the university with its city neighbors. Associate Dean Jones knows that the Psychology Department has a suite of four small rooms with comfortable chairs and coffee tables that it uses for one-on-one counseling sessions which would be perfect, and he calls Professor Willing, chair of the Psychology Department. Professor Willing is excited for her colleagues in the History Department and informs Associate Dean Jones that they would be more than happy to allow History to use their facility any time they are not doing counseling sessions. She sends Associate Dean Jones a schedule of available times (before 10:00 a.m. and after 2:00 p.m. on Mondays and Wednesdays, after noon on Fridays, and all day Saturdays and Sundays). Professor Willing also points out that the rooms are equipped with tape recorders and if the history researchers wish, they can record their sessions if they bring the correct size tapes along.
>
> Associate Dean Jones is sure that Professor Eager will be thrilled with this news. The researchers have space for their project and will not have to buy new tape recorders, thus saving grant money for other uses. He e-mails Professor Eager with the happy news and copies Professor Willing on the message. Professor Eager hits "reply all" and states that this is totally unacceptable. She wants the space from 10:00 a.m. to 2:00 p.m. on Tuesdays and Thursdays for the use of the History Department, and she adds that the dean's office needs to learn how to set priorities and to tell Psychology to vacate the space during that time. Needless to say, Associate Dean Jones sees this response as ungracious and unprofessional and hopes, for the good of the college, that Professor Willing is not reconsidering her generous offer.

Is there anything Associate Dean Jones could have done to avert this situation? How does he salvage it now that it has been created? In reality, other than asking if History had any special time constraints attached to the request, there is very little Associate Dean Jones could have done beforehand. Given this, the real issue now is what Jones can do to prevent the situation from escalating out of control. The answer to this question is dependent on a couple of things. First and foremost, how experienced is the chair of History? If the chair is very new to the job, Associate Dean Jones might use this as a mentoring/teaching moment. Perhaps Professor Eager is unaware of how her response sounded; asking her how she would feel in Professor Willing's position could be enough to make her see the error of her ways and to apologize for her poor choice of words and overzealousness. Additionally, it is worth pointing out to Professor Eager that e-mails can be and are frequently forwarded and can quickly become toxic, so this kind of inflammatory language should be avoided.

If Professor Eager has been around long enough to know better (or is new but unwilling to change her position), the situation becomes more complicated. Professor Willing may have a sense of humor and may not be insulted but, rather, find the whole situation amusing (you will be surprised how often this actually happens). If this is the case, Associate Dean Jones can point out to Professor Eager that beggars cannot be choosers and she owes Professor Willing an apology (yes, you do need to play the parent on occasion and remind people of their manners). If, on the other hand, Professor Willing is regretting her altruistic behavior in the face of this type of treatment by an experienced chair, Associate Dean Jones can thank her profusely for her generosity and let her off the hook by absolving her from her original offer.

Then comes the issue of what Associate Dean Jones can do with the grant and how he accommodates a researcher whose chair just made his life a little more difficult. The first step is to do a quick inventory of the possibilities. For example, if History has a conference room (perhaps not as comfortable as the small rooms with couches and chairs but serviceable), the interviews could occur here with the purchase of a tape recorder from grant funds. This may require History to eliminate other activities it would have held in the space but, as Professor Eager once said, leadership (of her department in this case) needs to figure out what is important and what has priority. In fact, a very successful method of getting your point across and in dealing with complaints is to repeat someone's own words back to them. Alternatively, Associate Dean Jones could find space off campus for the grant and charge the rent to the grant if allowable and to the department's operating budget if the grant does not allow this. This latter action may limit the department's ability to do other activities. It is true that either of these actions is punitive to the entire department for the actions of one person. However, it is critical to remember that rewarding (or even ignoring) bad behavior begets more of the same, so it cannot be ignored. On occasion, it may be necessary to inconvenience (but not harm) a small group to help a larger group in the future by changing the interaction. Never, however, go so far that these actions shift from inconveniencing to punishing the innocent members of the department in an effort to teach the chair a lesson. It is counterproductive and likely to backfire.

CONFLICT WITHIN UNITS: VIEWS OF THE FUTURE WITHIN A DEPARTMENT

In the example above, there was clearly one person who was a team player and one who was not. What happens when there are two intractable groups who fervently believe that what they are doing is the best for their department, the school, and/or the university but whose views of the future are very different? We frequently see this within departments. One of the areas in which these differences come to the fore is in hiring decisions, because they represent long-term investments that affect the future direction of a department, as illustrated in the following case study.

> The Department of Natural Disasters was allowed to search for a new tenure-track faculty member. They wrote the description in broad terms, asking for individuals with active research in the area of natural disasters in the United States. The four-member search committee narrowed the applicants down to twelve individuals from whom they requested reprints, letters of reference, and teaching statements. However, they could not decide which three individuals to bring to campus for an interview. Two members favored one group and the other two favored another group. The impasse lasted so long into the hiring season that all of the top candidates accepted jobs at other institutions. Tempers began to flare and the conflict started to affect other areas of the department. The chair of the department finally calls and tells you (as the associate dean for faculty affairs) that they have to cancel the search and will try again next year. At the same time the chair asks you what to do about the growing divide in the department. Upon investigation, you discover that the Department of Natural Disasters has two types of researchers: one group looks at the physical manifestations of a disaster (i.e., geologists, physical geographers, climatologists, volcanologists, seismologists, etc.) and the other deals with how people react to disasters (i.e., cultural geographers, sociologists, urban planners, anthropologists, etc.). These differences in emphasis mirror the divide on the search committee.

What to do? Your task as the associate dean is to help the department reach a consensus and form a plan that allows them to move forward before the factions become permanent and the department becomes dysfunctional (see chapter 9). Your efforts to try to heal the divide that is beginning to form should start now, rather than waiting until the search begins again next year. Because the two groups represent very different research perspectives, there are several things you should investigate. The questions you ask may be affected by how well you understand the field and the size and diversity of the research emphasis within the department, but a combination of group and individual discussions is probably called for.

Your first step should be to investigate whether it is possible to write an ad to attract individuals who bridge the divide. The pool will inevitably be smaller but the person hired into the position will have twice as many individuals with whom to potentially collaborate in research and curriculum. This is particularly important in small departments where you may have only one individual in each area of specialty. The downside of this kind of broad but shallow coverage is that individuals often feel isolated and/or marginalized within their own departments and thus seek research collaborations in other departments or other institutions. This is not necessarily a bad thing but has the potential to eliminate a shared interest that helps unite the department. Further, without a faculty person to bridge the divide, you end up with specialized classes that only one person can teach, placing the department's curriculum in jeopardy when an individual takes a sabbatical, goes on parental or medical leave, or retires. Thus, hiring an individual who overlaps several others, especially if he or she can bridge a theoretical or methodological gap, can result in a strengthening of ties within the department, which opens up the possibility of new research collaborations and a more sustainable curriculum within the unit.

The bridging of perspectives is not always possible. If this is the case, you need to determine if there is a unified view of where the department is heading and a plan for how to get there. Do *not* assume that just because faculty are in the same department that they all think the same thing; ask them. You will be amazed how few departments actually have discussions about the future and/or have developed a strategic plan that lays out goals and how they plan to implement them. Yes, we can hear the groans at the mention of strategic plans as we say this, but they are important. We understand the frustration. Many universities continuously develop new strategic plans. Faculty and midlevel administrators will frequently tell you that a tremendous amount of effort and time was put into the development of the last strategic plan but it seems that the plans are never implemented, or at least not in a timely manner. But large institutions like universities are like aircraft carriers—stopping and changing directions is not something they do on a dime; it takes numerous complicated steps and considerable time. The result is that the faculty members that sit on committees to create the new strategic plan are lucky if they see progress on one or two of the initiatives outlined in the several-hundred-page document in a five-year period. That does not mean we should do away with strategic plans; after all, having a sense of the direction in which you are heading in is better than constantly reacting, especially in times of resource constraints. Additionally, written plans help keep you on track when there are personnel changes in the department, school, or university.

A certain amount of frustration on the part of faculty at how slowly change occurs at the university level is to be expected. Conversely, departments are much smaller and more nimble (like speedboats). Changes in directions called for in departmental strategic plans, therefore, are much easier and quicker to implement. Importantly, the planning period provides a structure in which individual faculty members can talk about their hopes, dreams, and aspirations for both themselves and their departments. These conversations are absolutely necessary to create a shared vision of what the department should and can be, both now and in the future. These conversations rarely happen in the absence of strategic planning because, generally, individual members of departments are so busy making sure that the day-to-day operations run smoothly. They give high priority, as they should, to their own classes and research projects, so they do not take the time to talk or even think about issues of departmental visions and goals.

There are a number of ways to get the conversation about the future of the department going—all-day retreats are common, but weekly planning meetings are equally effective as long as everyone puts them on the calendar and commits to coming. If you are not comfortable working with the department to facilitate this type of conversation, there are certainly people in your school or your university—usually in programs in communication, public administration, or organizational psychology—who can facilitate. Look into the possibility of hiring facilitators to provide support to the department if it is needed. Once the plan is fleshed out and everyone agrees with the long-term plan, it is easy to move to the discussion of hires. The discussion should not start out with what the next hire should be, or the hard work of consensus building may get thrown out the window. Rather, the conversation should begin with a discussion of what the next five hires should be to meet the goals of the strategic plan. If individuals realize that others are aware of their concerns and that a hire in their area is coming, they may be willing to concede that another area needs the hire sooner. Those decisions must always be referenced back to the strategic plan. The commitments to those who agreed to delay their own self-interest must be honored in the future. In fact, even discussions about replacement hires should be referenced to the plan unless everyone in the department agrees to deviate from it. If the plan is not followed, trust will be lost by individuals who feel they are being punished for having been team players, and they may not be so willing to participate in setting strategic goals in the future.

MANAGING YOUR MANAGERS—LEADING YOUR LEADERS

In addition to conflict between groups of faculty that can arise over issues of the future of a program, conflict can and does arise between staff members and between faculty and staff. One of the most common areas is between supervisors and the individuals under them. Specifically, in your position as associate dean you are likely to oversee/manage faculty and staff in your school. Given that you came from the faculty ranks, it is highly likely that you were never trained in all the skills supervisors need to deal with conflict, motivating unmotivated employees, dealing with poorly performing individuals, etc. Further complicating the situation, you will oversee (or at least serve as a mentor for) people who in turn oversee other individuals; these managers/leaders are likely to have just as little training in this area as you did. If you are very lucky, you will be blessed with a team that all gets along together and is highly productive. In the real world, however, things are frequently not quite that smooth, as the following case study illustrates.

> Associate Dean Good Intentions is in his office one wintry day, looking forward to a quiet afternoon remarkably free of meetings. He plans to work on a manuscript that has been awaiting a few minor changes to make his editor happy. Just as he settles down with his cup of coffee, the phone rings and the caller ID shows it is his favorite contact in Human Resources. He picks up the line expecting at most a five-minute diversion. Unfortunately, a short diversion is not to be. It appears that the program assistant in the Department of Interpersonal Communication has filed a hostile work environment complaint against the chair of the department for belittling her in a faculty meeting and screaming at her in her annual evaluation meeting. While Associate Dean Good Intentions is still on the phone with HR, the chair of the department (Dr. Bad Communicator) storms into his office stating the program assistant is incompetent and demanding her immediate dismissal. Although Associate Dean Good Intentions knows the program assistant is not now and has never been a stellar employee (often doing nothing more than the minimum required for her job), she has generally gotten the job done in the past. Needless to say, screaming at others is not acceptable behavior and is actionable according to the hostile work environment policy of the university. Thus, the program assistant is entitled to due process procedures set up by HR (and in some cases, state civil services rules).

What is Associate Dean Good Intentions to do (other than kissing his afternoon of writing good-bye)? First and foremost, he must let HR conduct an investigation into the hostile work environment charge. At most institutions, if the investigation finds that a hostile work environment exists, plans for remediating the situation must be put into place. Sometimes this ultimately results in the employee moving to another position in the university, but often this is not possible due to financial constraints and lack of an open position that matches the employee's skill set. Alternatively, if the HR investigation finds against the chair, it might result in the removal of the chair from his position. If, on the other hand, HR finds that the chair may have used poor judgment but the situation does not rise to the level of hostile work environment, it often falls to the associate dean to intervene in the situation. In other words, the associate dean will be in the position of reestablishing a professional environment, ensuring that the work is done and that individuals are held accountable. Ultimately, the associate dean will need to mentor the department chair on how to manage the personnel within the department. In other words, Associate Dean Good Intentions is in the position of having to manage his managers. He must help the chair move from being a bad manager to being a good one, and if possible a leader. Until this occurs, the atmosphere within the department will continue to be toxic and the teaching, research, and service missions of the department will be severely hampered.

So what is Associate Dean Good Intentions to do? As in any circumstance when an associate dean is charged with solving a conflict between two individuals (or two groups of individuals), the first step is to collect the information so that he understands the full scope of the problem. That means the first step is to talk to the two individuals separately to find out their perspectives on the situation.

Associate Dean Good Intentions' conversation with the chair has two important purposes. First, the associate dean must find out from the chair of the department not only the situation that set off the confrontation (for that is usually just the straw that broke the camel's back), but also the long-term problems leading up to the confrontation. Second, he needs to make the chair aware of university policies on how to coach and evaluate staff members. Most universities require that an employee be informed of a problem in a professional manner and be given a chance to correct the problem (screaming at the employee in a yearly evaluation meeting and demanding her immediate termination does not fulfill this requirement). If the department chair states that he has done this, Associate Dean Good Intentions needs to ask for the documentation (another required step at most universities). Frequently, however, chairs just stop communicating with individuals that frustrate them as a conflict avoidance strategy. That means, however, that crucial steps have not been taken.

Associate Dean Good Intentions' conversation with the program assistant also should concentrate on two aspects. First, what has the coaching been like, has this problem been identified before, and if so, what steps has she taken to improve? Second, from the program assistant's perspective, what was the relationship like both before and after this confrontation? The response may be somewhat vague: "He is mean to me. He will not talk to me." This will require some probing on the associate dean's part to find out what exactly this means. He will need to ask for specific examples to illustrate what has been going on. It is also important to ask if there was a change in behavior and if so when it occurred.

Before meeting with the two together to work on a solution, Associate Dean Good Intentions also needs to make sure he understands both the program assistant's and the chair's job descriptions, as well as the culture of the department. For example, if all of the faculty members of the department are workaholics, the chair may unreasonably expect the program assistant to be one as well. Finally, he needs to check with HR, the finance department, the advising office, and the registrar to determine what is and is not getting done. Are there widespread problems with the way invoices are being submitted? Are there student complaints? Are contracts for temporary faculty or teaching assistants submitted incorrectly? Does the course schedule have to be redone multiple times? This last set of questions will help provide an independent view of the scope of the issue.

Once all the data are collected and Associate Dean Good Intentions feels he has a good handle on the situation, he should pull the two individuals together for a meeting with him. He should praise what each does well but outline where the problem is and have a discussion in which both are encouraged to participate about strategies to solve the problem. (Of course, he should have a solution in mind to offer if the chair and program assistant do not have workable ideas.) Once a solution is outlined, a timeline is needed that specifies what should get done when and by whom. Eventually, even if they do not like each other, they will be able to work together; predictability will make the working environment, if not pleasant, at least professional. Associate Dean Good Intentions then needs to check back to make sure the plan gets done according to the timeline—in particular, he needs to put a note on his calendar to check in several days before a task is due to be completed on the timeline, send a gentle reminder, and ask if there are any problems. Finally, he may wish to have a monthly meeting with the two individuals to check in and see how everything is going. Is the relationship improving? Are expectations and communication clearer? Once the day-to-day operation of the office becomes smoother, Associate Dean Good Intentions may want to propose additional projects (either projects that they work on together or two complementary projects they can work on individually) that will help strengthen some aspect of the department. Eventually, if all goes well and the stars align, the situation will start to improve, and Associate Dean Good Intentions' meetings with them can occur less frequently, and hopefully end altogether.

Even as we say this, we can hear a collective groan go up as you read this plan of attack: "I don't have time to babysit these two!" "Where am I supposed to find time in my day for yet another meeting just because these two cannot get along?" and so on. We would propose, however, that a schedule you control with expectations you clearly lay out for both parties will save time. It is much better to decide when and how to deal with these types of situations than to get constant phone calls from HR for which you have to drop everything and react, if for no other reason than it is extremely tiring to be in crisis mode all of the time.

Occasionally, no matter how hard you try, you will not be able to get the individuals involved to "play nicely." When this is the case, one of two things will happen. Either both will say, "Oh well, you tried," and other than the occasional e-mail, phone call, or visit to vent about the other's actions, they will coexist unhappily until one or the other changes jobs. Alternatively, one or the other may take your unwillingness to solve the problem they have presented to you as an indication that you refuse to support him or her. This frequently has a bigger impact when the individual who feels slighted is the chair, given the degree to which that position controls information going to the department faculty and thus may control perception of the relationship. Occasionally, this sense of persecution grows until the chair is convinced that the dean's office in general and you in particular hate him or her and are trying to destroy the department (do not roll your eyes, it happens). Depending on how the chair of the department relates interactions back to the faculty and their view of the program assistant's performance, the entire unit, or at least a large section of it, may feel as though the department is being treated unfairly. If this feeling of persecution becomes widespread, members of the department will begin to speak out about it in meetings and in conversations outside of the department.

It is always best if you can head off this type of paranoia, before it becomes widespread and deep-seated, by reassuring individuals along the way that you are there to help them and by checking back with them frequently. Sometimes, however, your first indication that this is actually happening is when someone from another unit asks you why you are punishing Department X. Sputtering protests and mounting counterarguments will likely result in quotes from *Hamlet* about protesting too much. On the other hand, you do not want to let the statement go without comment, either. This action might be interpreted as a cold and calculating confirmation of the accusation and concerns over where your unjust persecution might land next. Rather, a confirmation of a policy of equal treatment of all units, combined with a request for information, is warranted. In other words, never get down in the dirt—always take the high ground. This can be accomplished by stating something like the following: "It is unfortunate they and you feel that way as that is not my intent. In what way do you think Department X is being mistreated?" This statement acknowledges that you have heard the complaint without implying you think it has merit. Further, it reinforces your position of fair treatment and asks the person complaining to think about why he or she has made this assumption and about the information that either supports it or demonstrates that it is incorrect. In the end, however, you must trust that the people you work with are smart and will figure out what is going on when in possession of all the pertinent information.

TOOLS AND TAKEAWAYS

There is a high degree of unpredictability in the job of associate dean, and you are frequently in the position of having to drop everything to mediate disagreements between individuals and units. Sometimes these disruptions are easily rectified, but in other cases they take considerable effort to bring everyone to a consensus. There are several important things you should keep in mind while you undertake these activities.

1. *Dig below the surface to find the real source of the disagreement.* Rather than the immediate issue, disagreements between individuals and groups are frequently related to views of how the unit or campus should operate as a whole, including current and future allocations of positions, space, and other resources. Finding out what these different views are is the first step in mediating a conflict.
2. *Don't assume others have a full tool kit.* Many people in universities come into positions of leadership without the full set of skills needed to do their jobs (you are not alone in this fact). When mediating a dispute between a supervisor and an employee, you may be in the position of having to pass on to others the skills in conflict management, planning, and mentoring that you have gained as an associate dean.

Chapter 9

Trouble in Paradise

Dealing with Departmental Dysfunction

Every once in a while, you will come to work to start your day and your dean will pull you aside and tell you that he or she wants you to take on a leadership role for an existing project or unit (e.g., an academic department, a research center, or student support services or advising). There are several questions you should ask both your dean and yourself at this point (and yes, "Why did I get out of bed this morning?" is occasionally among them). Often, you will have heard about problems or issues associated with the project or unit in question prior to this point, but frequently you may not have all the information needed to accomplish the task at hand. Therefore, you need to find out some additional information so that you can plan accordingly. Take the following case study as an example.

> Through time the dean has noticed a drop-off in productivity from senior faculty in the Department of Conflict Studies. In addition, there has been a revolving door of junior faculty as well as increasing problems with student advising, including several instances of students believing they were ready to graduate only to find out they had missed several core requirements. This is a bit confusing because the chair seems so busy. He is on numerous committees, and faculty in other departments are constantly saying, "Poor Dr. Dedicated! If only he had better people to work with in his department!" In the last year, however, the situation has become worse. Faculty members of the department are rarely on campus and when they are, very public fights explode over apparently minor is-

> sues. After the last fight (occurring at commencement in front of a trustee and a reporter for the local paper), the dean has had enough. The chair is removed and you find yourself appointed as the new chair of a department far removed from your own field of study.

What do you do? How do you interact with the members of the department and what does the dean expect? Why is new leadership needed now, when it wasn't needed earlier? Associate deans are asked to add overseeing troubled units to their normal slate of duties for several reasons. Sometimes, as in this case study, the units are highly dysfunctional and need to be restructured. Other times, associate deans are asked to step into units because of personnel shortages (for example, if an interim director of student advising is needed because the existing director is retiring and there will be a lag time to conduct a proper search). Obviously, your approach toward a program or unit will be very different depending on whether the director was fired because of charges of sexual harassment or financial misconduct or if there is simply a time lag in hiring a replacement for a retiring director who is leaving the unit in good standing. On other occasions, an associate dean may be asked to step in as the acting chair of a department because the only tenured person in the department (at your university, tenure is a requirement for being the chair) is going on a sabbatical. Yet another approach is needed to lead the department in our case study, where fighting between factions within the department has become so public and disruptive that the students and junior faculty are being negatively affected. In short, caretaker positions in stable units demand very different approaches and considerations from the leadership of a troubled one.

ACTING AS A CARETAKER OF A STABLE UNIT

Taking on units that are basically stable and productive either during an ongoing search or because the current leader is on leave or sabbatical may seem like a fairly straightforward process, but there are, nevertheless, a few issues you should attempt to understand clearly from the beginning and incorporate into your approach. One of the first is who chose you to lead the unit. Was this a unilateral decision by the dean, was the decision made with consultation with only the current leader of the unit, or was the whole unit consulted in the process? Additionally, you should ask if there is someone within the unit who both meets minimum qualifications for taking the position and wishes to have the position but was passed over in favor of you. If there is a person like this in the unit, the situation may not be as stable as you originally thought, and some sleuthing to learn the back story is warranted. If the unit views you as someone who has been imposed on them from the outside, there may be resistance or resentment directed toward you with regard to the tasks you must undertake or ask the members of the unit to undertake, regardless of how small or straightforward they may be.

It is always better to have wide consultation within and outside of the unit prior to the dean's making a decision to put an associate dean at the head of a unit. If that has not occurred and you inherit the above situation, one of your first actions should be to meet with the members of the unit to ensure that the individuals you have to work with are on board with your leadership position. Failure to do this as your first act may mean that you'll find it difficult to accomplish the tasks required of you and that considerable stress will be added to your workdays. Minimally, heed Stephen Trachtenberg's (2007) advice and do not expect gratitude for your hard work in the unit—that will only lead to disappointment. On the other hand, Holton (1998b) reminds us not to expect opposition and interference from everyone, either. Most of our faculty members and staff are, in fact, hardworking; they care deeply about their students and research and are dedicated to their department, school, and university.

Let us assume that your new unit is thrilled with your appointment. There are still a number of things you need to know to be effective during your time in this position, particularly given the fact that this is probably a task added on top of your already busy schedule. First and foremost, you must determine the priorities of both your dean and the unit. These are frequently not the same thing. One of the major determinants of how your actions will be directed and perceived by the dean and the unit is the length of time your role as interim head/director/chair is likely to last. Stepping in for a month while the current director is out on leave for hip replacement surgery is very different from taking over the unit for a semester or an entire academic year. The longer the period you are to serve as head of the unit, the more likely it is that the tasks expected of you by the dean and the unit will diverge. For example, your dean's desire may be as simple as making sure classes get scheduled, routine personnel actions occur, and the number of complaints he or she hears about are kept at a reasonably low level. In addition, the unit may have begun a new initiative that needs considerable investment of time and intellectual energy to plan, initiate, and grow, and the unit is counting on you to flesh out the plan for this initiative and launch it. If the unit and the dean have such divergent perspectives, a conversation with the dean (and possibly the unit) is necessary immediately. Following these conversations, you need to draw up a realistic plan of action that takes into consideration the goals you are expected to achieve, the amount of time you are expected to devote to these goals, the manner in which the permanent members of the unit will be involved, and the anticipated time line for goal completion.

Once your focus and tasks have been agreed upon and the unit and the dean are on board with them, your job is to accomplish these goals as professionally and efficiently as possible and resist the urge to get diverted in a way that will make the reentry of the "real" leader difficult. Remember that you are a placeholder assigned to keep a train that's on the tracks moving in the right direction and help it not to lose momentum nor be diverted onto another track.

STEPPING INTO TROUBLED UNITS

In the case of troubled units, however, the train, at a minimum, is on the wrong track or, at worst, the train is off the tracks and has been dismantled by vandals. This is very different from the situation above, as reflected in the case study. In the case study, you are asked to step into a leadership position in a unit because vital tasks are not being completed (student advising); the unit is out of compliance with college, university, and state or federal regulations (workload); the unit is not participating in strategic plans of the larger university (mentoring of junior faculty); and/or factional fighting within the unit has reached a point where the unit is no longer functioning (hostile work environment and faculty absenteeism punctuated by public fights). In other words, a department (or other type of academic unit) is placed into academic receivership because it cannot function adequately and it has demonstrated that it is unable to manage its affairs. In this case, leadership of the unit is transferred to an individual who is not a member of the unit, regardless of the number of individuals in the unit who are qualified and willing to take the position. The new leader is charged with cleaning up the unit and will very likely face resistance from within it.

As with stepping into stable units, there are a number of issues you need to understand immediately. Some of these issues mirror the questions asked for stable units, such as how long you will be the interim director/chair/head. Others, however, are more targeted at the source of the unit's problems. First, is the dean making a change in leadership unilaterally or did the unit members demand a change in leadership due to factional fights? Related to this, what were the factors leading to the dean's decision to change unit leadership at this time (both the immediate, precipitating issue as well as the long-term issues)? The answer to this question will give you insight into the dean's primary concern and should help you frame your thinking about what to do and how to approach it. Second, how do the members of the unit feel about your coming into the unit? This will affect how you will interact with them and the amount of consensus building you will need to do from the very beginning. Typically, when a unit is in receivership, its members lose some of their self-determination, at least for a while, as the interim leader re-creates necessary processes and policies and restores a climate of professionalism. There may be limits, however, to what you can do in this regard, so it is important to find out what you are allowed to do under the bylaws of your school and/or university, collective bargaining agreement, and governance systems.

Leading a troubled unit is considerably different from leading a stable, productive one, (even a stable unit whose members are not thrilled about your presence). First and foremost, it is essential that the dean's goals for the unit (and frequently the provost's, chancellor's, or president's goals) take precedence in setting your agenda as the interim leader, even if they are in conflict with the goals of the unit (or the goals of some faction of the unit). Therefore, the first thing you must figure out is what the dean's goals are (Stone 2009). Rarely is the goal to make the members of the unit feel warm and fuzzy; actually, you must be prepared to "play the heavy" on occasion. The more vague the dean's goals are (e.g., "Make them get along and stop calling me"), the harder your job will be. Conversely, specific goals about compliance, assessment plans, research productivity, and program development are more concrete objectives around which methods of attack can be developed. Therefore, before you can make a plan of action, considerable discussion needs to occur between you and the dean, and this discussion must continue throughout your tenure as the head of the troubled unit. This will not only provide feedback to the dean on progress but will also be a good opportunity to discuss new goals and issues as they arise. Because the dean has not eliminated the program, he or she feels there are things within the program worth saving. It is important to recognize these, for they may serve as a basis on which to build within the unit.

A recent survey of universities and colleges (Stone 2009) demonstrates that academic receivership may be more common than is generally assumed, and that by far the most common reason for its occurrence is faculty incivility. Faculty incivility is a broad category and includes both active bullying and factional fighting, as well as more passive, behind-the-scenes sabotage that paralyzes departments (Gunsalus 2006; Higgerson and Joyce 2007; Lucas 1998; Twale and De Luca 2008). Therefore, regardless of the goals the dean lays out in terms of curriculum and research, the restoration of civility and collegial behavior is likely to be of paramount importance, and conflict management will be a major undertaking while you lead the unit. Fortunately, conflict management in higher education, after being ignored for decades, has recently become a major topic of conversation in the literature. Because conflict management is an important issue not only in taking on troubled units but also in much of what we do as associate deans, we will cite the literature rather heavily in this section to give you a wealth of resources to tap into.

CONFLICT MANAGEMENT

It is important to realize that not all disagreement is harmful (Cheldelin and Lucas 2004; Coffman 2005; Graff 1998; Higgerson and Joyce 2007; Lucas 1998). On the contrary, disagreements carried out in a professional manner lead to discussions about the most efficient manner in which to conduct department, school, and/or university business, and academic discussions lead to the discovery and dissemination of new knowledge. However, disagreement that rises to the level of incivility is not productive and must be addressed.

Many of us are ill equipped to deal with and manage conflict when we enter the position of associate dean because we grew up in an academic culture that vacillated between rewarding and ignoring this behavior. The rewards come in a system that trains and actively rewards academics (in the form of publications, grants, and promotions), from the early stages of graduate school throughout our entire careers, for being critical of the ideas and research of others. Most of this critique is done at a professional level and does not rise to the level of disruptive incivility or bullying, but the fact remains that being a team player who praises rather than critiques is not a behavior that is rewarded in academia (Lucas 1998). Added to this professional training, there is a history in higher education of avoiding conflict rather than dealing with it head-on. In the past, when conflict has reached the level that it is disruptive to units and students, the disruptive faculty members have been moved into different departments with the assumption that isolating the parties involved solves the problem (Graff 1998; Sturnick 1998). However, this merely delays the issue rather than solving it. Frequently, ignoring conflict results in increased conflict in the end because the bad behavior has, in one sense, been rewarded (by moving the perpetrator to a new position) and the perpetrator has suffered no negative repercussions. The result is the development of long-standing feuds between faculty and staff and a situation in which every debate devolves into an issue of personal attack based in age-old animosities (Berryman-Fink 1998; Coffman 2005; Graff 1998; Gunsalus 2006; Sturnick 1998).

The lesson to be learned from this situation is that faculty may be able to avoid conflict by looking for jobs elsewhere or working from home on days they are not teaching, but administrators do not have that luxury.

Associate deans who are faced with leading a department in receivership must confront it head-on and resolve it (Dowdall and Dowdall 2005; Coffman 2005; Gunsalus 2006; Lucas 1994; Twale and De Luca 2008). Despite this, you cannot start your stint as chair of the department by telling the faculty to stop acting like six-year-olds (as much as we all wish we could). Long-standing, deeply entrenched factions do not develop overnight and will not be resolved overnight. They need to be tackled in a careful and deliberate manner.

The most important thing to remember when dealing with hostile factions and bullies is that it is paramount that you remain calm and professional, no matter what happens. Do not react defensively, even when incivility or bullying behavior is directed at you (Higgerson and Joyce 2007; Sorenson 1998; Sturnick 1998). Beyond this, it is important to be able to recognize types of difficult personalities and behaviors so that you can catch bad behavior early in the interaction. Several experts in the field of conflict management have attempted to create personality typologies of individuals frequently involved in disputes and ways in which to minimize their impact (Gilley 2003; Higgerson and Joyce 2007; Sorenson 1998), and these are summarized in table 9.1.

Although each of these lists appears very different, there are commonalities. Gilley's (2003) shopworn faculty member, Higgerson and Joyce's (2007) indifferent soul, and Sorenson's (1998) dropout are all long-term members of the university who are burned out and disengaged. They put forth minimal effort and object to change because it disrupts their well-established routines. While these individuals can be disruptive to a department and cause resentment among those who have to pick up the work they are not doing, they are frequently not openly involved in conflict themselves. Rather, they need to be brought back into the fold as productive department members through engagement and encouragement (see chapter 10). Compliment their past accomplishments and ask them about their current interests. Once you find out their interests, ask them to share their wisdom and enthusiasm by participating in a commit-

Table 9.1. Types of personalities frequently involved in conflict

Gilley (2003)	Higgerson and Joyce (2007)	Sorenson (1998)
The Subversive	The Pot Stirrer	The Blocker
The Obstructionist	The Troublemaker	The Exploder
The Cynic	The Prima Donna	The Complainer
The Incompetent	The Drama Queen	The Sniper
The Lazy Person	The Confrontation Junkie	The Bully
The Shopworn	The Passive	The Saboteur
	The Indifferent Soul	The Dropout

tee or task force. Sometimes, people just want to know somebody cares and values them.

This is very different from individuals who actively undermine others and their units like Gilley's (2003) subversive; Higgerson and Joyce's (2007) pot stirrer, troublemaker, and confrontation junkie; and Sorenson's (1998) blocker, exploder, sniper, bully, and saboteur. These individuals often attempt to control information and divert it for their own purposes. Open, frequent communication through multiple channels (one-to-one and one-to-many) through multiple media is one way to deal with this. Additionally, find out what types of issues these individuals are most likely to act out about, so you can anticipate their behavior and stop it before it starts. This, however, is not always possible. Once the damage is done you need to stay cool, calm, and collected—that is, do not get angry and do not get defensive. Remember that no matter how bad the behavior and no matter how justified you might be in losing your cool, if you do so, it will cost you precious credibility. Instead, stand up to the bullies and bad behaviors calmly, firmly, and consistently and let them know (one-on-one to start with but publicly if necessary) that this type of behavior is unacceptable. At the same time, make sure to praise them publicly when they behave well. Beyond this, personal integrity and consistency are your best weapons. Take the high ground and remember that you work with very smart people; sooner or later they will figure out who is worth listening to and who is not.

Regardless of the personality types involved, there are steps that can be taken to both understand the root cause and resolve the conflict within units. First and foremost, remember that the issue is probably more complicated than it appears on the surface and the precipitating event is usually just the straw that broke the camel's back rather than the root of the problem. Additionally, you must look not only at the individual conflicts but also at the departmental culture in which they have occurred and the university-wide culture in which they have been tolerated to understand how the situation has devolved to its current state (Coffman 2005; Hoppe 2003; Sorenson 1998).

A number of authors (Coffman 2005; Gmelch 1998; Holton 1998a, 1998b; Sorenson 1998; Sturnick 1998) offer detailed plans on how to approach the issue of warring factions and bullies. These approaches are compiled into a single presentation below, but if you find yourself in this situation you might want to pull these original resources, as well as the volumes on faculty personality types discussed above, for more detailed information.

A first step in dealing with conflict is taking the time to understand what the source of the conflict really is. Conflict in a unit is rarely restricted to the instance that set off the latest round of battles and got the unit into receivership. You need to explore the breadth and depth of the underlying issues, and to do this effectively you must talk to all the relevant parties (the individuals involved in the conflict and other members of the department, as well). If you talk to only one individual, you will get only one side of the picture, and there are always two sides to every story. Additionally, you must remember that individuals may have different information (or different perceptions of the situation). By gathering information from multiple sources, you see where the redundancies are (i.e., the facts everyone agrees on) and where the differences in information or perception are (i.e., the cause of the disagreement).

Once you understand both the commonalities and the differences, you can then start conversations (both one-on-one and in groups) about the issues. Begin with the aspects everyone agrees on and reframe the differences. The reframing allows you to keep the focus on the facts rather than the personalities, to ensure that everyone has the same information, to identify possible common interests that were not evident before, and to present different ways of viewing the situation or perceiving it in a positive light. From there, brainstorming of solutions or plans of action can occur. Just as important as coming up with a plan of action, however, is to make sure that all parties follow through and implement the plan. This means setting a timetable and agreeing upon mechanisms for judging whether the plan is successful and mechanisms for evaluating progress in the future.

You may be saying to yourself, "That sounds nice and logical, but sometimes there are people out there who just will not let you move forward." That may be true sometimes, but we believe such people are rare. What we have presented is a way of structuring interaction to help move a troubled unit forward, but it does not always work; sometimes the problems are too deep and too entrenched. This is why the ongoing conversations with your dean are so important. Your dean's involvement cannot stop with setting the goals for the receivership. Conversations between you and your dean about the unit must be ongoing and at set intervals so that, collectively, you can evaluate progress and determine if the goals need to be reworked. In the extreme case, the dean may decide that despite what he or she originally thought, the unit cannot be saved and should be disbanded under the rules set out by the school and/or university bylaws and governance systems.

GOALS AND OBJECTIVES FOR THE UNIT

Let us assume, for the moment, that you are successful in managing the conflict within the unit (and this does happen more often than you think, if you are deliberate and strategic about your actions). The next question is how to accomplish your dean's goals and, in so doing, bring the unit back to a functioning state where it can be released from receivership. We live in a litigious society, and we work in universities with rules that constrain our actions due to collective bargaining agreements and/or principles of faculty governance. In other words, your power to do anything substantive and permanent may be tenuous at best. We do not mean to suggest that the situation is helpless and you are on a fool's errand. Rather, we wish to reinforce very strongly that what you have to rely upon is the force of your personality, your ability to persuade, and the power of policy (Hoppe 2003). That means you need to know policy well, including what you are and are not allowed to do in terms of rewards, punishments, and procedures. Equally important is for you to know what the members of the unit are and are not allowed to do in terms of resistance and participation. Additionally, you need to be aware of your interaction style and how that style affects others. Some of us are straightforward, no-nonsense people who say it the way we see it, and others are more skilled at subtleties and at connecting to the individual through indirect conversational conventions. There is not a right or wrong personality, but you need to understand what you are and are not comfortable doing in terms of interacting with others—because members of the unit who are opposed to your presence will certainly be able to spot a weakness in approach and exploit it if they wish to hinder progress. Regardless of how you handle it, it is wise to remember Steven Sample's advice: "Don't humiliate an opponent unless you are sure you are able, and want, to eliminate him altogether. Otherwise you'll simply make an enemy for life" (Sample 2002, 99).

Once you have seen progress in conflict management and you are beginning to achieve the dean's goals for the unit, it is important to engage the members of the department in strategic planning and goal setting to establish a firm foundation on which to build the future of the unit. This process has the added benefit of reinforcing the idea that there has been progress and that there is the possibility that the department members may move out of receivership and regain control of their unit in the future. Additionally, it gives them a reason to continue to improve departmental relations and functions, beyond the desire to keep their jobs.

TOOLS AND TAKEAWAYS

One of the most difficult things to get used to about being an associate dean is the lack of predictability in the day-to-day workings of the school and the dean's office. Being asked to step into and redirect a dysfunctional academic unit is, on one hand, one of the most critical jobs you might face as an associate dean, but it also is an incredibly disruptive task for you. The other tasks on your plate get crowded if not mothballed, any research and scholarship you have been trying to do as a faculty member gets pushed further back on the burner, and your ability to plan day-to-day is essentially removed at first as you move the situation from crisis mode to some semblance of stability. How do you keep positive and focused in the face of all this? In addition to the tips in chapter 8, we recommend the following.

1. *Remember that it is not forever.* It is important to think about the end game for dealing with a challenging task such as being put in charge of a troubled unit; there will be an exit strategy, and to a large degree, you can be its architect.
2. *Do not assume anything.* Do not assume that you know all the nuances of the situation. Talk to all of the parties involved and collect as much information as you can to get a clear and complete view of the situation.
3. *Set clear goals.* By setting clear goals for the unit through conversations with your dean, working carefully and respectfully to guide the unit toward these goals, and empowering the unit to return to self-governance, you can work through the disruption and succeed in your task.
4. *Accept and deal with conflict.* Ignoring factionalism and conflict within the unit will only make your job harder. Understand the sources of conflict, identify the players, and lay out a path to resolving the conflict, or at least insulating the rest of your and the unit's work from its damaging effects.
5. *Maintain communication.* It is crucial to maintain clear and frequent communication both within the unit you are overseeing and with the dean. Constant communication serves to move the process forward, engage all parties in the process, and ensure transparency.
6. *Be patient.* Remember that one reason you became an associate dean was that you enjoy and are good at supporting the school and moving departments and faculty forward; the service you do when rehabilitating a struggling unit is one of the most tangible examples of this support.

Chapter 10

The Inmates Are Running the Asylum

Getting Hostile and Unproductive Faculty and Staff on Board

As we have mentioned in a number of other chapters, the vast majority of faculty and staff are productive, engaged, and committed colleagues. Of course, these are not the people who will take up most of your time and energy as an associate dean. Unfortunately, you will spend the majority of your time with the other (albeit relatively small) segment of the faculty and staff who are divas (though not necessarily justifiably so)—high-maintenance, entitled, hostile, unproductive, disengaged, disruptive, and so on. In short, these are the individuals who the chairs of your departments claim are keeping your institution from being a great university because you, the associate dean, will not let chairs fire these unproductive and difficult faculty without due process. Clearly, developing strategies for bringing these people back into the fold of the productive and collaborative, or alternatively, minimizing the damage they can do, is in your own best interest as well as that of the university. Depending on your collective bargaining agreements, tenure system, and HR office, you, in fact, often will not be able to terminate these individuals—and, depending on your merit evaluation and reward system (see chapter 5), you may have little in the way of penalties to impose in response to lack of productivity and/or obstructionist behavior. This means you'll need to take a well-thought-out and often very different approach to dealing with these individuals in order to make the situation better and not exacerbate it. Needless to say, how you handle hostile faculty will be very different from how you handle unproductive colleagues, but in approaching both, it is critical to think of ways to encourage desired behaviors while discouraging undesired behaviors. The following case study illustrates the complexity of these types of situations.

> Spring is in the air and that can mean only one thing—it is time for annual merit evaluations of all of the faculty and staff in your college. The chair of each of the departments makes an appointment with the dean and the associate dean for faculty affairs to review what their faculty members have accomplished over the last year and to argue for a pay increase based on merit for each faculty member. The chair of the Department of Overachievers arrives with each staff and faculty member's yearly evaluation. Across the board, the members of the faculty are highly productive: all have applied for grants (several received grants, others are reworking their proposals for the next round of submissions), have published in scholarly journals, published monographs, and given papers at professional meetings. Additionally, the faculty members are active in service at the department, school, university, and professional level and regularly assess their classes to make sure that they are meeting the teaching mission of the department. The chair of the department is rightly proud of her department's achievements. In addition to the yearly pay raise, the chair proposes to you that if the department members' course loads were reduced from four classes a year to two they could produce even more research. However, faculty members are concerned about the students getting the classes they need to graduate and understand the need to contain cost. They are proposing to increase the average size of their classes from thirty students to seventy-five students and to use their portion of indirect cost recovery from their grants to hire their graduate students to hold study sessions for the students who may be challenged by this new format. The dean agrees, and the next year the Department of Overachievers receives an increase in external grant funding, publishes more articles, and has assessment data to demonstrate that their new class and study session format is a success.
>
> Later that year, the chair of the Department of Underachievers meets with the dean and associate dean. The chair informs the dean and associate dean that none of the faculty applied for grants and only one faculty member published a peer-reviewed article in the last year. Further, it is evident that senior faculty members of the department do no service, the department has yet to implement an assessment plan for student outcomes, and their classes are very small and frequently are cancelled due to low enrollment. When asked to explain this lack of productivity, the chair declares that it is because they are treated differently from other departments—for example, they have to teach four classes a year and the members of the Department of Overachievers have to teach only two. The chair states that this is an obvious example of the dean favoring one department over the other and attempts to make the case that, considering the teaching load of the faculty of her department, they did an excellent job on all fronts—in fact, she thinks it is fair to suggest that the one faculty member who did publish is probably one of the best scholars at the university if we consider quality over quantity of scholarly work. She goes on to state that the dean simply does not appreciate all the intangible things her faculty have contributed to the school in the face of

> the inequitable treatment they receive at the hands of the dean's office. Although the dean and the associate dean respectfully and carefully attempt to correct this department chair's misperceptions, she is resistant and is infuriated when the dean does not offer her faculty more than the base pay raise allocated for faculty. Although the chair works to retain her composure, she ends up leaving the meeting quite angry and vows to rally her faculty to correct this injustice.

There are various types of individuals illustrated in this example: stars that produce, unproductive faculty, and entitled faculty who see themselves as victims of an unfair system. Additionally, there is a disconnect between the department's internal perception of itself and an objective review of the data for the Department of Underachievers that the dean and associate dean are unable to correct despite careful and thoughtful discussion with the chair. How each of these situations and individuals is dealt with differs considerably, and it is often the job of the associate dean to do the heavy lifting in terms of bringing challenged faculty and units back to a place where they are productive and aware of what is expected of them relative to what they are doing. Much of this "rehabilitation" occurs through mentoring programs, the tenure process, post-tenure review, and occasionally through disciplinary action (though this last option is frequently very limited depending on the nature of the merit policy and/or the collective bargaining contract at the institution).

DISTINGUISHING THE STARS FROM THE DIVAS

The first step is to distinguish the truly productive faculty and staff from those who perceive themselves to be productive but are, in fact, unproductive. This is actually not as easy as it sounds. First, the more heterogeneous your school is, the more variance you can expect in what is deemed high scholarly productivity in different departments as well as what is deemed excellent job performance for staff. For example, whereas it may be reasonable to expect several coauthored articles a year from individuals in some of your science departments, you may anticipate one high-quality novel from your English faculty or one book from your history faculty every two to three years. Additionally, although the chair of the Department of Underachievers was going a bit far with her argument about "quality versus quantity," most of us would agree that fewer, high-quality, first-tier publications are preferable to a slightly larger number of fourth-tier publications. Productivity in teaching is also difficult to measure, although assessment designed around program goals is quickly becoming a mechanism that allows us to deal with disciplinary differences. Measures like class size, however, will differ for pedagogical reasons and can complicate evaluation of course quality, especially if student feedback is used.

So, how do you really know what the problem is with a faculty member who, at least on the surface, appears to be disengaged and/or unproductive? How do you know if someone really is a victim of circumstances that are keeping him or her from performing at the expected level, as opposed to someone who baselessly blames everyone else and the institution for a lack of progress? How do you distinguish someone who is a true star (productive, professional, collegial) from one who is a diva (someone who is demanding and high-maintenance, who may or may not be productive)? Finally, how do you know when complaints of a thing like unfair treatment, such as those leveled by the chair of the Department of Underachievers, have substance, as opposed to the chair's simply blaming policy and the dean for his or her own lack of progress to deflect responsibility from the department and faculty in question?

Key to answering these questions is understanding and clarifying, when necessary, the performance criteria for each faculty and staff position and for your academic departments. For faculty, the tenure criteria established by the primary unit are often the appropriate yardsticks against which to measure faculty productivity. These criteria are helpful not only for pre-tenure but also for tenured faculty, because they lay out a definition of what is meritorious in research and teaching in a particular field, and these definitions do not change overnight or just because an individual receives tenure. For staff, the official job description that goes along with each position serves a similar role. The benefit of tenure criteria and job descriptions is that they tend to be discipline- and/or job-specific and reflect, for example, the differences in activities and scholarship in the disciplines of English and chemistry. At many institutions, additional criteria exist for yearly merit evaluations for faculty and staff that set benchmarks for performance that are related to, but not always the same as, the tenure criteria and the job description. If this is the case, these criteria should also be used to evaluate objectively what people are and are not doing, and how well that maps onto the expectations of their positions. If faculty or staff are not meeting these expectations and no extenuating circumstances can be identified that account for the situation (such as the closing of a press for faculty or the implementation of a new computer system that required considerable additional training for staff), then you have an issue of low productivity and poor job performance (see below).

The above, of course, is predicated on the assumption that you have clear, written criteria for faculty and staff performance. Unfortunately, however, written criteria are missing at many schools, and the lack of criteria is the fodder of lawsuits. If you are at a university that lacks these types of documented criteria there may be little you can do about your unproductive personnel and units in the short term. Rather, you should work with your dean and the governance groups in your school to begin the process of establishing performance criteria and expectations for faculty and staff and to get these written down and approved by all involved. Realize though, that the development and approval of such documentation is likely to be a slow and contentious process because you are asking for a change in the institutional culture from one of ambiguity to one of accountability. Despite this, we urge you to undertake this task, as it is in situations in which the criteria are either nonexistent or ambiguous that the disconnect flourishes between the administration's perception and the faculty or staff member's perception of his or her productivity. That means that in addition to changing the culture, you also will need to deal with these very different views of reality, likely by using data and information from peer institutions, professional organizations, and scholarly research on faculty and staff evaluation, when it exists.

Unfortunately, clear, written, appropriate performance criteria are not always sufficient to prevent the sort of situation described in the case study above. Even when you have such criteria, you can still end up with a situation where faculty or staff are unhappy and feel unappreciated for their efforts. These individuals are often referred to as high-maintenance or entitled, and they may or may not be stars based on their performance. If they are really stars, then Bryant's (2005, 78) wonderful quote comes into play: "It is easier to work with faculty who act like prima donnas if they sing like prima donnas." We refer to these prima donnas that can sing (i.e., deliver the goods) as true divas. Of course, there are plenty of people who believe they are divas and act that way but do not have the scholarly chops to warrant the title. In the case of the real divas, however, your dean may be fairly generous with resources and time and extremely tolerant of their occasional outbursts and journeys into unreality. You may agree with this approach and the accompanying rewards due to the diva's productivity, but that does not mean that even the real divas do not occasionally irritate the devil out of you, and it is the associate dean who usually gets bombarded with their e-mails and phone calls—which include demands, complaints, condescending advice to you on how to do your job better, and so on.

So what do you do about high-maintenance individuals, regardless of their productivity? We find Chambers' (2004) insight helpful in this area—specifically, that high-maintenance individuals are basically people who micromanage you from below. The same tactics you would use for a dean who micromanages you (chapter 4) can be put into place. Figure out what aspects of your interaction with the individual you have complete control over, what you have partial control over, and what you have no control over. Generally speaking, you have no control over the high-maintenance behavior (after all it has been rewarded for years, so it is well entrenched), so do not waste your time and energy attempting to change it. You have complete control over the way you react to their behavior, however, and by extension you have partial control over the interaction. It is very liberating when you realize that you do not have to act on every one of their complaints or suggestions. Of course, you must remain professional in your interaction with the simple response of "Thank you for pointing that out to me" or "That's a great suggestion—we'll have to look into that" and then move on to the next thing on your calendar. If this is not sufficient, an "I will be sure to pass that suggestion on to the dean" can be powerful (do tell your dean, though, because the person will likely ask the dean about it at some future date). A general rule of thumb for dealing with complaining faculty and helping you feel that you have reframed the situation rather than simply being a punching bag for every disgruntled diva you deal with is to ask the diva for a solution to go along with the complaints and ask what he or she might be able to do in the diva's department, for example, to facilitate some of the changes he or she is seeking. For example, you might ask, "How would you handle that?" or "Could you put your perspective of the issue and possible solutions in a memo to me that I can give the dean?" For about half of the high-maintenance faculty, that will be the end of the conversation.

The above discussion has concentrated on the interaction rather than the issue of productivity. For highly productive faculty this is not an issue; they tend to be self-directed. For those who have become unproductive, however, mentoring and, ideally, consequences for continued poor performance (see chapter 5) may be required.

THE UNPRODUCTIVE FACULTY MEMBER

In addition to mentoring junior faculty members (which is what we usually think of when the word "mentoring" is mentioned), associate deans are often charged with increasing productivity from mid-career and/or late-career faculty and staff who have become disengaged or are perceived to have stalled. Sometimes this is true of an entire department. Regardless of the scale (individual versus a unit), this is an important issue that we all too often ignore in higher education but that we should deal with head-on (Higgerson and Joyce 2007; Sorenson 1998). From a purely market perspective, failure to remediate poor productivity in faculty results in a loss of expertise/productivity for the school, but it goes beyond this. In effect, it is a unilateral renegotiation of the workload in the work contract by the individual, in which the acceptable workload becomes lower for the disengaged individual than for the rest of the unit. If ignored, this can lead to frustration and loss of morale for the other individuals in the unit who must then pick up the slack. This may result in retention issues or decreasing productivity of the unit as a whole, as others begin to ask, "If there is no consequence for the individual who does less work, why should I kill myself doing all this work?" Conversely, individuals may disengage because they are actively discouraged from being engaged and active by others. In other words, disengagement may be an indication of dysfunction within the unit, or at the extreme, result from the presence of a bully (see the extreme results of this situation in chapter 9).

Being alerted to this problem in faculty or units can come in many forms: little progress noted on annual evaluations, or questions from chairs/supervisors about how to get rid of a particular individual through a transfer to another department or program, firing, or forced retirement. Before acting too quickly to reprimand the individual or unit, however, it is important to realize that disengagement is more complicated than it can initially appear, and that data gathering on your part is essential. To begin with, disengagement can appear in all aspects of the individual's job responsibility (these individuals are often referred to as "deadwood") or in just some areas of their job duties. An example of the latter is a full professor who is still active in research but does not participate in service and has no graduate students working with him or her, or the staff member who is loved by all of the students for his or her attention to their individual issues and their knowledge of contacts in other offices but who refuses to learn the new software needed to collect data on the students for evaluation of their graduation status. Additionally, the reasons the disengagement has occurred can vary considerably, and this affects the approach that you, as an associate dean charged with dealing with the issue, should take. The specifics of the reasons are as varied as the individuals involved, but they can generally be grouped into three big categories: (1) a mismatch between what the individuals or unit perceives to be their contributions versus what others perceive, (2) structural issues within the unit that discourage engagement of individuals and result in low morale, and (3) problem individuals or units who refuse to fulfill their job requirements. What you personally or the dean's office generally can do about individuals in these situations in terms of disciplinary action, the merit system, or workload assignment may be constrained by governance and/or collective bargaining agreements of your university; however, something as simple as taking the time to understand each individual situation and being careful and thoughtful about the way you communicate and interact can make a significant positive impact (Baldwin et al. 2008;

Sorenson 1998). Here are some specific suggestions for approaching each of the above situations.

Correcting the Mismatch between the Perceived and the Actual

When conducting research, anthropologists are acutely aware that how they see the world or particular events is very different from the way in which the people they study see the world or particular events. The anthropologist, as an outsider, frequently views and interprets an interaction from an "objective" and empirical perspective and often does not know the full history of the participants involved in the interaction. These views may be informed by scientific measures of climate, resource availability, resource use, political organization, and so forth. These views can be contrasted with the meaning of an interaction for the people themselves and, therefore, the manner in which they react. You may be asking yourself, "Why are they dragging me through an introductory lecture on how anthropologists study cultures of which they are not a part?" After all, the faculty and units we are talking about in this chapter are firmly ensconced in American academic culture just as we are; because we share the same culture, there should be no problem in everyone seeing a particular issue the same way, right? In reality, however, there are frequently considerable differences in the way various individuals within a university view a situation because of their differing frames of reference. These differences can be exacerbated by the different missions that administrators, faculty, and staff believe they have relative to the university. It is important not only to recognize this fact but, like the anthropologist, also to attempt to determine what these differences in perception are and use them to help understand why a faculty or staff member or unit is engaging (or failing to engage) in a particular way.

As Holton (1998a) rightly points out, individuals act on perception of situations rather than some outside objective measure. They need to see a situation as an opportunity that should be embraced rather than a problem that should be avoided, and they need to see that interacting or engaging in a very different way is possible as well as beneficial before they will change the way in which they are behaving. Unless those of us who are attempting to change behavior understand how the faculty and staff members or units perceive situations and the possibilities that may or may not be associated with them, we cannot work effectively to change their perceptions, and, as a result, encourage them to change their behavior.

A great example of a situation in which the context and perspective of an individual change across time and greatly affect how they behave is the life cycle of a faculty member. Junior faculty members who are making the transition from graduate student to faculty member are simultaneously dealing with a change in role (from student to teacher), learning a new institutional culture (having come to a new university), developing new classes (which they may have never done before), and setting up a research agenda. Most of us in administration recognize that this can be a very stressful period in a faculty member's career, and considerable support and mentoring are usually present to help junior faculty become established and thrive as they move toward tenure. Unfortunately, however, mentoring stops the minute an individual gets tenure at most universities. For some faculty this is not a problem, as they have figured out their research career and understand their institution well enough to continue to thrive. For others, however, the picture is much more problematic. They spend the early part of their careers striving for the goal of tenure, and then promotion to full professor. The result is that they reach the highest faculty rank they can achieve at a relatively young age and suddenly realize that they will be doing the exact same thing for the rest of their careers that they did as an assistant professor, albeit with a bit more service thrown in (Baldwin et al. 2008).

Faculty may wish to shift the direction of their research but require training in new methods to accomplish this goal. Alternatively, they may feel increasing difficulty connecting with students and keeping up with new innovations in technology and pedagogy, as active learning replaces the tried-and-true lecture format. Mentoring seminars designed for junior faculty are inappropriate for more senior faculty members because they have already mastered the basics of how to set up a syllabus, how to deal with disruptive students, how to manage time, how to set up a research agenda, and the like, and so a different approach is needed. Similarly, staff members are frequently expected to be up to date automatically on all the latest software programs and changes in national standards of advising, data collection, or state regulations on budgeting, but they may not know how to obtain these new skills. So how do you help these individuals? To help develop some interventions, ask yourself if your institution has mentoring programs for mid-career and late career faculty and staff. If so, how many of your faculty and staff actually know they exist? Mentoring later in an individual's career often occurs in a very different manner; specifically, peer mentoring or peer coaching is more common (Huston and Weaver 2007). In peer mentoring, two or more individuals at similar points in their careers are paired to discuss issues, evaluate each other's work, and share information on resources, methods, and techniques. Sometimes this is done informally (one staff member calls another up to ask them if they have used the new budget software) and at others more formally (faculty members observe each other's classes and discuss how new technologies can be introduced to enhance student learning). Or sometimes in monthly get-togethers faculty and/or staff share best practices on a particular topic. For research, faculty might wish their peer mentors to be individuals outside of the university but within the area of study they wish to explore.

Regardless of how this occurs, it is crucial for unproductive staff and faculty members to understand the possibilities and to believe that they are in an environment where they will not be punished for trying new things (which have the possibility of failure). Often, creating this environment is less about monetary resources than about taking the time to find out what individuals need and helping them to make the connections.

Structural Issues Impacting Engagement

Occasionally, you will find an individual who is aware of the resources available but has disengaged in all or part of his or her job anyway. This is particularly disheartening when it occurs in individuals who were very active in previous years. Before assuming that the individual no longer cares or is lazy, you should look at the unit in which they spend most of their time. Ask yourself the following questions: Are other individuals in the unit also disengaged? If so, is it only individuals in a particular area or of a certain age? If so, this may be more indicative of the climate of the unit than anything else. You must determine if the individual has been marginalized by the unit rather than willingly disengaging. For example, if a staff member's ideas are frequently dismissed or ridiculed in staff meetings or if graduate students are told that particular faculty members are old-fashioned in their approach to research or mentoring, those individuals have been marginalized and may stop participating in certain activities and concentrate their efforts elsewhere. In extreme situations, you may find a bully whom individuals attempt to avoid, and the result is disengagement. If these conditions exist and are not counteracted by the dean's office, the unit may reach a level of dysfunction that is so high that the unit has to be put into receivership and run by the dean's office itself. Chapter 9 explicitly deals with these situations.

Even as we dispense these philosophical jewels about reengaging faculty and staff by showing them resources they did not know existed or fixing structural issues, we can hear the chorus of cries out there saying, "Give me a break! Yeah, there are a few out there who just need to have their eyes opened to the possibilities or to protect them from hostile environments, but what about all the others?" We hear you loud and clear. It is important, however, to determine if there is a mismatch in the perception of the individual and/or unit of the situation in terms of resources, structural supports, and possible avenues before you assume the worst. Those who have misperceptions about expectations but really want to succeed can be educated relatively easily, which allows both you and them to move on once the ball starts rolling. Protecting those who find themselves in hostile environments is a bit more difficult, but again, a plan of action can be developed, sometimes in conjunction with your HR office. For those (few) faculty and staff who are incompetent, lazy, refuse to perform their job duties, or simply do not have a clue (i.e., the 5 percent of staff and faculty we spend 95 percent of our time dealing with), the approaches are somewhat more complicated.

Reengaging Individuals or Units Who Refuse to Perform Their Jobs

As with the other situations we talked about above, individuals can fall into this category for a number of reasons. The easiest case to deal with is the staff or faculty member who is a long-term member of the institution experiencing burnout from the long years of service. Individuals in this situation frequently are bored and feel that those around them are always asking them to do more but do not appreciate their past contributions and accomplishments (Armour et al. 1987; Gilley 2003; Higgerson and Joyce 2007). These individuals might want to know why they have to keep proving themselves after all of their accomplishments. Crucial to reengaging these individuals is a sincere expression of gratitude for their efforts and an attempt to discover the things they are still excited about (and there is always something). Once that is determined, get them involved in those activities—have them head a committee for an issue they are interested in or discuss the possibility of differentiated workloads/assignments so that the parts of their job that they are still passionate about are emphasized, expanded, and rewarded.

Conversely, there are those few individuals who truly are bad employees and refuse to do their jobs no matter what steps you take. How you deal with these individuals depends entirely on the nature of your governance system and, if you have them, collective bargaining agreements. In these instances, your best friend is your personnel/HR office. In almost every instance there will be a way to give an individual a measurable goal and/or duty, and if they do not meet those expectations, corrective or disciplinary action can be taken. How often this action has to occur, the manner in which your evaluation can be appealed, and what corrective action or sanction can be taken (the extreme of which is stripping of tenure or termination) varies considerably from university to university. Because taking these actions incorrectly can impede your desired outcome or put you and/or the university in a legally liable position, it is of utmost importance to call the experts in the personnel system into your activities early and to work with them consistently. As we said, the professionals in HR are your best friends in this instance.

TOOLS AND TAKEAWAYS

Dealing with disengaged and unproductive people and units is, without question, one of the most frustrating and unpleasant aspects of being an associate dean. The good news is that usually there are reasons behind bad behavior, and if you are creative, there are a number of ways in which you can help bring people who are no longer part of the team back into the action.

1. *Figure out whom you are dealing with.* Are you dealing with stars or divas? Are the people who seem unproductive, difficult, or disengaged simply passing the buck and blaming others while they do as little as possible, or are they basically hardworking people who, for some reason, are in a bad place? How you deal with the former is very different from how you deal with the latter.
2. *Understand the why.* Take time to discern what is behind the unit's or the person's disengagement. There are three major things we've seen that typically underlie these situations (see above).
3. *Make the investment.* Unless the person or unit you are dealing with is simply willfully shirking responsibility, take the time and energy to provide resources, mentoring, connections, and support for the person or unit in question. The attention and investment are likely what is needed to reinvigorate the situation in a positive way.
4. *Call in the big guns.* In the event that you have people who are intentionally disengaging or who, despite substantial investments, remain unproductive and/or insubordinate, use your campus resources to help you plan and execute next steps. Contact your HR office, the collective bargaining unit, legal counsel, and your campus faculty and staff affairs offices to understand and correctly implement corrective or punitive actions. Although we hope you never find yourself in this situation, if you do, be meticulous about doing these sorts of things by the book and documenting every step you and your dean take.

Chapter 11

I Know Your Parents Think You Are Brilliant, but You Still Have to Follow the Rules

Working with Students in an Atmosphere of Entitlement

The role of associate deans in the area of student services varies considerably from institution to institution. At some institutions, student conduct, advising, and outreach to parents is in the hands of professional staff, but at others these issues are overseen by associate deans. Even if your role is more restricted to issues of program development and curriculum, you will often be the first person a faculty member contacts with an ethics issue or the one a student contacts to complain about the advising office or an issue in a class. In some instances, you can redirect these issues to others who are charged with overseeing the offices that handle them, but many associate deans are pulled into these discussions and end up taking a fundamental role in dealing with them. Thus, understanding the policies, procedures, and organizational chart of your institution is crucial. The following case study illustrates how quickly and unexpectedly you can be confronted with such a situation.

> Associate Dean Earnest has just returned from lunch during finals week to find a student and her mother waiting for him. The student, Honesty Defined, and her mother are there because Ms. Defined wishes to add a class she has been sitting in on all semester. When Associate Dean Earnest explains that the deadline to add the class passed several months before, Ms. Defined's mother steps in to explain that an exception should be made for her daughter because she is a very good student, has done all of the work with an A average, it was a simple clerical error on her daughter's part, and her good friend Regent Helpful assured her there would be no problem.

Let us congratulate Associate Dean Earnest on being dive-bombed by a helicopter parent. The helicopter parent is a well-known character in admissions and advising offices throughout the country (though not as well-known in the faculty ranks) and is a reflection of the changing nature of students at universities today. Before we go further, we do want to stress that most students, like most faculty, are hardworking individuals who are never in trouble, and their parents are supportive and expect their children to take personal responsibility for their actions and to follow the rules. That being said, the small minority of students who do not fit this profile (just like the small minority of faculty) are the ones with whom you will spend the majority of your time, sometimes with parents in tow.

In any situation involving a student (with or without accompanying parent), one of the first things you need to figure out is whether the student has a legitimate issue (e.g., Ms. Defined submitted her registration material on time and has paperwork showing that, but for some reason it was not processed) or whether the student is trying to game the system (e.g., Ms. Defined was making sure that she had the grade she wanted before adding the class). In instances where a parent is present, understanding the role the parent is playing is critical as well. In some circumstances, the parent will have been recruited by the student to help, and in other situations the parent may have inserted himself or herself as an unwelcome player in what the student had wanted to handle alone.

Before plunging into the questions that you should ask yourself about this particular situation, there are a number of things you need to understand about the nature of today's students and their parents. There are several excellent references about these issues. From a student service perspective, we recommend the volumes edited by Daniel and Scott (2001) and Carney-Hall (2008) in the New Directions in Student Services series, and Margaret K. Nelson's (2010) volume titled *Parenting out of Control*. For a more popularly oriented, yet very informative book we recommend Howe and Strauss's (2000) volume on the millennial generation. As helpful as these volumes are, it is important to remember that today's college students (both graduate and undergraduate) are not a homogeneous lot in terms of age or life experience. For example, although many undergraduates are entering higher education right out of high school, others are coming to college after being in the workforce for a period of time or having a family. Further, the expectation of receiving an undergraduate degree in four years is increasingly disappearing as more students are working to help pay for their college educations, thus reducing the number of academic credit hours they take in any given term.

Having made these cautionary notes, however, a number of issues are important to keep in mind regarding today's students. First, students often communicate differently than today's university faculty and administrators did when they were at the same age and/or stage. Second, their relationships and communications with their parents are different and often much faster than in previous generations. Finally, the relationship between universities and students' families is not the same as it was a mere ten to twenty years ago. The upshot of all this is that whereas in prior generations universities and faculty were, to some degree, venerated by students and families who believed that it was largely their job to meet the university on its terms, the reverse is true today; many students and families expect that the university will meet them on their terms rather than those of the university. The impact of these changes is so profound that some institutions have hired individuals specifically charged to communicate with families and to encourage them to move to the position of supporting the student rather than intervening on their behalf, as part of the overall development of the student (see Coburn 2006 for an example of such a program).

In terms of differences, let us start with the issue of how students communicate and how that can lead to issues in their education with regard to knowing what the deadlines and policies are. Many departments, schools, and universities feel they are at the cutting edge of communication because of their investment in web page design and their use of e-mail as an official means of communication. However, as explained in Dan Carnevale's 2006 article in the *Chronicle of Higher Education* ("E-mail Is for Old People"), we frequently are not as cutting-edge as we think. Carnevale's interviews with students illustrate that they frequently skip e-mail in favor of social networking sites like Facebook and MySpace or more immediate communication media such as texting or Twittering. In this atmosphere, communication is immediate and frequent. If you are sitting there reading this and saying, "I suddenly feel very old and out of touch because I don't know what it means to say you Tweet," you are not alone and there is hope. Most universities have student services and IT departments with experts who can help get the message out about deadlines and other important issues in a variety of media. Additionally, if your university has a *consistently* articulated policy that students must check their e-mails, the students will do so. By *consistently* articulated we mean that it is stated by faculty and staff and included on syllabi, in orientation material, on advising sheets, and in other means of communication, and that the policy is followed and enforced. Finally, many institutions have found it helpful to have instructors insert information about the academic calendar and policies on their syllabi and on their Blackboard sites so that the students are exposed to the information in multiple venues, reducing the possibility that they don't know or understand policies and procedures.

Today's students differ not only in the media in which they choose to communicate, but also in how they relate to each other, their parents, and the university, which is all very different from what we did when we were their age. Some of this is related to generational differences that result from the historical, social, political, and economic context in which each of us was raised. Students currently in our colleges and universities are referred to as the millennial generation. These are individuals who were born from 1982 to 2002 and came of age (graduated from high school) at the beginning of the new millennium (Howe and Straus 2000). These are children born to the last part of the baby boomer generation and, until recently, as a whole they have experienced greater affluence, ethnic diversity, and protection through participation in structured activities than their parents. Their parents are frequently older, better educated, and have learned the process of advocacy and, at some level, distrust of individuals in positions of authority early in their lives. You might be sitting there thinking, "I can understand these students. I am the same generation as the parents and have millennial children myself." You have to remember, though, that as an associate dean, you are the person in a position of authority and represent the school and university. That means that although you may be able to empathize with both the parent and the student, you play a different role in the interaction. Added to this relationship dynamic are changing financial models and a consumer approach to higher education.

The financial model that both universities and students now work under is considerably different from models of the recent past. As state contributions to higher education shrink (in some cases to a level that makes public universities look more like private institutions), students and their parents are paying an increasing amount of tuition. This is occurring at the same time that numerous other issues compete for these resources; therefore, a more consumer-oriented approach is present. A common question for admissions staff is, "Why should I go to your school instead of another?" Increasingly, the answer is not framed in terms of the quality of your educational programs but in terms of value of the educational experience for the tuition dollars spent. These discussions are reinforced by discussions in the political arena about accountability and national rankings of institutions in the popular press. Whether these are good changes or not is a hotly debated issue. Regardless of what side of the debate you fall on, everyone agrees that an unfortunate side effect to this framing of the value of a university experience is a consumer approach to higher education in which the customer is always right.

Another way that the nature of interaction has changed is the active encouragement of parent involvement in K–12 education because, as studies show, clear increases in student success occur with parent involvement at this level. It is unreasonable of university personnel to expect that a behavior on the part of parents that has been successful and rewarded for twelve years will suddenly stop overnight. It is also unreasonable to expect students to assume that parental involvement is not an expected part of the process, just as it was in their high school. In other words, helicopter parents are often reacting to a call or e-mail from their child; thus, development of student skills in problem solving needs to occur at two levels: student and parent.

That brings us to our last cautionary note prior to delving into the questions Associate Dean Earnest should ask about the above situation: the Family Educational Rights and Privacy Act of 1974 (FRPA). FRPA was established to both ensure students access to their academic records and to ensure their privacy with regard to that record (see Bryan and Mulendor's 1992 volume, an excellent resource on this topic). The issue of privacy comes up most frequently, and is often focused on whether, in the absence of written permission from the student, anyone else has access to the student's record outside of the university. Do parents who are helping pay tuition have a right to know about the student's academic performance (including grades, ethics violations, conduct issues, etc.)? This is actually a more complicated issue than it appears on the surface. All schools can release directory information about students, but how much and what kind of other information the university can release to family members in the absence of written consent from the student depends on individual institutional policy and can vary considerably from university to university. Your particular university's policy will affect how much you can talk to the student about his or her case with the parent present in the room, as well as what you can tell a parent who approaches you on his or her own.

So, how does all this relate back to Associate Dean Earnest's situation? Keeping all of the issues discussed above in mind, the first thing to remember is that there are two sides to every story and you cannot make up your mind before looking into all aspects of a situation. In other words, every student is entitled to due process. Did the student make a good faith attempt to add the class by the deadline (and can the student document these attempts)? Were there circumstances beyond her control that kept her from completing the process prior to the deadline? Was the student told by the instructor during the semester that she was not on the class list and that she needed to check into the situation? Alternatively, did the instructor tell the student to not worry about the fact that the student was not on the class list because the instructor would take care of it? The answers to these questions will affect how you proceed. The other issue affecting your behavior will be the nature of the policies concerning academic issues in your school and university. Does your school or university have a petition policy for these types of issues? If so, has the student followed the appropriate steps in the process (e.g., is the student required to appeal to the chair of the department before approaching you)? If you turn down her request, does she have the right to petition your decision to a committee? If so, how do you inform the student of her rights? If your school does not have a petition process, we strongly recommend that you work to create one. These processes ensure that all students are treated fairly and that their rights are protected, while still holding them to a standard that they will be expected to follow in the workplace after the completion of their degree. It will also protect you, to some degree, from legal action.

In summary, Associate Dean Earnest's job is to be respectful of the student, the parents, and the school's and university's policies. Key to navigating unexpected situations involving students and parents is keeping an open mind, listening carefully, and making sure you have your facts straight. To ensure this is done correctly, Associate Dean Earnest may wish to collect all the information, and tell the student he will investigate and get back to her in the near future rather than rendering a decision on the spot. Regardless of the ultimate solution, you need to remember that even the most annoying helicopter parents are there because they are trying to support their children, and although those efforts may not, in the long run, serve to ensure that their children will develop the ability to take personal responsibility as we would like all students to do, your job as an associate dean is to make sure that all involved, including you, are treated fairly and with respect.

WORKING WITH STUDENT SERVICE OFFICES ON STUDENT ISSUES

Sometimes, unfortunately, there are students who are out to game the system, and in so doing they are knowingly manipulating, bending, and outright breaking the rules. When this happens, the student's actions are rarely confined to just your school, and you need to work with individuals in other schools and/or in student support services. This is illustrated in the following case study.

> Assistant Professor Enthusiasm has recently been made the graduate program director of his department. He is very excited about the opportunity to create some efficiency in the procedures for interacting with graduate students as a way to help the students navigate the confusing regulations so they can concentrate on their classes and research. Associate Dean Old Hand is glad to see the dedication and careful record keeping instituted by Assistant Professor Enthusiasm, something that was lax under his predecessor. About two months after becoming the graduate program director, Assistant Professor Enthusiasm calls Associate Dean Old Hand in utter frustration. Assistant Professor Enthusiasm has been working with a graduate student who he had assumed was just befuddled by the rules and needed some help getting on the path to the com-

> pletion of the program. Student Master Manipulator has been working on his master's degree (requiring thirty hours of class work and a thesis) for six years and has been on and off probation for poor grades several times. In looking at Manipulator's transcripts and talking to the faculty, Assistant Professor Enthusiasm discovers Manipulator has attempted ninety-six hours but due to failures and withdrawals has completed eighty-seven hours. Unfortunately, the majority of these hours are lower division undergraduate classes, none of which can be counted toward his graduate degree. Manipulator is still lacking required courses and has not produced a research proposal for his thesis project, despite having been told to do so in writing by the department several times. Assistant Professor Enthusiasm wants Associate Dean Old Hand to immediately suspend Manipulator from the university.

The first thing Associate Dean Old Hand needs to do is calm Assistant Professor Enthusiasm down and assure him that he will investigate the situation before acting on it. His next step is to determine if Manipulator is technically in good standing. We are aware that many of you may balk at the suggestion that this is necessary. We hear the cries of "How could he possibly be in good standing with ninety-six attempted hours for a thirty-hour master's degree?" This question, though, is actually more complicated than it sounds. First, has the department ever actually defined "good standing" for graduate students in terms of progress toward degree completion? If it has defined it, has the unit determined what happens to students who are not in good standing (i.e., what actions does your policy allow you to take)? Associate Dean Old Hand's investigation should start by examining the program's catalogue descriptions and/or published student handbook. You frequently hear the statement "The catalogue is your contract with the student." In reality, not every policy at the university is written down in the catalogue; rather, most are referenced there and are actually housed in detail elsewhere. The exception to this is the section of the catalogue dealing with specific program rules and graduation requirements. In some instances, these are clear-cut and the consequences for not meeting certain benchmarks are explicit. The vast majority of programs, however, will be far from clear-cut. If this is the case with Assistant Professor Enthusiasm's program, Associate Dean Old Hand should work with the faculty involved to develop their rules and catalogue content for future students. He cannot, however, apply rules that were developed after the fact to this particular student.

Associate Dean Old Hand's next step is to determine what, if any, rules or policies exist for his school, the graduate school, or the university as a whole. Most institutions have time limits on graduate degrees and consequences of going past these limits. For most, time limits are generally attached to classes—for example, no class older than seven years can count toward graduation without recertification of the content knowledge. Some universities have graduate school rules that state a student will be dismissed from the university if the student does not complete his or her graduate studies in a specific length of time. Assistant Professor Enthusiasm and Associate Dean Old Hand will need to work with the dean of the graduate school and his or her staff to determine if such explicit rules are in effect. If specific rules do exist, due process generally requires that a letter be sent to the student (either by Associate Dean Old Hand or by the dean of the graduate school) telling the student that he or she is in violation of the time limit and giving the student a set length of time to finish. The letter also must explicitly state that the student will be dismissed from the university if he or she does not finish by the time stated. In other words, you must tell the student in writing what the problem is, what the student must do to correct it, the timeline to complete the stated tasks, and the consequences of not completing the work on time.

In addition to working with the department and the graduate school to investigate academic policies relating to student issues, Associate Dean Old Hand should contact the director of financial aid immediately to determine if financial aid fraud is occurring. Unfortunately, some students view student loans and stipends as sources of income rather than as aid in pursuing and completing a degree program. As long as they are students, they feel they are entitled to additional loans and do not need to begin repayment. Many financial aid packets, including most loans, limit to 10 percent the number of hours a student can take beyond those required for the degree; for a thirty-hour master's program, this rule would put the maximum at thirty-three hours, not ninety-six. Before you throw up your hands in disbelief that a student could ever actually get away with taking this many additional hours given this restriction, stop and think about the limitations of your own student records system. How easily do the different units dealing with student records (admissions, transfer credit evaluation, registrar, faculty, advisors, scholarship office, etc.) actually coordinate? How many activities tied to student records must be processed in such short time periods during the academic year that the ability to run audits is precluded? Given these issues, it is not surprising that students like Master Manipulator could drop through the cracks. Associate Dean Old Hand should give the director of financial aid a heads-up about the student. If financial aid fraud is occurring, this is probably the easiest and quickest issue to fix. When Master Manipulator loses his access to additional loans and is required to start repaying the ones he has already taken out, he will either drop out of the program or suddenly begin to make progress.

DEALING WITH POLITICAL PRESSURE REGARDING STUDENTS

Unfortunately, there are times when individuals outside of your school apply political pressure to change an academic decision. Sometimes the student knows about these actions on his or her behalf (and may have even requested them), and sometimes the student does not know. Sometimes the student is unaware that others have taken up his or her cause (for example, the regent who plays golf with the student's father). At other times, students may renew their own efforts with the backing of the person exerting external pressure. Additionally, the person who is bringing the pressure on you to change your decision may be acting independently, without knowledge of the political "big wig" who is cited, as the following case study illustrates.

> Associate Dean Integrity has the honor of coordinating a scholarship committee for the School of Business every year. The committee is made up of faculty and representatives from the local business community and is charged with awarding a very prestigious fellowship to five deserving students in his school. The winners are honored at a banquet attended by the faculty of the school and the members of the state Chamber of Commerce. The actual amount of the scholarship is not that large, but the prestige of winning it is considerable and is recognized throughout the region; it often leads to internships and/or job offers. Associate Dean Integrity is thrilled because this gives him a chance to work with and award the true stars of his program.
>
> The committee meets and ranks the students. There is universal agreement on the five students who should be awarded the fellowship that year. Associate Dean Integrity sends the list of awardees to the president of the university, as is the custom. Later that day, he receives an e-mail from the executive assistant to the president asking him if there is any way the committee could reconsider the application of Jane Doe, who works in the president's office. The executive assistant notes that the president is very impressed with the student and has taken a personal interest in her career.

The answer to this request is very clearly no. It would be unethical to respond in any other way and punish a deserving student by favoring one less qualified regardless of her political connections. What Associate Dean Integrity does beyond this response depends on how he feels the request was made. If it is a simple query for information, explaining the process in his response to the executive assistant would be appropriate. If, on the other hand, Associate Dean Integrity feels political pressure is being brought upon him, he may wish to copy the president in his e-mail response. If Associate Dean Integrity feels the request is made in such a way that he is being ordered to violate his ethics, he may wish to say that he considers the request unethical. The result of this will be one of three things: (1) an apology from the executive assistant for a poorly stated e-mail and assurance that an unethical request was not the intent, (2) no response and the matter will be dropped, or (3) increased political pressure. At a minimum, Associate Dean Integrity should inform his dean of the situation so the dean is not blind-sided. Hopefully, the dean's immediate response will be that he or she has Associate Dean Integrity's back and will fight the good fight. If not, Associate Dean Integrity may wish to consult chapter 16 of this book, which contains advice on what to do when it is time to move on from the dean's office.

TOOLS AND TAKEAWAYS

Working with students is a highly gratifying aspect of our profession, and knowing that we have helped a deserving student achieve his or her goals gives us great personal satisfaction. That being said, however, problems involving students can and do arise. Keep the following things in mind if you are charged with student affairs in your school:

1. *Accept the brave new world.* Understand that the communication styles, expectations, and approach of today's generation of students, regardless of chronological age, are different from those of previous generations. Accepting this and learning to meet students (and parents) where they are rather than demanding that they behave differently is key to solving problems related to students.
2. *Determine motivation.* Spend the necessary time to figure out if the student has a legitimate issue. Many who come to you will have an honest problem they need help solving, but others will come to you in an effort to manipulate the system and take advantage of you and/or situations they are facing.
3. *Be flexible yet firm.* Where you determine that a student has a real issue, do whatever you reasonably can to help the student solve the problem. If there are things you can be flexible about that will help the student, do them, but only if you are willing to do them for others as well. If there are things you "really shouldn't" do to help the student, don't do them—be firm in your resolve.
4. *Have integrity.* It is not uncommon to find a regent, chancellor, president, or dean involved in trying to solve a student problem either because of personal relationships or interest or because of political pressure. In these cases, stick to your guns and follow policy (remember, policy is your friend!) and if those above you want something done, respectfully suggest that the higher-level person make the necessary changes.

Chapter 12

Call Me When the Fire Trucks Have Left

Defining and Responding to Crisis

Part of an associate dean's job is managing the crisis of the day. However, you will quickly discover that what constitutes a crisis to others (e.g., "I need you to move me into another classroom because mine is cold") does not necessarily require you to go into crisis mode to resolve the issue. Further, sometimes delaying action will allow the "crisis" to lose steam and solve itself. This is particularly true regarding the initial reactions people may have to unexpected situations. Such occurrences can spark a panic response that results in people defining the situation as a crisis when it is really not. Given some time to calm down and reflect on such a situation, many individuals will take a more even view and find a solution or a workaround. This is not always the case, however, and there will be times when very real crises arise, which require immediate and decisive action. Sometimes these arrive without warning, such as when a faculty member has a car accident and will be unable to teach his class for the foreseeable future or the science building is on fire. Still others build gradually, allowing for planning and reflection on your part. You may be able to anticipate some crises by reading the daily paper (to learn, for example, that the state is doing a midyear rescission of funding to higher education). Finally, sometimes a situation is not really a crisis involving true risk, but there is great concern about how a circumstance may be interpreted or appears externally.

CRISIS AS PUBLIC IMAGE

Many faculty members feel the attention that administrators pay to the image of their institution in the public sphere is unimportant, preferring to concentrate on more substantive intellectual issues. The fact is, however, that universities must consider how external communication occurs and, at times, take care to manage their images. To be clear, we are not arguing that institutions of higher learning should trade in substance for image. Clearly, intellectual substance is the basis for the long-term health of an institution. It does not take long, however, to learn that public image can be an important contributing factor to the health of a university or college. How an institution is viewed in the public eye can affect fundraising, student recruitment, and budget allocations. It cannot be ignored, as the following example illustrates.

> Several of your faculty in the Department of Tropical Weather Predictions have requested school funds to travel to and present scholarly papers at a national conference to be held in Hawai'i. Given the nature of the research, the location does not raise any red flags for you, so you approve the request. The faculty members follow official protocol in arranging their travel, and use their own credit cards to pay for extra tickets for their spouses. Again, no red flags are raised by your procurement office. At the end of the week of the conference, you open the morning paper to headlines stating that a reporter followed your faculty while they were in Hawai'i and recorded that they attended the meeting for just one hour (the hour in which they presented their paper) and spent the rest of the time on the beach, playing golf, and shopping with their spouses. By the time you reach the office, there are outraged phone messages from the trustees, the provost, and your dean wanting to know why you allowed such an obvious exploitation of state funds to occur and how you are going to keep it from ever happening again.

Is this a crisis? In terms of public relations, the answer is yes, but in terms of university policy, the answer is most likely no. Is it more than this, however? To answer this question, you need to ask several questions and consider the complexity of the situation. To begin with, you need to ascertain if this is just a matter of a few faculty members with bad judgment or if a larger systemic problem exists. One of the biggest problems with investigating these issues after they have "gone public" is that you have to sort through the considerable rhetoric that may have been generated by the press and your institution in order to get to the heart of the issue. In this particular case, is it a question of whether the faculty members broke the policy or is it that there is a problem with the existing policy? If it is the former, conversations with the faculty members, their department chair, and depending on how the policy is written, a possible reimbursement of the travel funds to the university may be warranted.

You might also wish to determine how often this type of behavior occurs in the school (or in a particular unit within the school). If, on the other hand, it appears that there is a problem with the policy or if no clear policy exists, the conversation should be broadened considerably, bringing in discussions with the finance office, the board of trustees, and the faculty governance committees. The point is, you cannot work toward resolution of a "crisis" until you know the severity of the crisis, including its pervasiveness, its depth, and its source(s). Unfortunately, the literature on crisis management in higher education is scant at best. The good news is, however, that information on methods of intervention for conflict and crisis management in the business world, although not originally directed toward higher education, can help us sort out these issues effectively (Buller 2007; Chu 2006; Sorenson 1998; Sturnick 1998).

So what do you do when faced with a crisis? First, do your best to avoid reacting immediately in fear, anger, or panic. Take a few deep breaths and wait to respond. After you and your dean have calmed down from the initial shock of the apparent crisis (remember, no one likes to be blindsided), have a conversation with the dean about what his or her concerns are. In some cases, such as the case above, you may wish to have some information at hand going into this conversation. For example, how often do faculty members in your school travel to meetings, and what policies currently exist for the approval of the use of school funds for travel? After presenting the facts you have about the situation to your dean, find out the scope and depth of his or her concern. For example, has the dean been given an order by the provost to investigate all travel in the school, or is he or she dealing primarily with public relations issues tied to this particular event? Based on this, discuss with your dean the type of intervention that is appropriate for you to undertake. What are the expected outcomes of intervening in the situation, and what would happen if you did not intervene? Is the objective to manage the public image, or is it to change the way the use of school funds for travel is approved? By structuring your conversations in this way, crisis management is transformed into rational and calm conversation about policy implications and enforcement. The result is a lowered stress level, avoiding a knee-jerk decision that all might regret later. For example, if the dean revoked the use of school funds for all research-related travel for all faculty members effective immediately in response to this incident, the research mission of the school would be significantly hampered. Moreover, such an action might violate collective bargaining agreements that are in place, and faculty groups might charge the administration with restricting their academic freedom by removing access to venues at which they must disseminate their work. By transforming the crisis into a conversation of policy rather than a reaction to public pressure, you can ensure that cooler heads prevail and undertake an examination of policy and practice. After that is completed, reasonable expectations for process and conduct can be established and agreed upon by all, and the crisis will have been resolved.

Of course, you may be a bit skeptical that this approach will always be effective. In fact, we can hear stifled guffaws and mutterings of "Are they nuts?" as you read this. Of course, we are not guaranteeing that everyone will walk away from discussions such as those described above happy, or that the public image problems suffered by your institution will be alleviated by a scintillating policy review. Rather, we are saying (and the conflict management literature we cite above is pretty clear on this issue) that it is much easier to resolve these issues in calm, cool conversations with reference to policy and procedure than when everyone is in crisis mode and demanding immediate action against a particular individual or unit. One of the biggest parts of managing crisis is managing hysteria. That is the take-home message for this chapter. To do this, first manage your own panic and anger and then manage the panic and anger of others by collecting and disseminating solid information and having solution-focused conversations.

CRISES AFFECTING LONG-TERM INSTITUTIONAL HEALTH

What about when the situation is more than just a matter of public appearance and is actually a threat to your unit or university? Massive budget cuts, dramatic drops or rises in enrollment, and threatened or actual loss of accreditation can dramatically affect the long-term health of an academic unit. These are crises that we can usually see coming, either because they are tied to the overall health of the economy or because we know the benchmarks we must meet and where we are struggling as an institution. Just because these crises can be anticipated, however, does not mean they can always be avoided. This is where strategic planning comes into play and can provide an anchor in the chaos of such crises.

We assume that at most universities, mentioning strategic planning results in groans and dread of an activity most people hate. It is frequently labor intensive and rarely results in immediate changes that people can see. The result is a perception that the results are not worth the work involved and that planning will make no difference. Taking the long view, however, gives a different perspective. Having a strategic plan with well-defined goals that everyone agrees upon helps administrators move out of a role of reacting to the crisis of the day and move into a proactive role that ensures the long-term sustainability of the institution. For example, budget cuts do, unfortunately, result in the elimination or postponement of some projects. Having a solid grasp of what is core to the unit not only helps administrators prioritize some activities over others but also helps the students, staff, and faculty understand the budget-cutting actions. This does not mean everyone is happy, especially the individuals whose projects are postponed or cut. You must remember, however, that you tend to work with very smart people in institutions of higher education, and if they understand the reasons why the dean's office is cutting some places but not others and the timing of when their project might move back into the forefront, you are less likely to face open revolt.

CRISES AFFECTING INDIVIDUAL HEALTH AND SAFETY

Unfortunately, not every real crisis is one that can be anticipated or dealt with as a matter of public image. Real emergencies do arise and are a serious threat to the health and safety of the people on your campus. What do you do when a tornado sets down on campus, or a student attempts suicide in the residence halls, or a police pursuit of an armed suspect moves from the surrounding city onto the campus in the middle of class change? How about when you have an active shooter on campus or a faculty member has a psychotic break in a meeting? Although these episodes can be highly stressful and emotionally draining, the good news is that you do not have to deal with these issues alone. You do, however, need to know your part in dealing with them and carry out your duties calmly, quickly, and predictably, or the crisis may escalate. In recent years, violence on high school and university campuses around the country has led to the formation of committees concerned with emergency preparedness. Although these committees are initially formed to focus on dealing with threats of gun violence, they frequently move on to plan for other types of emergencies, such as natural disasters. The key to success of the plans these committees make is that everyone must know what to do when an emergency occurs. All involved must execute their responsibilities correctly and in a timely manner.

In that vein, we suggest that when you first take the job as associate dean, you find out who on your campus is in charge of public safety. Contact campus security and the head of the emergency preparedness committee to determine the role you are expected to play in these plans when they are activated in response to a crisis. It is also important for you to know the roles of others with whom you work with in these plans. Find out how you will be contacted when an emergency occurs, and whom you should contact. Once you have gathered all the above information, make sure that it is disseminated to everyone who needs to know it. Just as everyone in your unit needs to know what to do in case of a fire to safely evacuate a burning building (hence fire drills), everyone also needs to know what processes will be activated when other types of crises arise. This information needs to be salient and clear enough that when and if an emergency occurs, everyone will know what to do and will do it correctly and quickly.

To facilitate this, make up a one-page quick reference sheet telling everyone what to do in case of an active shooter, a bomb threat, a fire, or a tornado/earthquake/hurricane/blizzard that you can e-mail and give out to people and post in public places. At our university, the institution has put these sheets on the back of our campus phone books and posts them in classrooms, offices, residence halls, elevators, and restrooms. If your campus has not come up with these plans, suggest that a committee with representatives from the academic units, student services, facilities management, risk management, and campus security be formed. Suggest that your dean talk to his or her counterparts in the other units on campus to begin a conversation with the provost about how to deal with emergencies such as the death or injury of a student, staff, or faculty member. The campus community will look to you, as an individual in a position of authority, to guide them through these events and help them heal afterwards.

WHEN TO HAVE YOUR LAWYER ON SPEED DIAL

We live in a very litigious society, so you should not be surprised when people threaten to sue you if you do not do what they want you to do when they want you to do it. How often this happens, of course, depends on your job in the dean's office as well as the size and makeup of your student body and faculty. At some point, however, we can almost guarantee that someone will tell you they will see you in court for a decision you make or an action you take (or decline to take). In fact, after you have been in the dean's office a while, you will notice that there is a cyclic nature to these events. New threats of lawsuits come around the time tenure decisions are made and grades are assigned. The following example serves as a case study.

Associate Dean Calm N. Collected is sitting at her desk one quiet day, concentrating on completing the grading of the term papers from the class she taught that semester. It is a good class, and the students' enthusiasm and performance reaffirm her faith in students and their desire to learn and explore ideas. Her feeling that all is right with the world is interrupted with an e-mail from a student who will not give his or her name and is not using a university e-mail account; the student is demanding a meeting with the dean. When Associate Dean Collected asks what the requested meeting concerns, the student's response is that he or she wants the immediate firing of Professor Reliable. When asked the nature of the complaint, the student responds, in a less than a coherent manner, that Professor Reliable is incompetent and needs to be fired right away. The student goes on to say that Reliable definitely needs to be replaced before the start of the next semester, when he would be teaching a required class that the student must take

> to graduate. He or she states that if Professor Reliable were competent and had taught the class well, the student would have aced the class after all the hours he or she had put in on the weekly homework assignments. Obviously, the problem is with Professor Reliable and his desire to ask picky little questions unrelated to anything the student sees as related to the important aspects of the class.
>
> Associate Dean Collected responds by explaining the process for grade appeals and how a student can file a grievance against a faculty member. She informs the student that these steps need to be taken prior to seeing the dean in regard to these issues. The student's response is that only an appointment with the dean will be acceptable and it needs to occur today. Associate Dean Collected explains that the dean is out of the office at a meeting of the board of regents today, but that if the student would like to begin the grade appeal and/or grievance process she will be happy to help him or her get the process started. The student's response is that Associate Dean Collected must get him or her an appointment with the dean today or he or she will sue the university and is, in fact, already in contact with a lawyer.

Is there anything Associate Dean Collected can do to deescalate the situation? Should she call the dean and tell him to come back from his meeting with the board to meet with the student? The answer to the first question is probably no. Associate Dean Collected attempted on two occasions to explain the process to the student and also explained that the dean was unavailable to meet with the student that day. Additionally, as we have stated elsewhere, it is generally a bad idea to break with set procedures and policies, no matter what the student threatens. As for the second question, we would not recommend that Associate Dean Collected attempt to call the dean out of a board of regents meeting unless the dean has left orders that he or she always be called when irate students threaten lawsuits (if this is the case in your school we recommend you read the section of chapter 3 relating to deans that are micromanagers). A heads-up e-mail to her dean (or a voice mail if the situation is particularly sensitive) is definitely called for. This is a situation when, especially in e-mail, you want to be careful what you say and how you say it. Remember that e-mail is forever, so stick to the facts and skip any commentary you might be tempted to include about the situation or your take on it.

So what should Associate Dean Collected's next move be in this situation? As a general rule, we recommend that anytime anyone mentions suing you or the university, you should contact your university's legal counsel immediately and forward him or her the e-mails. Do not avoid doing this because you think it is unimportant, an empty threat, or might go away. Generally speaking, lawyers would much prefer to know about a potential lawsuit that never materializes than to find out after a suit has been filed. Additionally, your university (and/or accrediting board) may have rules about when correspondence tied to student complaints in general and legal actions in particular needs to be saved and how. Finally, if ever in doubt, it is not a bad idea to run the wording of your response to an individual by the lawyers. It is much better to be safe than to have an unfortunate turn of phrase come back to haunt you in some future legal action.

That being said, you should not assume that the lawyer knows every detail of the university's or your school's policies and procedures. In forwarding e-mails to lawyers, you should give as much background as possible. A phone call may be the most efficient and confidential way to have this conversation. In addition to explaining the processes in question to the lawyer, you may also wish to include some broader background or contextual information. For example, Associate Dean Collected should include information about the home department of the faculty member in question. If there is a history of problems with the department or this professor in particular, this information should be included as well. Conversely, student evaluations praising Professor Reliable should also be included, if they exist. Associate Dean Collected also should tell university counsel if she has contacted the chair of the department to find out if he or she has been involved in previous discussions with students about the professor. If so, she should outline the nature of these conversations and their outcome. If, for example, a group of students was concerned that the professor's syllabus was not clear about grading policies, did the chair have a conversation with the professor to correct the problem?

If the lawyer suggests that you or the dean take a step that you do not understand or agree with, ask questions about it and explain your concerns. It may be that there is some process or rule unique to your unit with which the lawyer is not familiar that could alter his or her advice to you. Remember, however, that what the university's lawyers are focused on is federal and state law and the changes in these that impact higher education. Faculty, staff, and administrators are almost never as up-to-date on such things, and it is in this capacity that the office of legal counsel can be of great help. The reason the lawyer might be telling you to do something that is different from how issues have been handled in the past might be due to a change in these rules. Asking questions will help you figure out if you need to update your rules and procedures to be in compliance with the law and recent court rulings and will help you understand why you are being asked to take a certain action. Finally, if your university has more than one lawyer, chances are that each specializes in different things. For example, one might be an expert in the laws and rules governing students and another might focus on dealing with personnel and tenure issues for faculty and staff. Find out their specialties so you will know whom to contact when.

TOOLS AND TAKEAWAYS

At times, being an associate dean feels like being on the front line in dealing with the crisis of the day (or minute). Associate deans need to be well versed in handling various issues that might come through the dean's office and know when additional individuals need to be brought into the conversation. The following tools will help you do this.

1. *It is easier to manage a crisis if you are calm.* One of the first steps in managing a crisis is managing the panic it engenders. Redirect your reactions and the reactions of others from the particular instance that set off the crisis to policy and process. This action not only will help you figure out what steps to take but may also indicate changes that need to be made to prevent similar problems in the future.
2. *Crisis mode is exhausting.* Strategic planning does not prevent problems from arising but gives you a road map to solving them and keeps the emphasis on the big picture and long-term health of the unit rather than the crisis of the day.
3. *Know your emergency preparedness plan.* Individuals in the school and university will look to administrators to lead them safely through periods when their health and safety are in danger. Know your role in your university's emergency preparedness plan and carry it out calmly and efficiently to ensure everyone's safety.
4. *Call the lawyers.* Better to be safe than sorry on this one. Whenever a lawsuit is threatened, chat with your legal counsel to figure out what steps to take and how to handle and document the situation.

Chapter 13

Meet and Greet

Making Connections outside Your School

Although a great deal of your work as an associate dean will be concentrated within your own school, your school does not live in isolation. Rather, it is part of a bigger institution, and so creating connections outside of your school is just as important as developing and supporting connections within your own college. The nature of these relationships may vary considerably depending on your area of responsibility, but each one is an opportunity not only to achieve your goals as an associate dean, but also to provide a chance for others to get to know you and to establish important connections for your own career. The frequency of interaction with individuals outside your school and the number of committees on which you will be asked to serve will vary from institution to institution depending on which processes are centralized and which are decentralized. For example, if functions related to sponsored programs administration are centrally located at your university, you may not need to serve on any committees related to intellectual property, but if these functions have been delegated to each school and college, you may have to serve not only on the intellectual property oversight committee in your college but also as a representative of your college on the university version of this committee.

Early in your tenure as associate dean you should work to determine the areas of your job in which collaborations across the campus are needed and the individuals in those offices with whom you will need to work. Common areas that are centralized to at least some degree at most institutions are legal counsel, Human Resources, the final stages of the tenure processes, and some aspects of grants and contracts administration. Some areas that are completely centralized at some universities are decentralized and housed within individual schools and colleges at other institutions. These include undergraduate advising, graduate student affairs, student resources, and oversight of the core curriculum. Finally, you may have some areas of overlap where the actions of individuals in two or more units need to be coordinated so that their efforts are mutually supporting. For example, if your institution has a graduate school, honors college, or undergraduate university college, the members of the dean's offices of these units need to work together to ensure that programs are offered and students are served. You can make these contacts in a variety of ways, ranging from sending an e-mail introducing yourself to individuals with whom you will work to meeting people while attending university-wide functions or sitting on committees. What this means is that most of your actions outside of your school have the dual impact of both building your reputation and career and establishing and strengthening relationships between your school and other units.

Of course, committees are not the only way you meet individuals outside of your school. As mentioned above, during the early days of your position as associate dean it is best to determine what areas of your job require, or would be facilitated by, collaboration with individuals outside your school. Even if you have been in the job for a while and have not done this, it is not too late. In some cases, knowing what office to contact might be sufficient, but for many tasks you will need to foster relationships with individuals in other units. These individuals need not always be the ones who run the offices, but simply need to be the people with whom you will need to collaborate and who have the knowledge you need to accomplish your tasks. Remember also that the people you need to cultivate relationships with in order to do your job and develop lasting professional relationships are not always faculty; staff members are often the grease that makes the wheels turn. It is essential to treat them as the colleagues they are and show them respect and appreciation. For example, knowing the particular staff person in the grants and contract office who works with the agencies to which your faculty generally apply is probably more important than knowing the faculty member who is the vice chancellor for research or all the members of his or her office. Other offices you will have occasion to work with (depending on your specific duties) include Human Resources, legal counsel, the advising office, and your faculty affairs office. Again, think about what aspects of these offices are important for you to accomplish your job and reach out to the people you'll need to help you navigate the system when the time comes.

FRUSTRATING COMMITTEES

Having urged you to serve on committees to make connections and do tasks outside of your school or college, we'll be the first to acknowledge that committee work is, at least sometimes, incredibly frustrating. Because as an associate dean you'll frequently be asked or assigned to serve on committees that are charged with dealing with complex issues that affect the entire institution, your probability of experiencing a significant amount of committee-related frustration is high. Although some of these committees are ultimately rewarding and productive, you may end up on committees on occasion that never seem to end and never seem to accomplish anything, despite meeting every two weeks for months at a time. Such committees are, in a sense, exercises in frustration that you feel compelled to undertake every two weeks but always walk away thinking, "I must be missing something, because this just does not seem that hard to fix. What is wrong with these people?" If you are not in charge of setting the agenda, as in the case study below, what do you do to facilitate fulfilling the charge of the committee and building relationships between units while maintaining your sanity?

Because of Associate Dean Wisefellow's work with graduate programs in her home school, she has been asked to sit on a committee to form an overarching graduate school. The charge of the committee is to design a structure for the graduate school, including the role of the dean, associate/assistant deans, graduate faculty, and staff, as well as a set of bylaws governing committees and rights and responsibilities. Additional issues that must be addressed include what, if any, oversight role the graduate school will have when new programs are proposed, as well as minimum standards for admissions, graduation, and probation/suspension. Associate Dean WiseFellow is very excited about this opportunity because there are a number of issues that continually arise that she thinks this could address and she has some ideas she would like to discuss with others on the committee. Associate Dean Wisefellow attends the first meeting with great anticipation. The committee is given the charge by the provost, and then introduced to the special assistant to the provost, Professor Logorrhea, who will be heading up the effort.

It is now a year later. The committee meetings continue, every two weeks for two hours at a time. Unfortunately, there are still no recommendations on the structure of the graduate school or the rules that will govern it, nor is it clear when these tasks will be accomplished. The meetings are not at all contentious and the lack of movement on these issues is not due to disagreements over the direction in which the graduate school should go. Rather, the committee has never gotten to the point of discussing these issues. Meetings are disorganized and there is no direction that is evident; in fact, most meetings do not even have an agenda and are dominated by casual chatter among Logorrhea and others about issues in higher education. Associate Dean Wisefellow has become very frustrated with

> the lack of progress of the committee and the amount of her time that is being wasted. She is considering sending in her resignation letter to the provost, even though she'd had very high hopes for the committee.

Is resigning from the committee actually the smart thing to do? The answer, despite the frustration Associate Dean Wisefellow is feeling, is "Not necessarily." Whenever you as associate dean make a decision about anything, it is important to think of all of the possible ramifications of that action. Regardless of the original charge of the committee, there are certain things to remember. First, committee work is crucial for the university; faculty members know this as well as administrators. However, the actions an individual faculty member undertakes are viewed differently than the actions of a faculty member who is also an administrator. Specifically, when a faculty member resigns from a committee, it is often interpreted as a result of conflicting commitments or demanding schedules. Alternatively, when an associate dean either formally resigns from a committee or stops attending meetings, it is often interpreted as the entire school withdrawing from the conversation and as a condemnation of the purpose of the committee by the school rather than merely a response to its lack of progress by the associate dean. The unintended messages of your actions are just as powerful as the message you overtly send out, so consider them carefully.

Once you have become more visible in the institution as an associate dean, doing something like resigning from a provost's committee also has implications for your reputation and, potentially, your career. Although the committee is doing nothing and you feel that your time is being wasted, some are likely to interpret your resignation not as a commentary on the ineffectiveness of the committee but as an indicator of your impatience or inflexibility. Remember that only you have the real information on why you are leaving the committee; other people will fill in the blanks, and often will do so in a way that may not be flattering to you. Be aware that regardless of the real reasons for your resignation, the rumor mill may generate the impression that you are impatient and think your time is more important than anybody else's—which is not an impression you likely want to have floating around if you aspire to further leadership positions.

In addition to how others interpret your actions in representing the entire school's position on a topic, you need to remember that most new initiatives we attempt to undertake are at least partly a social and political negotiation. Different universities have different cultures and different governance systems, so the importance of the social and political negotiations varies some from institution to institution; however, they are always there to some degree. One of the main reasons that the social and political aspects of committee work are so important is that for most of us, the budget situation is frequently the elephant in the room as far as developing new programs or policies, creating and deploying new initiatives, and establishing new centers or components of the institution. Although a committee may decide to shunt a bunch of new faculty hires into one college to support its growth, that decision means that those funds are not available for something else, or in some cases, may be taken from another program or unit. This essentially means that the "creative work" done by planning committees, for example, is a zero-sum game. Thus, if you and your dean care deeply about an issue, you need to spend some time building support for that issue among your colleagues in other schools, rather than just going into the meetings with your guns blazing.

This is one part of the political equation, but another is that you also need to demonstrate that you are a team player for issues that other schools care about (assuming of course, that they are reasonable and are good for the institution as a whole). This shows that you and your school are collaborative and generates goodwill. You build these support systems both through one-on-one conversations (much the way you build coalitions among the faculty and staff in your own school) and by conversations that occur with your colleagues before and after committee meetings. Going to frustrating committee meetings demonstrates that your school is at the table and allows you to build relationships with your counterparts in other units in the university. These are people that you not only will work with on this committee but also are likely to work with again in the future, so the time and energy investment is well worth it. In other words, people have to know who you are and how you operate if they are to contact you about an important issue, ask for your support or advice on something, or lend support to your proposals in the future. The way others outside your home school get to know you is often through committee work, no matter how frustrating the committee may be.

Having said all that, we did hear a collective groan as we gave the advice to keep going to committee meetings that are mind-numbingly boring and a waste of time, even if there are important networking aspects of your continued participation. So, given that we are telling you that you have to keep sitting through these meetings, is there any way that you can positively influence their outcome? The answer is "Sometimes," and it is largely dependent on who is running the meetings and on whether you are willing to let that person claim the credit for the committee's success with the provost or whomever the committee is serving. The good news is that even if you are okay with letting the person running the meeting take the credit for its success (if that is something that is important to that person), the members of the committee will generally recognize and remember the truth—that you all worked together and that you were a voice of reason.

One way to potentially turn the work of the committee to a positive purpose is to use open conversations that occur within the committee to suggest a small related project or goal that will change the inertia of the group from standing still to slowly moving forward. For example, Associate Dean Wisefellow might ask a simple question like "Do we know how many graduate students we actually have in our various graduate programs?" This is a simple demographic question that seems innocuous but is actually important background information (the bigger the program, the more invested in the outcome of the process a school might be). Associate Dean Wisefellow might even volunteer to collect this information before the next meeting (an action which is relatively easy to accomplish by visiting the Institutional Research web page or talking to a member of the Institutional Research Department). After presenting this information to the group, Associate Dean Wisefellow can bring up an issue she is particularly concerned about (for example, the probation/suspension policy) by stating in the general conversation period that she is having an issue in her school and wonders how others are handling it. She should make sure that the school with the largest number of students speaks to this issue because they are likely to be the group with set procedures in place to deal with the larger volume of students. This discussion can lead to a comparison of methods so that a "best practices" list can be developed and serve as the basis for that part of the policy that the committee is charged with writing. Wisefellow has gently, through a relatively small amount of time and effort invested on her part, managed to gently push the committee toward its goal without being pushy or overbearing.

This is all well and good if the head of the committee is willing to let someone else subtly shift the committee's direction in this way. Many people charged with running a committee of this sort will be okay with this, because the success of the group reflects well on the person who chaired the committee when the critical policy was written and enacted. If, however, the head of the committee does not embrace this sort of process, merely sees the committee as a forum to pontificate for two hours twice a month, and will not let anyone else pose these types of suggestions, a different strategy is called for. Because Associate Dean Wisefellow still has to administer the graduate programs in her school, she could call her colleague in another school (either an individual with whom she has a good working relationship or her counterpart in a school known for setting up and consistently implementing good procedures) to discuss the issue one on one. With this as background information, she can begin to create a policy for her school through her school's governance system. If no other school has a workable procedure, conversations with the faculty within her school can be a good starting point. As for the semimonthly committee meetings, think of them as a good time to decompress, mentally order your day, write your grocery list, or outline an article (perhaps on dealing with frustrating committees). Just make sure you do this subtly with one ear to the conversation. Using old-fashioned pen and paper looks like you are taking notes, while Blackberrys and laptops make it look like you are checking e-mails. Remember, being overtly rude to the special assistant to the provost is never a smart political move, even if he is terrible at running meetings.

WORKING WITH FRUSTRATING INDIVIDUALS

There are other kinds of situations in which it is not a committee but an individual who makes work on a project highly frustrating. This creates immense stress. Unfortunately, it is not an unusual situation. The most common situation is when the person you are supposed to be collaborating with avoids doing any of the work, leaving all of it to you. This is very different from the disengaged faculty or staff member discussed in chapter 10. Rather, it represents a person who makes an effort to deflect the work and responsibility but does so in such a manner that others view it as appropriate and perhaps a good example of delegating workload, as the following case study illustrates.

In an effort to better the relationship between the university and the surrounding community, the provost asks the associate deans from the College of Community Engagement (Associate Dean Eager) and the College of Public Interaction (Associate Dean Delegator) to collect information about the types of programs the community would like the university to undertake. The provost suggests a first step is to collect information from various stakeholders in the community and develop a proposal for activities that should be undertaken (and their priority), and he requests that the proposal be ready in three months. Associate Dean Eager does not know Associate Dean Delegator well, but he has seen several presentations Associate Dean Delegator has made and is impressed with his passion and apparent expertise in the area of community engagement and interaction. Therefore, Associate Dean Eager anticipates a productive collaboration and sets up a meeting for the next week for the two of them to plan out a strategy and time line to complete the project.

Associate Dean Eager arrives at the meeting with some ideas about how to interview community members and a possible time line. He assumes Associate Dean Delegator will do the same and they can merge their separate ideas into the beginnings of a plan of attack. Associate Dean Eager is disappointed to find out that Associate Dean Delegator has not thought about the project over the previous week. However, Associate Dean Delegator seems happy with Associate Dean Eager's suggestions; they talk about the interview process and divide up an initial list of contacts in the community for each of them to contact and interview. They agree to meet in three weeks to compare results.

> At the next meeting, Associate Dean Eager arrives with exciting insights based on his discussions with the five community members he agreed to interview and looks forward to seeing if Associate Dean Delegator has found similar trends. He is disappointed to learn, however, that Associate Dean Delegator has not interviewed any community members because of a conference that occurred last week. They agree to meet in another two weeks with another series of interviews. Unfortunately, the next time they meet, Associate Dean Delegator still has no interviews (though Associate Dean Eager has managed to conduct four more). After two months, Associate Dean Eager has amassed 20 interviews and Associate Dean Delegator none. Associate Dean Delegator listens to the results Associate Dean Eager has come up with and some ideas for projects. Because of his familiarity and obvious excitement with the topic, Associate Dean Delegator suggests Associate Dean Eager write up his findings for the meeting with the provost the next week. Associate Dean Eager does so and sends Associate Dean Delegator and the provost a copy of the recommendations the day before the meeting. At the meeting with the provost, Associate Dean Delegator takes the lead and talks about the wonderful findings the project found and outlines the recommendations. Although Associate Dean Delegator speaks eloquently and the provost enthusiastically embraces all of the recommendations Associate Dean Eager put forward, Associate Dean Eager feels more than a little let down and used. As a result, he does not look forward to working on any future committees with Associate Dean Delegator.

Is there anything Associate Dean Eager could have done to anticipate how the working relationship with Associate Dean Delegator would turn out? The answer might be no. If Associate Dean Delegator is a "golden boy" (see chapter 5) of the administration, others who have been caught in and are frustrated with his style and approach will likely be unwilling to advertise their bad experiences. Is there anything Associate Dean Eager could have done to change the dynamic during the course of the project? Again, probably not, given that Associate Dean Delegator's behavior is probably of long standing and has been rewarded in the past. Likewise, confronting Associate Dean Delegator or attempting to embarrass him in front of the provost by asking him detailed questions on the interviews would likely backfire.

What lessons can Associate Dean Eager learn from this episode? The most obvious is to try to avoid working with Associate Dean Delegator again. If the provost asks the two to continue working on the project, Associate Dean Eager can cut his losses and bow out by saying, "I am really pressed with other projects and I know this is really important to you. As you can see, Associate Dean Delegator has a great grasp of the issues and I look forward to what he will do with this information in the future." Unfortunately, Associate Dean Eager might not be in the position to do this, especially if this would put his relationship with the community members that he interviewed, and with whom he works with on other projects, in danger. An alternative would be to respond to the provost's request by stating that due to the press of other commitments, Associate Dean Eager will not be able to actually meet with Associate Dean Delegator for the next couple of months. Associate Dean Eager could then follow this by reaffirming his commitment to this important idea and suggest a division of the labor needed for the next step right there, a future meeting time with the provost, and suggest the three of them meet with results at a specified date in the future. That way, Associate Dean Eager can concentrate on only his part and not worry about what Associate Dean Delegator is or is not doing. Will this make Associate Dean Delegator suddenly start working? Probably not, but at least Associate Dean Eager will not feel as abused as he does now.

There are a couple of good "rules to live by" that come from this example. First, never resort to sabotage or name calling and never try to humiliate someone else in public—it will inevitably come back to haunt you. Always take the high road—no one has ever considered being called classy or gracious an insult, but having the reputation of being nasty or bad-tempered generally is not desirable. Also remember that you work with really smart people and in the long run, they will figure out what is what and who is worth having on their team (although it may seem to take them a really long time to do so).

TOOLS AND TAKEAWAYS

Connecting with people and units outside of your school or college is at least as important as making connections within your own unit. Many of these connections are necessary for your job and will occur through committee work and by working with individuals. Although these interactions are essential, they are not always smooth.

1. *Know who it is that you need to know.* As you think about making connections, step back and think about your job as an associate dean and which people outside of your college you will need to connect with to get your job done. These are people you need to actively cultivate. Do not forget staff as well as other faculty and administrators.
2. *Embrace the frustrating committee.* When you find yourself on a frustrating committee, remember that as tempting as it might be to resign, it is likely not the right decision. Resigning not only reflects on you as an individual but also has the potential to reflect poorly on your dean and/or your school. Think carefully before stepping away.
3. *Take a deep breath.* When working with a frustrating committee or individual, remember why you are doing it and what the end goal

of the interactions is. Remember also that you did not create the frustrating committee, committee chair, or other individual you are working with, and that getting exercised about how frustrating the interaction is will likely only serve to further upset you and will not have a positive impact on the situation at all.
4. *Make it better*. Once you've taken a deep breath regarding the difficult committee or person, think about how you might be able to change your approach and help move the situation to a positive conclusion. Remember to be cognizant of the needs not only of your own college in doing this, but also of the other units and people involved. Be creative and respectful, and you are likely to come out of the interaction having accomplished at least part of what you had planned.

Chapter 14

Adapting to Change While Keeping Your Sense of Humor

Change is all around us. New software programs are developed and old ones updated to make tracking pay, employees, and students easier; deans, provosts, and university presidents come and go; new strategic plans are developed; key personnel in your office retire; and funding constraints require the introduction of new cost-cutting measures, including restructuring your office or your school. Although there will always be people within your school and university who will embrace the change and carry it forward, this is not true of everyone, and it certainly can complicate your existence as an associate dean. It is an interesting phenomenon of university life that despite the fact that we are surrounded by change and that we, as academics, are trained to research and learn new things, universities in general and many of the people within them seem particularly resistant to learning new ways of doing things or embracing new visions of the future of the university. The following case study illustrates this.

> Associate Dean Old Hand has overseen personnel issues in her school for some years and has long been concerned that the university handles issues like the hiring of adjunct faculty in a very casual way, sometimes processing contracts well after the start of the semester and frequently losing paperwork for faculty on medical leave or requesting the tenure clock to stop. Additionally, the university is largely out of compliance with state regulations on how to hire state employees. For example, departments in Associate Dean Old Hand's own school frequently attempt to forgo formal searches and instead hire graduates from their

own programs or individuals recommended by friends at other universities for research and adjunct positions.

However, two things have occurred simultaneously that give Associate Dean Old Hand great hope that the system will improve. The first is the hiring of a new director of Human Resources from the business world at the beginning of spring semester. The new director takes one look at the current system and immediately starts a major overhaul. The first step is to set definite deadlines for contracts and to establish templates with consistent wording, approved by the legal department, that are required for all new hires. This task is completed midway through summer session. Tied to this change in the hiring process is a second innovation. Specifically, the HR director implements a new computerized system designed to make communication and tracking of contracts easier and also creates electronic personnel files that are easier to update than the old paper files. The computerized system takes a full year to research, purchase, and implement. The second event that makes Associate Dean Old Hand's life much easier is the hiring of an HR coordinator (a new position for the school) charged with being the liaison between the Human Resources office and the school and overseeing all of the day-to-day issues tied to contracts, sick leave, and payroll. The person hired into the position, Ms. Conscientious, is extremely well organized, hardworking, and has experience with the new computerized system from her last university. Associate Dean Old Hand is thrilled with these additions and is looking forward to spending more of her time developing mentoring programs for the staff and faculty and less of her time tracking down lost paychecks and contracts.

Once the new system is in place, things become more regularized, with only one or two minor problems. For example, as a person coming from the business world, it takes some time for the HR director to understand the nature of nine-month contracts and the fact that some faculty are not present to answer his questions or undergo training on the new system year-round. In addition, having always worked with twelve-month contracts, he is mystified at first by the concept of additional summer compensation for faculty and department chairs who work for the university in the summer in teaching, grant-funded research, and administration. However, the HR director is pretty bright, and after a brief period of frustration for all involved, he adjusts his expectations regarding these issues and the new system seems to hum along quite well. The director, unfortunately, has more difficulty understanding the need for quick turnaround of contracts when an adjunct faculty member suddenly announces the week before classes start that he has decided not to teach for the university; but after three or four false starts this too is solved.

The introduction of the computer system is the next step in updating the HR system. It will cause closer adherence to the new HR deadlines and learning a new system by all faculty and staff undertaking a new hire (including adjunct faculty), and this is where the problems begin. The new system requires that explicit job descriptions and ads be written, submitted for approval, and then posted on the university web site for a minimum of three weeks. Needless to say, all of this requires training sessions for department chairs, department secretaries, and search committees. To facilitate the training, a series of workshops are scheduled which anyone participating in the hire is required to attend.

> This last part results in an outcry from the department chairs, and the complaints flood in to both Associate Dean Old Hand and the HR coordinator, Ms. Conscientious. First, Ms. Conscientious and Associate Dean Old Hand are bombarded with e-mails and phone calls from some (though not all) of the departments. These calls and e-mails escalate to such a high volume that Ms. Conscientious is having difficulty finding enough time to get her work done. Unfortunately, some of the calls also are verbally abusive, as the faculty and staff heap their frustration on Ms. Conscientious. As a result of the abuse, Ms. Conscientious is ready to quit. The frustrations of members of the school are fanned in public meetings by Dr. Naysayer, who complains about the increasingly corporate nature of the HR department and the HR director's attempt to impose conditions on positions he knows nothing about. At a schoolwide faculty meeting to address the issue, Dr. Naysayer rises to speak about the increasing workload pushed onto the faculty in general and chairs in particular and how this increased workload interferes with their ability to teach and do research. Dr. Naysayer's oratorical expertise is well known, and the audience gathers steam behind her impassioned pleas. The end result is that Associate Dean Old Hand's dean tells her he is tired of hearing the complaints from both the faculty and the HR office, and it is Associate Dean Old Hand's job to get the program implemented regardless of what she has to do.

What is Associate Dean Old Hand to do? Are there things she could do early in the process to smooth the transition? Given the current state of affairs, what should be her first step? It is easy to agree that the first thing she needs to do is to take the heat off her HR coordinator and, if necessary, deal with any bullies making Conscientious's life difficult. Next, Associate Dean Old Hand needs to go about the process of implementing system change in the school rather than relying only on the HR director's efforts at the university level. Luckily, there is a large body of literature on the nature of organizational change and how to bring it about (for recent summaries of the literature, see Bess and Dee 2008; Burnes 2004; Kezar 2009; McCabe 2010).

DISORGANIZATION AND CHANGE FATIGUE

The next thing that Associate Dean Old Hand needs to figure out is why there is resistance to the change. There are numerous reasons why this could be the case, and being aware of some of these ahead of time can lessen the resistance to new initiatives considerably. One of the most common points of resistance is that new initiatives, whether large or small, are often poorly coordinated on a campus and a lack of communication fuels confusion and frustration, creating resistance. Such initiatives can bubble up from the faculty and staff in your own school and from other staff groups on the campus, especially those specializing in student services. Other initiatives, perhaps related to the aforementioned ones (or not), simultaneously come down from above from the president's or provost's office. The result is a shotgun-like scatter of a large number of initiatives demanding change all at the same time, usually with little if any coordination or synergy. Individuals get "change fatigue" as a result, which is characterized by a sense of paralysis and inability to make any more adjustments to meet new and changing demands (Kezar 2009). This situation is most common when an institution tries to "get it right" by making frequent adjustments to a policy or process that seem to occur just as the people involved have made the changes necessary to comply with the previous version of the policy. You have probably felt this yourself at some point in your academic career. Ask yourself this: Have you ever had a week when you feel like you are bombarded with hundreds of new little changes and/or initiatives all at the same time, and you just want one day when you do not have to deal with one more new thing and things are predictable? If so, you have suffered change fatigue.

If this is the case with Associate Dean Old Hand's faculty, one of the first things she needs to do is sit down with her dean and figure out all of the new initiatives currently in existence and prioritize them. Chances are, the HR initiative will be near the top of the list given its legal implications, but are there other initiatives that could be put off or rolled together to relieve the change fatigue and lessen the workload? Tied to this examination, Associate Dean Old Hand should examine when the various initiatives are being rolled out. Do they require new work/training at stress periods that already exist during the semester (e.g., when grades are due, at midterms, right before the deadline of a major granting agency, in the summer when most of the faculty are gone, etc.)? If this is the case, can the training or implementation be moved to a time for which there are fewer conflicts in all of the tasks that need to be accomplished?

CHANGING THE CULTURE

What if all of this planning and prioritization is done ahead of time and there is still resistance to change? What can we, as leaders in the middle, do to ensure that a new initiative is successfully implemented? The first thing we need to realize is that change is difficult, and the bigger the change, the more difficult it is. Some research of change in the business world suggests that more than two-thirds of all new initiatives in business fail due to resistance to change (Burnes 2004). If an initiative requires a change in how the participants view their institution and their place in it, or if it is inconsistent with the culture of the school or university, resistance to the change is more likely because it requires not just the acquisition of technical skills but also a shift in relationships and the perception of the role and mission of the university (McCabe 2010). These shifts can engender fear and a sense of insecurity in the participants and result in some of the most vehement opposition to new initiatives.

In our case study, for example, Associate Dean Old Hand should determine if Dr. Naysayer and her followers believe this is a step toward making the university more corporate (read: "cold and calculating"). Do they believe that it reduces their ability to quickly react to changes in personnel when there is an unexpected resignation, while maintaining both a collegial atmosphere in the department and high-quality research and teaching (a conversation Associate Dean Old Hand has already had with the director of HR)? Is there a fear of a loss of control, power, or influence over the system? Alternatively, is there a fear of learning a new computer system ("When will I have time to do this and who will help me if I have questions, given that I do not have a personal contact in HR?")? Have the chairs had bad experiences in the past with how new procedures are taught by HR staff in their training sessions?

Once Associate Dean Old Hand knows the source of the fear that's getting in the way of making the changes at hand, she can work to alleviate the concerns. The first three are issues of how we view the university and our place in it and are the most difficult to alleviate. Alleviating these fears, or alternatively, instituting a change in vision/perception of the university, is a slow, incremental process resulting from numerous conversations about attitude at the grassroots level and accommodations and adaptations to differences in perception and attitudes. Researchers in organizational structure refer to these kinds of changes as emergent change (Burnes 2004). Failure to undertake emergent change will guarantee resistance to the new initiative in both subtle and not-so-subtle ways. Alternatively, structural change is initiated in upper administration and can be considerably more rapid. It tends, however, to work best with technical issues (like learning a new software program). In our case study, Associate Dean Old Hand should determine if the source of the concerns of Dr. Naysayer and her followers is really on the technical end, resulting in a refusal to participate in the HR training sessions or use the new software. If the issue is a matter of structural change (dictated from above), is there something that Associate Dean Old Hand can do to help make the change occur more smoothly? The answer is actually yes—in fact, Associate Dean Old Hand can do a great deal to help implement structural change. Specifically, although the structure of the change and the software program are structural changes from above, how they are learned and used can be more flexible.

One of the things we as faculty members know is that teaching is not something everyone can do off the top of their head and is not something that everyone is good at. In other words, is the person who wrote the computer program or the HR person in charge of compliance the best person to teach the department chairs and secretaries how to use it? The HR person, for example, may know his or her job and the content very well, but does he or she know how to teach? Because Associate Dean Old Hand comes from the departmental ranks, she may be able to anticipate many of the frustrations and questions that the chairs and secretaries will have. If the issue is how the training sessions are handled, a workshop team-taught by Associate Dean Old Hand and the HR person working together may be an excellent solution. Alternatively, Associate Dean Old Hand might be able to create a how-to manual with step-by-step instructions that take into account the way the departments think and talk about the hiring process rather than the jargon and methodology of the HR department. Associate Dean Old Hand's HR coordinator Ms. Conscientious can be a great help in bridging the language divide that frequently occurs between HR personnel trained in the business world and faculty trained in the academic world. What is important to remember is that before any solution can be found, the source of the problem and fears needs to be determined. Once this takes place, a plan of action can be put into place to facilitate the change.

TOOLS AND TAKEAWAYS

It's been said that change is the only constant, and that is certainly true in higher education administration. Not only will you, as an associate dean, be buffeted by change, but you'll also be charged with managing change within your unit. Here are some tips for making it go more smoothly.

1. *Recognize fatigue.* If there is a pattern of repeated tweaking of processes and policies that faculty have been required to follow for some period of time, do not be surprised if there is a real reluctance on their part to make yet another change. They are not trying to be difficult, they are just tired.
2. *Listen and learn.* When real resistance to change emerges, do some detective work to determine the basis for it. It may be confusion, fear, history, or a combination of these things, but knowing where the resistance is coming from is key to working through it.
3. *Provide support.* Once you know what the roadblocks are to facilitating the changes you are charged with making, design useful and well-placed trainings and support systems to overcome the fatigue and resistance. Acknowledging that people do not want to make change and understanding why helps you figure out the type of support they require in order to make the change occur.

Chapter 15

Burning the Candle at Both Ends

Drawing Boundaries and Defending Balance

This chapter deals broadly with creating and maintaining separation between your work and your personal life. There are many ways to accomplish this, and doing it consistently will go a very long way to keeping you effective, professional, and relatively content in your position as an associate dean. Two major areas are discussed: setting boundaries between work and home; and leaving work at work, both physically and psychologically. Although there is some overlap between these two areas, there are important differences as well. The first focuses on getting and retaining control of your time, and the second focuses on managing your emotions at and about things that happen at work. Together, these two components create a sound strategy for not only protecting a sufficient quantity of time for your personal life, but also ensuring that the time you do have is of high quality.

SETTING BOUNDARIES BETWEEN WORK AND HOME

As faculty members we become accustomed to blurring the lines between work time and home time. In part, we do this because we enjoy the freedom from having to punch a time clock for a work week that is 8:00–5:00, five days a week. It is all right if we leave work at 2:00 on Wednesday to attend our son's high school basketball game because we will be grading papers all day Saturday or will meet our colleagues for coffee on Sunday to discuss a possible new hire. Further, when inspiration hits for an article or a creative piece we are working on, we generally follow through on it, even if it does come at 9:00 at night. As noted above, however, much of this changes when you become an associate dean, because your presence in the office is needed during regular business hours to conduct your administrative duties. At first, you may continue to work at night and on the weekends after a full day doing administrative work, because you are used to it. Unfortunately, this extension of the work week can get easily out of hand, and before you realize it, you are working sixty and seventy hours a week, as the following case study illustrates.

Associate Professor Workhorse has just become an associate dean—an aspiration of his for several years. He is eager to do the same bang-up job as an associate dean that he has done as a faculty member, and he lets Dean Invasive know that he is available 24/7 to do whatever he needs him to do for the school. Associate Dean Workhorse thinks, of course, that weekends and nights are really his own time to spend with his partner and on his other interests, but he wants to make sure that Dean Invasive can count on him to do his job and support him as dean. Dean Invasive lets Associate Dean Workhorse know how much he appreciates his commitment but assures him that he is a big advocate of work/life balance, as he has a family himself. Dean Invasive takes down Associate Dean Workhorse's cell and home phone numbers in case of emergency. The dean assures Associate Dean Workhorse that he appreciates his dedication but does not anticipate contacting him at home.

Associate Dean Workhorse has been on the job for three weeks and is on the way home from work one night when Dean Invasive calls his cell phone. Assuming that something critical is going on, Associate Dean Workhorse quickly pulls his car over to take the dean's call. Dean Invasive apologizes for bothering Associate Dean Workhorse after hours, but he really needs some information. Associate Dean Workhorse, paying full attention, tells his boss that it is fine and that he is glad to help solve the problem. Dean Invasive then asks Associate Dean Workhorse if it is more appropriate to refer to non-tenure-track faculty in the college as "faculty" or "instructors," as he is preparing some remarks for a meeting he has with these faculty members at the end of the week. Associate Dean Workhorse is silent for a moment, waiting for the "emergency," and when the dean says nothing more, Associate Dean Workhorse answers the question. Expecting the call to end, Associate Dean Workhorse prepares to restart his car, but Dean Invasive goes on to ask about the history of faculty governance in the school and to recount how non-tenure-track faculty were involved in faculty governance at his previous institution. Associate Dean Workhorse listens patiently, and he is relieved to pull into traffic nearly thirty minutes after picking up the call. On the way home, Associate Dean Workhorse reflects on the conversation, first feeling proud that the dean wanted to talk with him, and second, squelching his frustration that his "off the clock" time was interrupted for a nonemergency that easily could have waited until the next day.

> Several months later, Associate Dean Workhorse has come to expect frequent nonemergency calls from Dean Invasive in the evenings, before work in the morning, on weekends, and on holidays. In addition, it is clear that Dean Invasive's expectation is that Associate Dean Workhorse will be on his e-mail and continuously available even when out of town on a family vacation. Following the interruption of a birthday dinner party for his partner by a one-hour call from Dean Invasive on a Saturday evening, Associate Dean Workhorse's partner loses it and loudly lets Associate Dean Workhorse know where he should tell Dean Invasive to stick his e-mail and cell phone. Associate Dean Workhorse is distraught, feeling torn between his partner and his boss in a situation in which he cannot make either of them, or himself, content.

Associate Dean Workhorse may have difficulty talking to the dean about work-home boundaries because of fear that by drawing and holding real boundaries between work and home he will be labeled as "lazy" or "lacking dedication" by Dean Invasive. He also may worry that if he insists on holding his boundaries, the dean will not consult him on something that really *is* crucial, resulting in a big mess that Associate Dean Workhorse will have to fix at a later date. Depending on his relationship with the dean, he also may worry that partitioning his work and home life may result in his being replaced in his associate dean job, damaging his reputation in such a way that it will preclude any future administrative positions. If you are in this latter camp, however, you should remember that associate deans generally put in long hours and perform unenviable tasks. In short, the job of associate dean is not often coveted, and Associate Dean Workhorse can likely be fairly secure in the knowledge that few others want to take on the load he carries. Moreover, it turns out that many people, including some of his associate dean colleagues, have and hold solid boundaries between work and home life, and feel no ill effects. Associate Dean Workhorse absolutely could have and still can establish and hold boundaries, and he will soon realize that not only will his personal life improve, but he will also be less stressed out and, therefore, more effective at work as well (Boenisch and Haney 1996; Sorcinnelli and Gregory 1987; Woverton and Gmelch 2002).

Repeat after us: "The weekend is a time to relax, recharge, do the things you want to do, and not work." We know this is hard, but there are major advantages to being a member of the "not working on the weekends" crowd. Sometimes associate deans fall into the trap of spending weekends interspersing checking and answering e-mails and trying to get caught up with family time and so-called relaxing. What they quickly learn is that on Monday morning they are neither caught up nor relaxed. In fact, they may actually be more frazzled when walking in the door on Monday morning than they were when they departed on Friday evening. There are ways to change this scenario so that you, your work, and your family are better off. Here are some important things to remember.

1. *The work will still be there on Monday*. You can pick it up where you left off on Friday when you return, but you will come back relaxed, recharged, and stress-free rather than exhausted.
2. *"Caught up" is a myth*. There is always something else you can do. What all administrators must learn to do is prioritize. The criteria for prioritization should include deadlines and project impact, but the point is that not everything must be done the second it comes across your desk/e-mail/phone.
3. *There are no true emergencies in the associate dean job*. We are not firefighters, police officers, physicians, or hostage negotiators; our fingers are *not* on the button for nuclear Armageddon. In reality, very little short of a fire or a shooter on campus is truly an emergency. If one of these true emergencies should occur, the dean's first call should be to a firefighter, police officer, physician, or hostage negotiator, not an associate dean.
4. *Nobody says on his or her deathbed, "I wish I had spent more time answering e-mails and doing administrative work."* Many people's doctors, on the other hand, do tell them to cut down on stress or they will be on their deathbed.

So what can you do to create and maintain a better work-home balance in your life? Well, to start, set and hold some very firm boundaries in your personal and professional life. Here are some suggestions to help you regain and maintain the balance.

First, simply do not do e-mail or make work phone calls in the evening or on weekends, period. The trick here is to communicate this to the people you work with to manage their expectations, especially if this is a change. Just let people know that due to family or personal obligations, you are unavailable for e-mail and phone calls after hours and on weekends. If you are an e-mail junkie (you know who you are!), it is important to do this cold turkey. Resist at all costs backsliding into the notion of checking e-mail just this once. E-mails are like potato chips—you can *never* answer just one. Turn the cell phone off (or if you need it for family reasons, change the number and give it only to family members). Turn the computer off. Once you have retrained yourself as well as the individuals you work with at your school and university, you can set yourself up with a nonuniversity e-mail account for your friends and families to communicate with you.

Second, set goals in your personal life just like you do in your professional life. If you set a goal of completing a training or publishing a paper or getting a promotion at work, you plan for it and work for it, right? Do the same thing in your personal life. For example, if you set a goal of learning to play tennis, take steps to meet that goal, just as you set and take steps to accomplish things at work.

Third, schedule dates with yourself and other people for nonwork activities. Just as you make appointments for work items or events, create calendar entries for personal and family time and activities. Plans are easier to break in favor of work if you do not have an appointment or firm commitment. Seeing the date on the calendar and knowing someone else is counting on your presence can help make the event real and harder to skip in favor of work.

Finally, decide what types of events you will consistently say "no" to and what kinds of events you will willingly participate in at night and on the weekend on occasion. To help you figure this out, decide what kinds of work activities you feel are important and/or rewarding enough to invade your "real life." In other words, prioritize your commitments. For example, if you get the occasional invitation to give a talk somewhere outside of office hours and you want to, then do it. Or if you enjoy the annual celebration dinner of the top students and/or faculty, then participate. However, get committees currently slated to start at 6:00 p.m. rescheduled, as dinner time is prime family/child/partner/home time.

It may be a little tough to commit to these actions and adjust the expectations of others as you set your boundaries, but once you have done it, you will find that you return to work on Monday rested, more effective in accomplishing your work, and less stressed and burned out, allowing the creative juices to flow. In short, by saying no and reclaiming your personal time, you will become more productive.

LEAVING WORK AT WORK: DEALING WITH WORK-RELATED EMOTIONS

Even if you are extremely good at maintaining boundaries between your work and personal time, your job as associate dean can still invade your personal life. Let's face it, there is a ton of stress involved in administration. In addition to the high workload and often unreasonable deadlines, associate deans are frequently on the front line for student complaints, conflict resolution between faculty, and mitigating the impact of new policies, procedures, and budget cuts (Grasha 1987; Selden 1987; Woverton and Gmelch 2002). The result is a high level of stress and tension that can, if allowed, permeate your entire life, as the following case study illustrates.

> Associate Dean Pensive is in charge of the college retention, tenure and promotion (RTP) committee, which has met and made its recommendations for the year. One decision goes against the vote of the Department of Metaphysical Studies, which is supportive of tenuring Assistant Professor Tepid, who has a weak teaching record and no publications. Associate Dean Pensive writes the RTP committee's letter explaining their recommendation against tenure, as her job dictates, and works with the committee until they are happy with the letter. Associate Dean Pensive then follows policy by discussing the decision with Dr. Tepid's department chair, Dr. Dubious, and sending copies of the committee's letter to Drs. Tepid and Dubious. During her conversation with Dr. Dubious, Associate Dean Pensive lays out the next steps for the RTP case and offers her help to the Metaphysical Studies faculty in responding to the issues raised by the committee's letter. Dr. Dubious acknowledges the next steps in the process and declines Associate Dean Pensive's offer of help. Associate Dean Pensive thinks nothing more of it until she is called into Dean Distant's office and informed that Dr. Dubious has filed a formal grievance against her for dereliction of duty on the grounds that Associate Dean Pensive neither explained the department's options in the case nor offered assistance to them. Dean Distant asks Associate Dean Pensive why she did not follow policy and reprimands her for her lack of professionalism in dealing with the Dr. Tepid case. Associate Dean Pensive is devastated, angry, and indignant, and leaves the office. On her drive home, Associate Dean Pensive replays the episode over and over again, berating herself for the situation and fueling her own anger and resentment at Dean Distant and Dr. Dubious. Although she is able to continue to hold it together at work and function well in the subsequent days and weeks, she lies awake at night ruminating over the situation and holding on to her anger and frustration. Her anxiety and dissatisfaction grow and spill over into her personal time and life.

We have all been in Associate Dean Pensive's shoes to some degree. After a hard day at work, you leave the office, get in the car or on the train, and the tape loop keeps playing and playing: "So-and-So is such a jerk! I have to find a way to deal with him." Or you might see yourself as inadequate and say, "What am I going to do about getting that report done? I do not have time!" Alternatively, you might realize the situation is unreasonable and say to yourself, "I wish they had given me more time to get that data together—two days just is not enough time." Finally, after you have been unfairly blamed, you might say, "Why didn't I come up with a better comeback?" It seems endless. Once you walk in the door at home, the loop may slow down or pause while you deal with the tasks of dinner, cleaning the kitchen, and perhaps connecting with spouse and/or children, but even then, the background noise of work stress can invade the precious time you have at home. Then, of course, when the lights go out, the quiet of the night can give rise to massive rumination about work worries, fears, and problems, robbing you of the sleep you need to awake refreshed and actually ready and able to take on and solve these very challenges. What can you do to break this cycle?

We all need and want to do a good job at work, but to do that, we need to leave work at the office as much as possible. Find ways to depersonalize what happens at work and reduce the sometimes significant level of stress you may feel. Succeeding at this takes a combination of disciplining ourselves to leave work where it belongs (at work) and learning to deal with conflict and difficult people effectively. We must learn to do this if we are to preserve our emotional energy and investment for our relationships, families, and ourselves. These steps are, of course, easier said than done, but understanding the nature of stress and our psychological and physical responses to it can help.

Gmelch's (1987) study of stress among university faculty is helpful. Gmelch argues that there are four parts to the stress response. By understanding these we can mitigate the stress that results from a particular issue to some degree. The first and most obvious part of the process is the actual stressor (in Associate Dean Pensive's case, the dean's and department chair's reactions to the committee decision). This action by itself, however, is not sufficient to set an individual into a downward spiral of sleepless nights and stress-induced high blood pressure. Our own perception of the stressor is the second crucial piece in the puzzle. If you feel you do not have the resources, institutional backing, or power to deal with the situation, stress is heightened. In our case study, Associate Dean Pensive's reaction to the department chair's action would likely be much different if she felt she had the dean's support. The third factor of the stress response is the size of the disconnect between the resources and institutional support that you have versus what you feel you need to address the issue. The greater the disconnect, the more intense the mental and physical response to the situation will be. The final aspect is the anticipated consequence of the event in terms of long-term relationships with others with whom you work and your career.

Given that we often cannot prevent the stressor from occurring, how can we modify our perceptions of the situation and its consequences to mitigate the stress that inevitably results and thus stop that downward spiral we mentioned? First and foremost, give yourself time to decompress when a stressful event occurs. Go for a walk, or go over to the local coffeehouse and look at a section of the newspaper (the comics or sports page is always a good choice—avoid the help wanted ads). You need some psychological "down time" so you can get some perspective. If it is the end of the day, this may mean driving home without the radio on and talking yourself down from some of the stresses you have experienced, writing in a journal about your day, or reading a good book on the bus or the train to help reset from the day. We all probably have been seen in traffic yelling (seemingly at no one) at the top of our lungs while we vent about the situation at work. We may look a little crazy to the people in the next car, but we are generally much happier and more relaxed when we get home for having gotten our frustration off our chests.

Second, given that the major portion of the stress reaction is related to our perception of the event and the disconnect between what is needed to deal with the issue and our access to those things, you need to take time to analyze the situation. We recommend following Boenisch and Haney's (1996, 92) model of "boxing your worries." This process consists of analyzing the situation, breaking it down into its constituent parts, and putting the various parts of the issue into different areas of a box dictating where control lies and how important the task is. We illustrate the process with Associate Dean Pensive's situation.

In other words, Associate Dean Pensive should concentrate only on things that fit into Box A. She needs to let go of the parts of the situation in Boxes B, C, and D.

Third, reduce stress in general by setting and maintaining those boundaries we talked about. Do not work at night and on weekends. Many of us work at night and on weekends because we feel like we should, not because it is really necessary. However, this is actually counterproductive because working after hours only exacerbates the feeling that you have too much to do. This is a major source of stress for most people (Seldin 1987). Additionally, because you are tired and burned out, you are less productive when you are at work and less able to address major stressors when they arise. If you are already in a high level of stress, you are more likely to perceive a large disconnect between your ability to address an issue and the skills, time, and resources needed to do so.

Table 15.1. Associate Dean Pensive's worries boxed.

A: Things I can control that are important	B: Things I cannot control that are important
Associate Dean Pensive can control her response to the actions of Dr. Dubious and Dean Distant. Part of her response should include giving the dean and the individual investigating the grievance process documentation demonstrating that appropriate process was followed.	Included in this area is Dr. Dubious's grievance complaint. However, Associate Dean Pensive must have faith in the system and trust in the integrity of those she works with. In other words, she needs to let the process take its course.
C: Things I can control that are not important	**D: Things I cannot control that are not important**
If it is not important, Associate Dean Pensive needs to ignore it, even if she can control it. It will only use up valuable time and energy to waste time on things in this category.	If something fits in this category, it is a waste of time and energy. Associate Dean Pensive should not even think about it.

This means do not check e-mail once you get home, even if you tell yourself that your intention is only to clean out the spam and you will not look at anything else—because you always do something else (remember those potato chips!). It might be particularly tempting for Associate Dean Pensive to do this, thinking it will mend fences and/or clarify her actions, but it will backfire if for no other reason than it only reinforces the stress of the day. Box the worries, decompress, and be ready to take action at work the next day. Then move on.

Fourth, work to depersonalize the stressful aspects of your workplace. When you take things personally, emotions come into play. The fact is that emotion rarely has any constructive place in our careers and can, in fact, muddy the waters of what we do. Think of the number of times you have had to calm down angry faculty or staff members or work to reduce conflict between individuals in your school due to anger, jealousy, pride, frustration, or defensiveness. At all costs, avoid falling into the same trap. That means do not take the actions of others personally, even when they include a personal attack. You may not be able to control how someone else talks about you, but you can control how you react to him or her. So take the old adage "It's just a job" to heart and repeat it to yourself over and over. Even if someone is personally attacking you, as in the case study above, remember that professional people do not operate that way. You need to ignore these actions and always act in a professional manner yourself. The bad behavior of others is a diversion from a real issue. Also, remember that you work with smart people and, in the long run, those around you will figure out what's what, who's who, and just how good you really are. In effect, we are telling you to always take the high road. Always err on the side of giving people the benefit of the doubt, and always do the right thing, even if it is tempting to do something vengeful, retaliatory, or manipulative. Always ask yourself "Would I want my parents/children/spouse to see me now? Would they be proud of what I'm doing?" If the answer is no, stop and change course. We are not telling you to be a doormat. Rather, we are telling you that you should dictate your own behavior, rather than allowing the person attacking you and your work situation to determine how you react. The person attacking you is probably attempting to make himself or herself look better by trying to devalue you. Don't allow that to happen.

To help you do this, remember that process is your friend. If a situation or person at work is problematic, find out and follow any process that exists and document every action to deal with the problem instead of just trying to head it off by short-cutting the process. For example, Associate Dean Pensive should have copies of her correspondence on the case (the letter to Dr. Tepid telling him the committee decision, e-mails between herself and Dr. Dubious, notes on the conversations with Dr. Dubious on the phone including time and date). She should make copies of this material and give it to her dean and to the individuals investigating the grievance. The other thing to remember is that time really is your ally. Take the time to learn about a situation, get your emotions under control, let others cool off, and weigh the possibilities in resolving a conflict or meeting a work demand. Do not rush into things. It is better to say "I'm sorry, but I need a little more time to investigate the policy" than to jump to a conclusion that is hasty or wrong.

TOOLS AND TAKEAWAYS

The balance necessary to do a good job as an associate dean while retaining control over your personal time and life is often difficult to achieve, but doing so should be at the top of your list. Here are our top tips on how to create and maintain the essential equilibrium between work and life.

1. *Respect yourself*. This may sound trite, but it is a mantra that's easily put aside in the face of "taking one for the team" and "going the extra mile." Be clear about what you will and will not do, and be consistent in your messages and your actions to show your dean and the people in your life that having boundaries is important. This will help you function better all around.
2. *Be flexible*. Having said that, it is important to have clear boundaries, and use good judgment in bending them. If you have a "no work functions on the weekends" policy but your dean calls you on Friday night to say that his wife was admitted to the hospital suddenly and he needs you to attend a student function in his stead on Saturday morning, it is probably wise to see if you can work out some way to make that happen. After all, you would hope the dean would do the same for you if the situation were reversed.
3. *Analyze the situation*. In work circumstances when your boundaries are challenged, step back and determine whether you can control the situation—as well as whether you should. This approach helps you determine your response and the intensity of it, and helps you gain and keep perspective on whether a perceived emergency really is one or not.
4. *Take your time*. When in a stressful situation that challenges your bounds of patience and/or balance, take the time necessary to get all the information you need and to consider the realities of the situation before taking action or responding. Virtually nothing requires an immediate response, and well-considered words and actions will help you grow and maintain your credibility and support your own boundaries.

Chapter 16

Moving On

Life after Being an Associate Dean

Although there are many individuals who have long careers as associate deans, many others leave the dean's office after a while, either to move into a higher administrative position or to return to the faculty. This happens for a variety of reasons. Sometimes, a new dean who comes in wants to bring in new associate deans to form his or her leadership team; sometimes there is a realignment of staffing or priorities in the dean's office that shifts your job in a way that does not work well; and sometimes (perhaps most often) it just becomes clear to you and possibly others that it is time to go and move on. This insight may be tied to the realization that it is time for you to take on new and different challenges in higher education administration or in your research area. Alternatively, you may wish to go back to your faculty roots as you near retirement. Finally, the decision to leave the associate dean position may be tied to differences in priorities, approach, or style between you and your dean that make your working relationship less productive. Regardless of the reason, deciding on and making this transition can feel awkward, especially if becoming an associate dean was something you aspired to achieve. Deciding to move on to a different administrative position at your own or another university or returning to the faculty represents a considerable change in your career trajectory and everyday life, and there can be some anxiety around such a situation. There are many things to consider at this transition point. First, how do you decide it is time to leave the dean's office and move to a different position? Second, if you are leaving for some reason other than a job offer, what will you do next and how do you actually leave? Finally, what can you expect in the aftermath of being an associate dean?

KNOW WHEN TO EXIT

Making the decision to leave your job as associate dean may be easy for some, but for many it is a difficult decision for several reasons. First, most of us came to these jobs with the idea that we had a contribution to make to the school beyond our faculty positions. While an associate dean, we served as good stewards of our schools and universities by making a positive impact on students, staff, and faculty over the long run. In other words, we care about the long-term health and sustainability of our institutions. When you care about something, it is hard to walk away from it, and you may feel like you are abandoning your post. This sense of duty creates a level of guilt about not staying in your position that may feel as if you are shirking responsibility or bailing out of the job. It is possible that you have never resigned from anything in your life, which can make this an even more unsettling decision. This may be intensified by the reaction of others, who will try to talk you into staying, citing unfinished work on future projects. Second, most of us came to these jobs because we are good at what we do. We are organized, able to start and finish things, not shy about speaking our minds (respectfully and professionally, of course), and okay with taking responsibility and making tough calls. We also, most likely, are pretty sure that we will be hard to replace when we leave the dean's office, and so, worries about succession may cloud our thinking about exiting. Finally, once you have been an associate dean, what you do next is not always clear, and the choice of what direction to go when you leave the dean's office can be a daunting one. Your options are really two (unless you are eligible for retirement): you can either move into higher levels of administrative work, or you can return to the faculty. Each has its advantages and challenges, which we will discuss later in this chapter. Regardless of the reason you decide to leave, the choice is not an easy one for many individuals.

The above factors are likely to feed your decision to leave the dean's office, but in addition, unless you are dismissed or there is an organizational shift, a large part of your decision to leave may be tied to how effective you feel in your job as associate dean, how constrained you are in it as your knowledge and skill levels grow (prompting you to apply for a deanship or other administrative position at your own or another institution), and/or how supported and valued you feel in your job. Undoubtedly, there will be a few (okay, maybe many) days in your job as associate dean when you get in your car or on the train at the end of the day and say to yourself, "That's it! I've had it. After a day like today, I am through with this stupid job. I am quitting." Sometimes these feelings last for only a few minutes or hours, and other times, they last for days or weeks, but they may eventually subside. It is important to distinguish momentary frustration and anger from sincere burnout and readiness to move on. Consider this case study.

> Professor Fairweather became associate dean for faculty affairs in the College of Liberal Arts and Sciences eight months ago. The end of the school year is now upon her, and she has had a pretty smooth ride until now. Suddenly, it is time for annual merit reviews, reappointments, staff evaluations, and determination of faculty and staff raises. At the behest of Dean Dodgy, Associate Dean Fairweather sends out the necessary forms and dates to the department chairs to get faculty and staff evaluations done, and she sends along a datasheet that Dean Dodgy has asked the chairs to fill out, which documents the scholarly activities of the faculty and staff members in their unit on a single summary sheet. The datasheet focuses on the categories of grants, peer-reviewed journal articles, book chapters, conference presentations, review articles, and peer-reviewed abstracts for documenting scholarly work. Fairweather is stunned when, after she sends this sheet and request out to the department chairs, she begins to receive a series of extremely angry e-mails and voice mails from the chairs and some faculty in the humanities; they express resentment concerning the definition of scholarship she has sent out, which they believe has dismissed outlets of scholarly work in the humanities—specifically, books, novels, monographs, poetry or short story collections, readings, exhibitions, and so on. Some faculty, in fact, are so upset about the matter that they contact Dean Dodgy to say that Associate Dean Fairweather is insulting them and is not fit to serve as an associate dean because she is so insensitive to the work done by those in fields other than her own (she is a chemist, as is the dean). The dean, instead of taking responsibility for the datasheet, responds to the complainants, copying Fairweather, asking her to explain why she framed the datasheet as she did and asking her to correct it to meet the concerns.
>
> Needless to say, Fairweather is beside herself upon reading the dean's e-mail, as she feels she was merely complying with his request. She feels as though she has been thrown under the bus by the dean. Up to this point, she has felt supported by the dean and has been enjoying her work as an associate dean, so this is a real shock! Moreover, she does not feel a great drive to return to her classroom or lab at this point, but she is so enraged by this event that she spends the weekend seething about the injustice of the situation and penning her letter of resignation to the dean.

Can you relate to Fairweather's feelings? Is she making the right decision? In some cases, she might be, but in this case, we would argue that she is throwing the baby out with the bathwater. Sure, she may feel that it is not fair that the dean put her in such a difficult position. Given that she is generally enjoying her job as an associate dean, however, and does not have a strong desire to return to the faculty, nor does she feel she has amassed enough experience to apply for the position of dean at another institution, should she really throw in the towel at this point?

This case study is included to illustrate the peculiar nature of the associate dean's position. That is, you are frequently following orders but are perceived to be implementing new procedures unilaterally. Occasionally, associate deans get caught in the cross fire and appear to be blamed by both sides in the ongoing e-mail communications of the school. The question to ask yourself is whether this happens once in a while or is frequent enough that (1) you lose credibility, (2) you lose self-respect, and/or (3) you cannot be effective in your job as associate dean. If this is not a frequent issue, take some time to think things through about the situation. Go for a walk, work at home for a day, anything to create some distance and perspective. It is critical not to make any decision about what to do, or what to say for that matter, when you are as upset as Fairweather is in the case study. Once you have calmed down, a face-to-face discussion about how the communication of the dean's request to the chairs could have been handled differently is in order, so that this type of reaction does not occur in the future. If, on the other hand, this is a frequent issue, then maybe it is time to think about applying for a different job or returning to the faculty. In making your decision, weigh the good against the bad before cutting the cord. Typically, when you leave a job like this, you cannot come back to the same job. That means you need to think about where you want to go next in your career and what is the best way to get there. In other words, think long and hard before you resign, because the ramifications may be considerable. What do we mean by that? Well, here is some advice for how to separate the wheat from the chaff to decide when you really need to leave and when you just need to chill out and go with the flow.

How do you know when your level of boredom, burnout, and/or unhappiness or dissatisfaction in your job as an associate dean has reached the point of no return, and you are better off leaving your job than sticking with it for a while longer? Although there is no tried-and-true formula to know for sure, if you notice any of the ten signs below, it could be a very good indication that it is time to leave your associate dean position and either move up the chain or return to the faculty.

1. *You are frequently sick in the absence of a diagnosed chronic medical condition.* Stress-related illness like migraines, insomnia, depression, high blood pressure, anxiety, or frequent colds and infections or other illnesses are all signs that your job worries are taking a toll on your physical health. Alternatively, if your friends and family notice something is wrong, that you are "not the same person you used to be," or that something is bothering you, it is a

major sign that your work is causing you stress to the point that your mood and health are suffering. If your health is suffering physically, emotionally, or both, your job may not be worth it.
2. *You feel your values and ethics are frequently challenged.* Maybe your dean or school has priorities you do not believe in or your dean's vision is out of sync with your own. Whatever the reason, if your values and ethics are being violated at work, you will have a hard time feeling fulfilled in your job or justified in your career choice.
3. *You are not challenged intellectually.* If you would like the chance to use your problem-solving, public-speaking, mentoring, fundraising, and (you fill in the blank) skills, but you are stuck doing busywork or dealing with crisis after crisis, or the job has become routine, with little intellectual engagement, rather than an exciting career, it is probably time to apply for a different type of job in higher education administration. A job that is not challenging you and allowing you to use the skills you have developed may be a hindrance in the long term. If you feel that your skills and personal career goals are being marginalized in your current position, it may be time to look for other work options. Realize, of course, that this may require moving to a different university if those challenges include becoming a dean or a provost or taking another administrative position.
4. *There is no room for advancement.* If your university's workforce or leadership structure is stable, it means that your career will not be able to advance. An environment that offers no room for you to move up or take on more responsibility unless someone else retires may put you in the position of looking for a new position at a different university.
5. *You feel belittled or discredited.* If your colleagues are condescending and your opinion is not respected by members of the dean's office, the upper administration, or the faculty and staff members of your school, it may be time to move on. If you are not asked to attend important meetings related to your area of responsibility or you feel your work does not make a difference to your school or university, it may be time to consider other options, especially if your relationship with your colleagues has been damaged beyond repair. Many disagreements can be resolved, but if, for whatever reason, your relationship with your colleagues has been irreparably damaged by the exclusion or derision you feel directed at you, it may be time to bail.
6. *The school or university is in serious trouble.* It is important to work in a stable, reputable environment. An organization that is

constantly reorganizing, downsizing, or changing leadership may not be a good long-term career choice. The same goes for an organizational structure that provides no rules or procedures to protect employees (or provides rules and procedures, but they are not followed) and the administration is unwilling to work to change the situation. If this is the case, it may be time to apply for a position at another university for the long-term health of your career.

7. *You dread going to work every day to the point that the thought of it makes you sick.* This is a sign that your job is not meeting your needs—financially, ethically, or motivationally. Life is too short to spend it being miserable.

8. *Your family circumstances change.* A change in your personal life (marriage, having children, caring for elderly relatives, etc.) may make it necessary to find a new job because of location, finances, or a need to spend more time at home.

9. *Your office is an emotionally abusive environment.* A work environment that is hostile, is led by abusive management, and/or offers no route to solve grievances is an emotionally abusive one. This type of atmosphere could lead to physical and mental suffering that if not addressed can have an adverse impact on your health. If you are in this situation and can find no recourse through your ombudsperson or the grievance process, you should seek another position immediately.

10. *A better opportunity comes along.* There may come a point in your career when a new opportunity presents itself. For example, we have all been approached by headhunters and/or members in upper administration of our own institution telling us about intriguing new opportunities and asking us to apply. When this happens to you, make a list weighing the pros and cons of each position, and if the new job comes out on top, do not be afraid to make the switch.

YOU HAVE DECIDED TO RESIGN YOUR ASSOCIATE DEAN JOB—NOW WHAT?

If you think resigning your position as associate dean is the right decision, there are a couple of major things you should do before actually taking the leap. Most likely, part of the reason you are a good associate dean is that you are skilled at contingency planning and weighing options, so do not neglect to do that for yourself as you face this transition. First and foremost, if you have a partner and/or family, discuss your thoughts about resigning with them before you do anything concrete.

Although it is your career, your partner, spouse, or family will be affected by this change. There may be financial fallout from your decision that will impact them, so it may be necessary to make some budgetary shifts or do some planning or economizing to accommodate your loss of income. Alternatively, if you are applying for a position at another university, it may involve moving to a new city. Your spouse and family will likely experience some collateral stress when you go through a job search, take a new position, or return to your academic department as a faculty member.

This may sound redundant, but stop again and think hard about all your options. If you are unhappy with your current position, is resigning really the best solution? Although there are plenty of times when it is, sometimes there may be another way through a difficult period that will leave you in a better position. Can your current job situation be improved by talking honestly and directly to your dean about what your concerns are and what is not going well? This is a sticky wicket, of course, if part of the reason you are considering resigning is because you do not work well with your dean. Regardless, if you have this kind of conversation, remember that once you say something it cannot be taken back; consider your words carefully and think about how you want to present your concerns. If you have already had this kind of conversation with your dean or you know it will just make things worse, be sure you have researched other options for positions or discussed returning to the faculty with your department chair. Know what you are going to do next one way or the other. Whatever decision you make, try to stay positive about it. It will make it easier to find a new position or reenter the faculty ranks, or to improve your view of your position as associate dean if you decide not to leave.

LOOK BEFORE YOU LEAP

So, if you are going to end your stint as associate dean, what are you going to do next? This may seem like a simple question, but when you are right in the middle of deciding what your next steps are, the answer may not be so obvious. You can certainly think about what you would like to do and how you can attain the level of professional and career satisfaction you are missing now, but if you stay in academia, you basically have two options: (1) move up into a higher administrative or leadership position, or (2) return to life as a faculty member. Each of these options has distinct advantages and challenges that may affect you differently, depending on where you are in your personal and professional life when you make this decision and what you decide for your ultimate career goals. These goals are not the same for everyone, and so there is no single right decision.

Option 1: Seeking a Higher Administrative Position

A key factor in this decision is really being honest with yourself about where you are in your personal and professional life and what your goals for the next five to ten years are at this point. There is no right or wrong decision here, because everyone's goals are different. The important thing to realize is that decisions you make in the short term may affect your ability to achieve long-term goals. In other words, do not shut a door or burn a bridge on the way out that you may need later on. Additionally, how you position yourself in your next job may eliminate possibilities down the line. For example, if you decide that you want to move up the chain and become a dean, vice president, or provost, you need to understand that you will be essentially be kissing your life as an active scholar good-bye (or at least severely curtailing it), and it may be very difficult in the future to restart an active research program in the field in which you were trained, especially if you are in an area that requires substantial grant funding. Although some individuals in high administrative academic positions manage to maintain some level of research and scholarship activity, the demands of these higher positions are typically so great that it is impossible to give the necessary effort to research and scholarship that is required to run studies, mentor students, write grants, go to conferences, and publish manuscripts. A research hiatus of a few years can be utterly deadly as far as being able to compete for grant funding, although there are a few mechanisms for "reentry" funding for people in career transitions. Alternatively, you may wish to change your research focus to that of administration in higher education (though, believe us, this is not as easy as it sounds if your former training did not deal with organizational issues in some way).

It is also likely that you will largely give up teaching when you go into a very high administrative position, although there is more flexibility here. Some very successful college presidents, for example, do not have active research programs, but they prioritize teaching one undergraduate course section per year. This can be an enormously rewarding thing to do, because first, it keeps the administrator connected to the real work of the institution, and second, it makes him or her visible and accessible to the people who really drive the whole enterprise, the students. The take-home message here is that typically, being an associate dean is one of the last administrative positions in which you can sustain some semblance of life as a "regular faculty member" by doing some teaching and scholarship; positions higher than associate dean typically do not allow for these activities, and some expressly require that you commit 100 percent of your time to administrative work twelve months of the year and expect that you will mothball your scholarship while you serve in the position at hand. If you are ready to largely give up your life as a scholar, moving up may be the right decision for you right now, but if you still have aspirations regarding your research and scholarly work, you may wish to delay climbing the administrative ladder to a later point in your career.

Another aspect of taking on a higher administrative position relates to your personal life and goals. You have already experienced the substantial loss of flexibility in controlling your time that came with becoming an associate dean; after years of determining your own schedule for the most part as a faculty member, you suddenly had numerous regular meetings, emergencies you had to accommodate, late nights you had to work to complete important reports or institute new programs, and events and conferences you had to attend. Further increased pressure on your calendar is a given aspect of moving into a higher administrative position. To illustrate, when we asked a colleague of ours who is a dean how many nights per week he was out for university-related events and business, he responded, "Eight." To do the job of an upper-level administrator well, especially at a larger institution, you need to be prepared to commit time to your work over family. If spending time with your spouse, children, and/or other family members is something that you want to be involved in regularly, it may not be a good time to take on a higher administrative role, as the requirements of the position will very likely conflict with your desire to spend quality time with your family. Remember that if you are hardworking, have integrity, and stay engaged, upper administration will be an option for your career later in your life, but as a parent, you will only have one chance to go to the sixth-grade spelling bee or kindergarten graduation. If being a parent or being a caretaker to an aging parent or ailing spouse is important for you at this point in your life, taking on a higher administrative position may not be a good choice right now, but it could be in the future when your personal circumstances change.

As long as you do so with your eyes open, moving into a higher administrative position may be a logical next step after being an associate dean. This could take the form of moving up into a position in your current institution or, more likely, moving to another institution. If you do decide to do this, here are some things to consider as you are positioning yourself, as well as while applying for your next administrative position. First, ask yourself what skills you possess and, equally important, what skills you need to develop. Use this as a productive opportunity to take stock of your skills—something many of us do not do often enough. Do not limit yourself to skills you are using right now as an associate dean. For example, although fund-raising is not something you have done for the university, you may have participated in it with a charity with which you are involved. Additionally, you may not supervise individuals in your current associate dean position, but maybe you do supervise while running a research project. You will want to talk about these skills in your application letter to give search committees a view of your expertise beyond what is listed in your CV. Equally important is to think about what necessary skills you lack for the job to which you aspire. Are there workshops you can attend to help you achieve these? Alternatively, can you volunteer for a committee at your current university that will expose you to these issues to prepare you for future positions? Finally, read the professional literature on higher education administration so that you are informed about the issues you will face in your new position; we can guarantee you will be asked about them if you make it to the interview stage.

Second, ask yourself how well you cope with major changes in your life. Change is one of the most difficult things anyone faces in life, and there are few changes more significant than a career change. Think about how you faced major changes in the past and what stress they caused you. Also, look back at the decisions you have made in your life and whether they turned out well or not. If you have made poor decisions in the past, can you make this decision more effectively? What did you do well last time that you can use again now?

Third, you need to prepare yourself to actually apply for and, hopefully, to accept your new position. Is your network up-to-date? We all rely on our networks of friends and colleagues to help us make a career or institution change or to find out about new positions; getting your name out there and letting people know you are interested in new opportunities is half the battle. If you feel you need to update your network for the change you are contemplating, supplement your discipline-specific professional organizations with professional organizations tied to higher education administration. Attending their meetings and volunteering for committees will help build the network you will need to make this change in the direction of your career.

Once you get the job, make sure you get a mentor. Someone who is working in or has worked in your new academic position can be very helpful in getting you through the rough patches in a new career. This person does not have to be a president or at a super-high level, but he or she does need to be someone who is successful and satisfied in his or her career or administrative position and can be helpful to you as you make your change. For many of us, this person is our current dean, or some other person with whom we work within the administration of our university. Remember that as well as guiding you through the pitfalls and successes, mentors had to apply and interview for their current jobs, so they can give you advice before you get your new job as well as once you are in the position. Tied to this, you should review your job-hunting skills (and a mentor can help here, too). If it has been a few years since you actively applied for a new position, you probably need to tune up your job-hunting skills a bit. For example, you may need to go back to the drawing board in creating a solid administrative CV and cover letter (these look very different for administrative positions than for faculty positions). You may have no familiarity with online job searching resources and be out of touch with the professional job boards and publications where jobs are likely to be advertised. You may be rusty in negotiating a new salary or starting package. None of these things should dissuade you from making the move up the administrative ladder you are considering, but you will have to polish up your job-seeking and interviewing skills to successfully make the change you are contemplating. Finally, be sure to send a thank-you letter or e-mail to all the people who support you in this change, indicating that you will be glad to return the favor in the future.

Option 2: Returning to the Faculty

For those not interested in moving to the higher levels of administration, a return to your former faculty role occurs. This transition, however, is not as easy as it sounds if you do not make preparations ahead of time, and it can be frustrating, as the following case study illustrates.

> Associate Dean Avid has had a great run in the dean's office, but he has decided it is time to go back to the faculty. For the three years he has been in the dean's office, he has learned a great deal and actually really enjoyed the job, but in the last nine months he has become burned out. He has been working under a new dean who frequently countermands decisions Avid makes. Avid is returning to his position as a professor in the Department of Integrative Psychochemistry and is preparing to rev up his research program again. Avid has a solid reputation as a scientist and has managed to maintain a federal grant and his lab and to mentor a couple of PhD students while in the dean's office, but his publication output has dramatically decreased. As he prepares to leave the dean's office, he makes plans to immerse himself in the substantial amount of scholarly writing he needs to do and sets a goal of getting three new publications reviewed and in press in the twelve months following his departure from the dean's office. In addition, his grant is about to run out, so he begins to lay the groundwork necessary to support a large grant submission, on which he will work in the months following his exit from the dean's office. Avid is excited about getting back to his scholarship and returning to the classroom, and he looks forward to his exit with anticipation.
>
> The fiscal year ends and, as planned, Avid's contract as associate dean expires, and he returns, officially, to being "just a faculty member" in the middle of the summer. As he packs his associate dean office, he is thinking of the papers he will write and the grant proposals he will submit in the next few months. However, the end of summer rolls around, and Avid has made little progress on his goals. This

> trend continues through the fall semester, and Avid begins to wonder if he made the right call by leaving the dean's office; he finds himself searching job boards for administrative positions and feeling surprisingly unsettled. Months pass, and although Avid slowly begins to regain his research productivity, within the year he is actively searching for a position as a college dean at other universities.

Is this case study surprising to you? We include it to illustrate that for many, the experience of being an associate dean is a career-changer, even if it is not immediate. In Dr. Avid's case, he knew it was time to leave the dean's office, and at the time, he was not convinced that moving into a higher administrative position was the right move for him, so he decided to return to the faculty. Eventually, he discovered that he was yearning for a leadership position and began a search for a position not as a "middle manager," but as an executive—in Dr. Avid's case, as a dean.

The other important point of this case study is that even for people who return to the faculty after being an associate dean and stay there, the expectation that there will be a seamless transition from one position to the other may be unrealistic. Although Dr. Avid had great plans, he had a hard time getting going, and in fact, it took him several months to get back on track with his writing and scholarship. This is to be expected and should not be a source of concern. Many leaving the dean's office will do so in part at least because of burnout, frustration, overwork, stress, or a combination of these. Given this, it is no surprise that the months following departure from a position as an associate dean may be characterized by a "refractory period" of sorts, in which the person has to recharge his or her batteries to develop the mental energy and excitement necessary to really change gears and engage in activities that were largely stagnant while serving in the dean's office. In Dr. Avid's case, one reason for this was that at his core, he was ready to be a dean, and thus he had a harder time reengaging than he might have otherwise. But even if this were not the eventual outcome, returning to a normal faculty life of research, teaching, and service with a largely unstructured schedule that is once again in your control can be a bit of a shock to the system. After having meeting stacked upon meeting stacked upon deadline stacked upon event stacked upon task force, regaining control over your own time commitments can take some getting used to (see Fish 2004 for a humorous view of the transition). In other words, be patient with yourself when you return to the faculty. It is natural to take a while to reacclimatize.

Here are a few tips to help facilitate the transition from the dean's office to the faculty once you know you are going to make the switch. Hopefully, you will have a few months to plan for this and can put the following things into place. Although these suggestions certainly will not alleviate the stress and ramp-up of the transition, they will help get your head back into your teaching and scholarship.

The first thing you should do is talk to your department chair. Let your chair know you are planning to return to the department. If you need a new office, this is something to work out, as well as teaching assignments and other duties you may want or need to assume when you return. Follow this up by quietly chatting with a few key individuals. As you get ready to depart, think about the people on and off the campus whose opinions you really care about. Contact them to reconnect over coffee or lunch and talk with them about your plans and why you are making this change. When you leave your position, there will be speculation about why among some, and it is wise to make sure the people who matter have the correct story. Ask them to keep this information confidential, however, until after you have told your dean. You do not want your dean to hear it through the grapevine before you have a chance to talk to him or her. It is discourteous, disrespectful, and will burn one of those bridges we talked about earlier.

Second, make sure your professional memberships are up-to-date. If you have let any society memberships lapse while in the dean's office, renew them. Tied to this, reconnect with your colleagues. Look for annual meetings of societies you belong to (or are rejoining) and attend the conference, even if you are not presenting. Just going to the sessions and seeing old and new colleagues will help you start thinking about your scholarship in a more active way, bring you up-to-date on what everyone is doing and perhaps give you an idea for a new research project. If you are in a field that is amenable to it, think about establishing new collaborations. A great way to give your research program a shot in the arm is to team up with someone who is doing complementary work where you can make a contribution. This not only gets you back in the game more quickly but also injects some newness into your projects. Contact people ASAP to see what might work. Finally, depending on your field of research and creative activities, try to write some grant proposals. In fact, if you can swing it, try to write and submit at least one grant application before you leave the dean's office if funding is an important issue for your scholarly activities.

TOOLS AND TAKEAWAYS

Whether you stay an associate dean in perpetuity or decide to transition either back to the faculty or up into a higher administrative position, you will have done a substantial service to your school and university and have learned a great deal in this role. Ultimately, however, your career is your own, and when, for whatever reason, it is time for you to move on, do it wisely, cleanly, and with confidence. Some simple strategies can make the transition out of being an associate dean productive and straightforward for all involved.

1. *Know when to go*. Pay attention to the feedback you are getting from the dean, the faculty, your direct reports, your family, your partner, and yourself. When the messages tell you that it is time to go, accept them and act wisely.
2. *Plan your exit*. Before announcing your plans to leave, give some thought to where you want to go next and what you want to do. Typically, people either move into a higher administrative position or return to the faculty and resume their teaching, scholarship, and service at that level.
3. *Communicate clearly*. Be clear with your dean and others that you are leaving to support your own career, not because of some ugliness in the college or with the dean (even if this is the case). Be positive about your transition. State that you are moving on for your own career as clearly and as often as necessary, but be aware that the rumor mill will generate myths about why you are "really" leaving. Be prepared for this, but, to the degree you can, control the messaging by sticking to your story.
4. *Be kind to yourself*. Expect that this will be a tough transition in some way. It may be financial, it may be your morale, it may be that you are having trouble getting back into the swing of being a faculty member, or it may be a combination of these and other things. Take care to set your own expectations appropriately and not to beat yourself up when and if things don't go as smoothly as you would like. Although you are close, it really is true that nobody's perfect and some bumps are to be expected.

Chapter 17

Lessons Learned

Distillation of the Principles of Leading from the Middle

After having read this book, you may be asking yourself why you would ever want to be an associate dean. Alternatively, if you are already in the job, you may be asking why you should not focus on chapter 16 and plan your exit from the dean's office as soon as possible. Our hope, however, is that you are doing neither of these things and that rather, you are walking away from this book with a sense of the balance between the considerable professional and personal rewards of the job and the challenges you may encounter. We would have not written this book or continued to serve as associate deans as long as we did if there were not many wonderful things about being an associate dean that extend far beyond those mentioned in chapter 3. As an associate dean, you have the chance to positively impact your school in many important aspects of its long-term growth and health. You will also have gratifying day-to-day interactions in which you can do things like help solve a problem for a student in crisis, mentor a faculty member with a terrific research project, and toot the horn of the underappreciated staff members who keep the place running. Aside from these altruistic activities, being an associate dean gives you an inside glimpse of the administrative workings of the university and allows you to build a personal network and set of skills to launch you on an administrative career. We hope this book provides a roadmap to the types of skills needed to do the job of associate dean and other administrative jobs confidently and competently. Just as you needed to develop skills and techniques to excel as a teacher and scholar, you need to become aware of and master skills that will help you successfully navigate university administration and take your administrative career to the next level.

DEVELOPING A TOOL KIT

We have pointed out a number of times in this volume that the skills and tools used by administrators are different from, and sometimes antithetical to, those we developed and were rewarded for as faculty. To start with, administrators need to develop perspectives of larger units and keep the big picture in mind at all times. This means that you must reverse the trend of ever-increasing specialization associated with advanced research and become a generalist. Further, you must be able to see the ramifications of your actions beyond the needs of you personally (or individual students or faculty) and your home department in every decision you make. If you cannot do this, you will be, at best, a manager rather than a leader and, at worst, completely miserable and possibly incompetent in your job. If you do succeed at taking the longer view, you will be able to successfully lead from the middle. This big-picture perspective is, however, different from the perspective of most students, staff, and faculty at the university. As a result, you should not be surprised when your faculty colleagues see and treat you differently when you become an associate dean (hence the reference to "the dark side"). This comes through in your interactions, with faculty in particular, in a variety of ways, but the general theme is that now that you are an administrator, you can no longer appreciate what it is like to be a "real" faculty member. This perception may affect the degree to which even close colleagues are comfortable confiding in you about things and/or the way in which your opinions, motives, and actions are interpreted by faculty as well as by students and staff. This is not necessarily something you can do anything about, but you should anticipate it.

Even after you manage to change your perspective from the specialized and narrow to the broad and generalized, you should expect an initially steep learning curve in mastering the various skills necessary to be an effective administrator. Remember that the abilities that made you an effective faculty member are not necessarily the same ones that will make you a successful administrator. You will need to shift consciously from being independent and perhaps a bit competitive to being collaborative and willing to let others take credit for things you work very hard to accomplish. Be prepared for great success, as well as for healthy doses of frustration and some disappointments. On the days when you feel like writing your resignation letter, step back and remember the big picture of why you wanted to take this job, and what you are getting out of it. Also remind yourself that the job is not forever, and that you can do anything for a relatively short period of time. Focus on meeting your obligations and making the best of even the bad days, as these may be some of the best opportunities for personal growth you will have.

In addition to a change in the way faculty and staff view and interact with you, your life will change in terms of the structure of your day. Suddenly, rather than getting to work every day and having the freedom to determine how you allocate your time between teaching, research, and service, you must report to and take direction from your dean each day. This is very different from the largely autonomous nature of faculty life and requires that you make a special effort to understand your dean's management and communication styles. The bottom line is that your schedule will lose much of its flexibility as it becomes populated with standing committee meetings and the need to be available from 8:00 a.m. to 5:00 p.m. to help students, staff, and faculty with issues that arise unpredictably. This change is complicated by the fact that you must do all of these things while maintaining your faculty duties and some semblance of balance in your life. To successfully juggle these competing demands on your time and retain your intellectual energy, you must develop some guiding principles and a host of new skills to solve problems and otherwise negotiate the everyday life of an associate dean. It is challenging, but we believe it is well worth the effort to do so.

BASIC PRINCIPLES TO LIVE BY

It is important to take a moment and do a healthy amount of introspection regarding your core values when you take on the associate dean role. We recommend that you write a personal mission statement and state the goals you have for the job and for your career and personal life over the short and long terms (three and ten years). We are fully aware that most of you laughed at us when we said this and will not follow our advice. Regardless of whether you do or do not write your mission statement and a list of personal and professional goals, there are a few things you absolutely must consider and decide on if you are going to be successful in the job.

First, you must figure out the relative importance of your personal and professional commitments now and in the future and act accordingly. Resist the urge to think that you can put your personal life on the back burner, and have the courage to draw and hold boundaries around your personal time. Remember that you are a person with a career and with a family and friends who love you. Although it is great to be a team player and support the school, the fact is that you do not have to sacrifice yourself, your career, or your personal life to be a great associate dean. This statement is not permission to blow off the responsibilities of being an associate dean and assume someone else will pick up the slack. You would not appreciate it if someone did that to you, so do not do it to someone else. Rather, we want to emphasize that maintaining balance between your life as a scholar and an administrator, as well as between your career and personal life, will make you a happier, healthier, and more productive person and associate dean. Exactly what the nature of that balance looks like and how you maintain it will be unique to your own situation, so it is important to reflect on and determine this for yourself. That being said, we strongly recommend you carve out research time during the week for your scholarship and hold your evenings and weekends sacred and free of work. It is important to realize as you do this, however, that occasionally real emergencies do arise (though not as often as you may think). Treat those in crisis (real or perceived) as you would like to be treated under the same circumstances, and be prepared to do what you can to help when the real need arises.

Second, when trying to decide what to do about a problem or how to respond to undue pressure in a situation, remember that no one ever considered being called a person of integrity an insult. Therefore, treat everyone fairly and equally and never play favorites. Aside from the ethical dilemma it creates, treating anyone preferentially simply creates more headaches for you and your dean in the long run. Additionally, it is critical to know the issues upon which you must take a stand (i.e., the hill you will die on) and those on which you can compromise. Issues upon which you may want to commit to standing firm are likely to involve protecting the long-term health of the institution and protecting vulnerable populations. Exactly what issues fall into this category will vary from individual to individual and will be based on your frame of reference and the areas in which you have in-depth knowledge. Give careful thought to these issues and clarify them in your mind.

Third, people may have negative and angry reactions to a decision you make or to a policy or procedure you must enforce; resist the urge to take their reactions personally. If you are consistent and there is a reason for your actions, people may not be happy at the moment, but they will appreciate that you have been thoughtful in your decision and considered all of the ramifications. They also will appreciate knowing exactly what the rules are and that you attempt to apply them fairly to everyone.

Finally, despite your best attempts, you cannot save people from themselves. Associate deans can do a great deal in terms of mentoring and arbitrating disputes between individuals and groups. One of the key elements in managing these situations is pointing out how actions and words can be interpreted in a way that was not intended and pointing out the long-term ramifications of the actions people are taking in a heated conflict. In the end, however, you cannot keep individuals who are seemingly intent on ruining their relationships or making bad decisions from doing so. All you can do when this happens is mitigate the damage to innocent bystanders and hope that all involved learn something in the process.

"STRATEGIC PLANNING" IS NOT A DIRTY WORD

Mention the words "strategic planning" to most people in academia and chances are you have visions of people hurling insults, erasers, and, if handy, rotten produce at you. The urge to react in this way occurs because most people think of strategic planning very narrowly. Specifically, they think of it as an institution-wide process that frequently results in a large report and little or no action. When strategic plans result in changes in how things are done, the changes are slow and may take eight to ten years or more to have a tangible impact. A fundamental problem with institutional strategic planning is that the expected lifespan of a dean, provost, or president at an institution is, on average, considerably shorter than eight to ten years. Each time an upper-level administrator is replaced, a new cycle of meetings on strategic planning is likely to occur, potentially replacing the actions of the prior round of planning. This can be frustrating, understandably, to faculty, staff, and associate deans. We encourage you, however, to broaden your perspective on such processes. Ideally, strategic planning is about bringing people together to discuss and agree on a view of the future, set some goals, prioritize those goals, and decide on a course of action to meet them. From this perspective, strategic planning is a good thing to do. Being part of such planning, and playing a leadership role when you can, will be a rewarding and fruitful experience for you personally and for your career.

Depending on the size of the group doing the strategic planning (individual, research collaborators, an academic department, the whole school, or the university), the length of time it takes to reach consensus on the planning and actually achieve the goals will vary considerably. Small groups are nimble and easily change direction, while large universities are cumbersome, policy bound, and take considerably longer to make a change. Regardless of the size of the unit and the nature of the goals, though, strategic planning has two distinct advantages. First, constantly being in crisis/reaction mode is exhausting and utterly unsatisfying. Strategic planning helps you switch into a more proactive role and demonstrate to yourself and to others that you (or the unit you are dealing with) are moving forward rather than standing still. Second, given that there is never enough time or money to do everything we want to do at once, strategic planning helps us prioritize our goals. Members of a unit will be much more willing to wait their turn for their issue to be addressed if they are sure their turn will, in fact, come. The prioritization aspect of strategic planning helps this occur.

ASSOCIATE DEANS ARE NOT SURROGATE PARENTS FOR STUDENTS, STAFF, OR FACULTY

Although it occasionally feels as if you are overseeing a group of children rather than adults functioning in a professional environment, your job is not to act as a caretaker or parent for every student, staff, and faculty member in the school. Yes, you will occasionally have to break up fights, discipline a bully, or listen to an incredible amount of whining and complaining. Remind yourself, however, that you are dealing with adults who must take responsibility for their own actions and their own lives. Be respectful and professional toward them and demand respectful and professional behavior in return. Serve as a mentor when it is requested or necessary, but remember it is ultimately the mentee's life and career, and therefore, he or she makes the decisions about what to do and must face the consequences. Above all, concentrate on facilitating processes and collaborations when it is helpful, but do not allow yourself to do other people's jobs for them, even if it would be easier to do so on occasion.

POLICY IS YOUR FRIEND

You cannot enforce rules or standards if no rules or standards exist, and you cannot reward excellence if you do not know what constitutes excellence. Find relevant policies at the department, school, and university levels; set up mechanisms to review them periodically; and update them if needed. If no policy exists for a commonly occurring problem, propose one. In the process of creating policy, remember that governance groups are not the enemy and they are not roadblocks to be avoided if at all possible. Rather, learn to treat governance groups as your partners in policy development. These groups can be of great help, and they do considerably more than just buy into your plan. Governance groups can serve as a source of collective wisdom and new ideas, if you treat them with respect and truly engage them in the process of policy development and approval. Alternatively, if you choose to, or appear to choose to, dismiss or disrespect these groups, they can actively hinder your progress.

Once you have found and/or established relevant policies, do not vary from them without a great deal of consideration. Once you grant an exception to a policy, you have set a precedent that you will have to honor for others in the future. If you fail to do this, your credibility will be weakened and your integrity will be called into question. In the worst cases, you also may find yourself on the phone with a lawyer hired by an employee who feels he or she has been treated unfairly. Remember above all else that outside of accepted policy, an associate dean has extremely limited power. What little power you do have is based on persuasion and personal capital. Every time you break from accepted policy, your capital is diminished, and you will get to a point that no amount of persuasion can make up the difference.

SOLVING PROBLEMS REQUIRES COMPLETE INFORMATION AND TIME

A large part of the associate dean's job is solving complex problems. When you are contacted about such a problem, the issue at hand will likely be presented as a crisis that requires you to drop everything else to solve or the world will fall apart. In fact, very few problems rise to this level, and if they do a call to campus security, the fire department, or some other first responder is generally in order. In fact, the first step in problem solving and crisis management is almost always managing your reactions and the reactions of others. This is a critical step to determine if a real crisis is occurring, and if so, what the facts of the matter are. Acting without knowing all of the facts or taking action while you are angry or afraid will almost always make the problem worse. The second step is sorting out fact from rhetoric to get to the heart of the issue. Your response to any issue of complexity should always be "Let me investigate the matter and I will get back to you."

Once you have a sense of what the problem is, begin to systematically gather any missing information and learn about what options exist to resolve the issue at hand. First, determine whether there is a policy involved or whether it is a conflict between individuals and the differing priorities of individuals and groups. If the problem is a conflict between priorities or individuals (the most common), do not assume you know what has happened or what everyone thinks about the situation. There are at least two sides to every dispute and subtle nuances that complicate virtually every problem. Figure out who is involved and the motivations and goals of everyone involved. Ask questions such as "Why has this particular issue become a problem this week when it was not a problem last week?" Above all, remember that the history of a policy, an individual, or a relationship is always an issue both in the perception of the situation and its possible solution.

Once you figure out the "who, what, and why" of the situation, think about broader connections that may be important in your approach. Can the issue be solved easily internally, or do you need to involve other units like student services, Human Resources, risk management, or legal counsel? After you have considered all of these options, you will be in a better position to formulate a solution and take steps to deal with the issue. A key piece of this is communicating your findings, the solution, and the steps to be taken to all of the relevant parties.

EFFECTIVE COMMUNICATION IS ESSENTIAL

It is hard for us to think of any single skill that is more important for your success as an associate dean than effective communication. Clear communication can go a long way in helping you build relationships and solve even the most complex situations you are likely to face. More importantly, by being proactive about communication you are likely to be able to keep many issues from ever bubbling up to the crisis stage. Poor or infrequent communication, on the other hand, can make a tense situation explode or create a problem where none exists.

So what does it mean to communicate well? There are the obvious aspects your parents taught you as a child. First, be courteous and say "please" and "thank you." Remember this even when you are asking people to fill out required paperwork several times a year. Second, be responsive to inquiries and answer e-mails and phone calls promptly. Do this even if all you are doing is to redirect a question or say, "I will have to research the issue and get back to you." The exception to the prompt reply rule is when the e-mail or voice mail is abusive, in which case you may wish to forward it to the person who deals with hostile workplace complaints at your university. Effective communication for your work in the dean's office, however, extends far beyond these fundamental childhood lessons. Infusing transparency into your communication is very important, although this can be hard to achieve consistently. We know that "transparency" is a common buzz word these days, but it is worth mentioning in this context. You will find that in many situations, the people involved will not have all the information that you do about an issue. This can occur either because they were busy and missed information that was shared in an announcement or e-mail or because they do not have easy access to the information. Many in the school will view you as an information portal for what is going on in the university. In other words, associate deans are often called upon for their ability to locate policies and procedures quickly. Additionally, because they have one foot in the faculty and the other in the administrative campus, they can translate the considerable jargon involved in official messages between the two groups. Finally, associate deans often act as a liaison between the departments within the school and the dean. In this capacity, it is critical that associate deans communicate information from and about students, faculty, and staff to the dean, especially if there is a problem looming, and also information from the dean to the students, faculty, and staff.

In performing these communication duties, you need to remember that people in different positions within the university may interpret the information in very different ways because their frames of reference and the missions associated with their positions vary greatly. When deciding how to talk to various people about thorny issues, be sensitive to these differences. Be careful not to assume that people do not need or do not want to know what is going on, and be sure to err on the side of giving too much clarification. Remember that in the absence of information, people often will assume the worst and may create complicated conspiracy scenarios in their head to fill in the blanks. Sharing information clearly and frequently can help defuse this phenomenon, so do what you can to inform all affected parties respectfully when change occurs.

Another key consideration in your communication is conveying pertinent information in a way that is accessible and clear. Give careful consideration to the medium you use for communication, as it will vary based on the message. E-mail is convenient and can avoid problems with misunderstandings as things are written down in black and white. A problem with e-mail, however, is that its intent can sometimes be misinterpreted as it lacks the emotional cues that are key parts of oral communication. E-mail has the dual problem of lacking these important emotional nuances and being copied and distributed. Thus, e-mail is probably not the best medium for communicating about a complicated or confidential issue. One-on-one meetings or telephone calls allow for clear confidentiality and clear communication about sensitive issues, but they are time consuming and sometimes difficult to arrange due to conflicting schedules. Despite the possible inconveniences of setting up meetings, in difficult situations personal contact is generally the best route of communication. Finding the right medium can go a long way to delivering your message effectively. Alternatively, choosing the wrong method of communication can interfere with the message and result in nascent problems bubbling up to full-blown-crisis level.

FINAL TAKEAWAYS

So how do we sum all this up? We hope that you will embrace and enjoy the great potential and many positive aspects of being an associate dean and use and adapt the tools we have presented in this book to deal with the problems that you encounter. Treat yourself and others with respect. Communicate clearly and frequently. Say thank you to others for a job well done, but do not get upset if no one says it to you. If you follow this advice, we think you will find leading from the middle a rewarding job and a great entry to the world of university administration.

References

Armour, Robert A., Rosemary S. Caffarella, Barbara S. Fuhrmann, and Jon F. Wergin. 1987. Academic burnout: Faculty responsibility and institutional climate. In *Coping with faculty stress*, edited by Peter Seldin, 3–12. San Francisco: Jossey-Bass.

Baldwin, Roger, Deborah DeZure, Allyn Shaw, and Kristin Moretton. 2008. Mapping the terrain of mid-career faculty at a research university: Implications for faculty and academic leaders. *Change* 40(5): 46–55.

Berryman-Fink, Cynthia. 1998. Can we agree to disagree? Faculty-faculty conflict. In *Mending the cracks in the ivory tower: Strategies for conflict management in higher education*, edited by Susan A. Holton, 141–163. Bolton, MA: Anker.

Bess, James L., and Ja R. Dee. 2008. *Understanding college and university organization*. Sterling, VA: Stylus.

Boenisch, Ed, and C. Michele Haney. 1996. *The stress owner's manual: Meaning, balance and health in your life*. San Luis Obispo, CA: Impact.

Bryan, William A., and Richard H. Mullendor, eds. 1992. *Rights, freedoms, and responsibilities of students*. San Francisco: Jossey-Bass.

Bryant, Paul T. 2005. *Confessions of an habitual administrator: An academic survival manual*. Bolton, MA: Anker.

Buller, Jeffrey L. 2007. *The essential academic dean: A practical guide to college leadership*. San Francisco: Jossey-Bass.

Burnes, Bernard. 2004. Emergent change and planned change—competitors or allies? *International Journal of Operations and Production Management* 24: 886–902.

Carnevale, Dan. 2006. E-mail is for old people. *Chronicle of Higher Education* 53(7): A27.

References

Carney-Hall, Karla C., ed. 2008. *Managing parent partnerships: Maximizing influence, minimizing interference, and focusing on student success.* San Francisco: Jossey-Bass.

Chambers, Harry E. 2004. *My way or the highway: The micromanagement survival guide.* San Francisco: Berrett-Kohler.

Cheldelin, Sandra I., and Ann F. Lucas, eds. 2004. *Academic administrator's guide to conflict resolution.* San Francisco: Jossey-Bass.

Chu, Don. 2006. *The department chair primer.* Bolton, MA: Anker.

Coburn, Karen Levin. 2006. Organizing a ground crew for today's helicopter parents. *About Campus* 11(3): 9–16.

Coffman, James R. 2005. *Work and peace in academe: Leveraging time, money, and intellectual energy through managing conflict.* Bolton, MA: Anker.

Daniel, Bonnie V., and B. Ross Scott, eds. 2001. *Consumers, adversaries, and partners: Working with the families of undergraduates.* San Francisco: Jossey-Bass.

Davis, James R. 2003. *Learning to lead: A handbook for postsecondary administrators.* Westport, CT: Praeger.

Dowdall, George, and Jean Dowdall. 2005. Crossing over to the dark side. *Chronicle of Higher Education* 52(5): C1–C4.

Fish, Stanley. 2004. What did you do all day? *Chronicle of Higher Education* 51(14): C2–C3.

Gilan, Gary L., and Alan T. Seagren. 2003. Six critical issues for midlevel leadership in postsecondary settings. In *Identifying and preparing academic leaders*, edited by Sherry L. Hoppe and Bruce W. Speck, 21–33. San Francisco: Jossey-Bass.

Gilley, Daryl. 2003. Bedside manner and effective academic administrative leadership. In *Identifying and preparing academic leaders*, edited by Sherry L. Hoppe and Bruce W. Speck, 95–102. San Francisco: Jossey-Bass.

Gmelch, Walter H. 1998. The Janus syndrome: Managing conflict from the middle. In *Mending the cracks in the ivory tower: Strategies for conflict management in higher education*, edited by Susan A. Holton, 28–45. Bolton, MA: Anker.

———. 1987. What colleges and universities can do about faculty stressors. In *Coping with faculty stress*, edited by Peter Seldin, 23–31. San Francisco: Jossey-Bass.

Gmelch, Walter H., and Vall D. Miskin. 1993. *Leadership skills for department chairs.* Bolton, MA: Anker.

Graff, Gerald. 1998. Administration in an age of conflict. In *Mending the cracks in the ivory tower: Strategies for conflict management in higher education*, edited by Susan A. Holton, 12–27. Bolton, MA: Anker.

Grasha, Anthony F. 1987. Short-term coping techniques for managing stress. In *Coping with faculty stress*, edited by Peter Seldin, 53–63. San Francisco: Jossey-Bass.

Gunsalus, C. K. 2006. *The college administrator's survival guide.* Cambridge, MA: Harvard.

Higgerson, Mary Lou, and Teddi A. Joyce. 2007. *Effective leadership communication: A guide for department chairs and deans for managing difficult situations and people.* Bolton, MA: Anker.

Holton, Susan A. 1998a. Academic mortar to mend the cracks: The Holton model for conflict management. In *Mending the cracks in the ivory tower: Strate-*

gies for conflict management in higher education, edited by Susan A. Holton, 221–238. Bolton, MA: Anker.

———. 1998b. What's it all about? Conflict in academia. In *Mending the cracks in the ivory tower: Strategies for conflict management in higher education*, edited by Susan A. Holton, 1–11. Bolton, MA: Anker.

Hoppe, Sherry L. 2003. Identifying and nurturing potential academic leaders. In *Identifying and preparing academic leaders*, edited by Sherry L. Hoppe and Bruce W. Speck, 3–13. San Francisco: Jossey-Bass.

Howe, Neil, and William Strauss. 2000. *Millennials rising: The next great generation*. New York: Vintage Books.

Huston, Therese, and Carol L. Weaver. 2007. Peer coaching: Professional development for experienced faculty. *Innovative Higher Education* 33: 5–20.

Kezar, Adrianna. 2009. Change in higher education: Not enough, or too much? *Change* 41(6): 18–23.

Lucas, Ann. 1998. Spanning the abyss: Managing conflict between deans and chairs. In *Mending the cracks in the ivory tower, strategies for conflict management in higher education*, ed. Susan A. Holton, 60–80. Bolton, MA: Anker.

———. 1994. *Strengthening departmental leadership: A team-building guide for chairs in colleges and universities*. San Francisco: Jossey-Bass.

McCabe, Darren. 2010. Taking the long view: A cultural analysis of memory as resisting and facilitating organizational change. *Journal of Organizational Change Management* 23(3): 230–250.

Nelson, Margaret K. 2010. *Parenting out of control*. New York: New York University.

Palm, Risa. 2006. Perspectives from the dark side: The career transition from faculty to administrator. In *Transitions between faculty and administrative careers*, edited by Ronald J. Henry, 59–65. San Francisco: Jossey-Bass.

Plater, William M. 2006. The rise and fall of administrative careers. In *Transitions between faculty and administrative careers*, edited by Ronald J. Henry, 15–24. San Francisco: Jossey-Bass.

Raines, Sherley C., and Martha Squires Alberg. 2003. The role of professional development in preparing academic leaders. In *Identifying and preparing academic leaders*, edited by Sherry L. Hoppe and Bruce W. Speck, 33–40. San Francisco: Jossey-Bass.

Sample, Steven B. 2002. *The contrarian's guide to leadership*. San Francisco: Jossey-Bass.

Seldin, Peter. 1987. Research findings on causes of academic stress. In *Coping with faculty stress*, edited by Peter Seldin, 13–22. San Francisco: Jossey-Bass.

Sorcinelli, Mary Dean, and Marshall W. Gregory. 1987. Faculty stress: The tension between career demands and "having it all." In *Coping with faculty stress*, edited by Peter Seldin, 43–52. San Francisco: Jossey-Bass.

Sorenson, Nancy L. 1998. The cutting edge: The dean and conflict. In *Mending the cracks in the ivory tower: Strategies for conflict management in higher education*, edited by Susan A. Holton, 81–96. Bolton, MA: Anker.

Stone, Tammy. 2009. Departments in academic receivership: Possible causes and solutions. *Innovative Higher Education* 33: 229–238.

Strathe, Marlene, and Vicki W. Wilson. 2006. Academic leadership: The pathway to and from. In *Transitions between faculty and administrative careers*, edited by Ronald J. Henry, 5–14. San Francisco: Jossey-Bass.

Sturnick, Judith A. 1998. And never the twain shall meet: Administrator-faculty conflict. In *Mending the cracks in the ivory tower: Strategies for conflict management in higher education*, edited by Susan A. Holton, 97–112. Bolton, MA: Anker.

Twale, Darla, and Barbara M. DeLuca. 2008. *Faculty incivility: The rise of the academic bully culture and what to do about it*. San Francisco: Jossey-Bass.

Trachtenberg, Stephen J. 2007. Lessons from the top. *Chronicle of Higher Education* 54(10): 59.

Woverton, Mimi, and Walter H. Gmelch. 2002. *College deans leading from within*. Westport, CT: Praeger.

Index

authority, its ambiguous nature, 64, 65, 68, 69, 98, 179

bullies, dealing with. *See* conflict management
bylaws, 75, 93

calendar. *See* time management
change, 27, 67, 143–48; change fatigue 146
collaborations, the importance of, 28–30, 67–68, 69, 133, 138; cross campus committees, 135–38; human resources, 47, 83, 86, 111; institutional research, 138; legal counsel, 129–30; student services, 118, 120. *See also* consensus; negotiation
communication, 68, 71–76, 107, 162, 180–81; building consensus and communication, 65–68, 93; conflict management and communication, 86, 94–98; dean's communication style, 4; e-mail problems, 72–73, 74–75, 76, 78–79, 115; public image, 124; response to abusive e-mails, 106; students, 115; your communication style, 5, 63, 65, 66, 74, 98. *See also* collaborations; conflict management; crisis
compromise, 26, 67, 78–79, 80–82, 137, 176. *See also* negotiation
conflict management, 11, 48, 57–58, 71, 79, 84–87, 89–90, 93–99, 111
crisis, 6, 86, 123–31, 152; definition of a crisis, 123, 124; emergency preparedness, 127–28; managing hysteria, 126; public image, 124–26

dark side, going to, x, 10, 12–13, 17–18, 20, 26, 64, 69, 73, 174
dean: avoiding blindsides, 74, 75, 122, 129; bias of, 42–43; strategic vision and goals of, 41–42, 91–92, 93. *See also* communication; leadership; management; micromanagers
decision making, 26, 45, 68, 101–2, 107–11, 117, 179–80. *See also* tool kits
departments: conflict in departments, 80–87, 89–90, 92–98, 110; working with chairs 55–56, 73, 78–87; your home department 3, 10, 64–65, 84

facilitating. *See* collaboration; consensus
faculty: facilitating collaborations, 28–30; governance groups, 75, 105; high-maintenance, 105–6; motivating faculty, 95, 104, 108, 111; stars vs. divas, 103, 111; working with, 69

golden boy/girl syndrome, 58–61, 139–41

human resources, 47, 83, 86, 111

incivility. *See* conflict management

leadership, 3, 24, 34; building consensus, 27, 65–68, 91; dean's leadership style, 4; leading vs. managing, 3–4; your leadership style, 10, 26, 91–92. *See also* collaborations; dean; management
learning a new position, 4–5, 24, 34, 64, 67–68

management style, 4; dean's management style, 4, 43–45; managing vs. leading, 3–4, 36–37; your management style, 10. *See also* dean, micromanagers
mentoring, for yourself, 16, 19, 32–33, 168–19; mentoring others, 28–31, 83, 106–17; mid-career faculty, 109–10; personal mission statements, 18–19, 27, 175; setting goals, 13, 16–17, 19, 20, 152–53, 175; staff, 109
micromanagers, 44–45

negotiation, 28, 83–87, 136–37

policies and process, the importance of, 48, 66, 68–69, 74, 93, 98, 117–18, 119, 124, 176, 178; communicating about, 68, 84; creating new policies, 75, 125, 178; setting precedents, 69, 129, 179

rumor mill on campus, 69, 136

staff, working with, 33, 83–87, 104, 107, 109–10; governance, 75, 105; motivating unproductive staff, 111; working with staff outside your college, 134
strategic plans, 177–78; dean's, 27, 41–42; department, 81–82, 97, 98; school and university level, 126. *See also* mentoring
stress, 32, 151, 152, 153–58, 162–64
students, 113–22; consumer model, 116; FRPA, 117; helicopter parents, 114, 116–17; millennial generation, 116; student complaints, 138–30; student support services, 118, 120

time management, 6, 11, 175; changes in your calendar, 6, 24, 170; maintaining a personal life, 14, 149–53, 157, 175–76; maintain research and teaching time, 11, 13, 41, 176
tool kits, 20–21, 34, 49–50, 61–62, 69, 76, 87, 98–99, 112, 122, 131, 141–42, 148, 158, 171–72

About the Authors

Tammy Stone, PhD, RPA, is a professor of anthropology and former associate dean in the College of Liberal Arts and Sciences at the University of Colorado Denver (UCD). She received her PhD in anthropology with a specialty in archaeology from Arizona State University and her certification from the Register of Professional Archaeologists, prior to coming to UCD. Stone has a distinguished record of teaching, research, and service and has served in numerous leadership positions on her campus, including chairing the Department of Anthropology, as well as two departments that were placed in academic receivership by the college, and as acting dean. Stone's academic background is concentrated in archaeology, with particular emphasis on the dynamics of factionalism and alliance formation in communities in Southwestern pueblos. She has published two books and eighteen peer-reviewed articles in archaeology and two peer-reviewed articles in higher education administration.

Mary Coussons-Read, PhD, is a professor of psychology and health and behavioral science, is former associate dean at the University of Colorado Denver (UCD), and is currently chairing two programs in receivership in the college. She received her PhD in psychology and neurobiology from the University of North Carolina at Chapel Hill and completed postdoctoral training in psychiatry and pediatrics at the University of Colorado School of Medicine prior to coming to UCD. Coussons-Read has a distinguished record of teaching, research, and service, and she has served in numerous leadership positions on and beyond her campus including chairing the UCD Faculty Assembly on the downtown campus and serving as faculty council vice chair. Coussons-Read's academic background is concentrated in psychology and mind/body health, and she has published more than thirty peer-reviewed articles in behavioral and health science. A special focus of her research is the neural-immune consequences of stress during pregnancy and how these changes can affect maternal and infant outcome. She is also active in her profession and in the community, serving in leadership roles for her primary scientific society and as a member of the board of directors and as incoming board chair for Smart-Girl, Inc., a Denver nonprofit providing leadership training to girls and young women.